Native Athletes
in Sport &
Society

Edited by C. Richard King

Native Athletes in Sport & Society

A READER

University of Nebraska Press

Lincoln & London

Chapter 3 originally appeared as "World Champions: The 1904 Girls Basketball Team from Fort Shaw Indian Boarding School," *Montana* 51:4 (2001): 2–25. Reprinted with permission. Chapter 8 originally appeared as "An Examination of Sport for Aboriginal Females on the Six Nations Reserve, Ontario, from 1968–1990," in *Women of the First Nations: Power, Wisdom, and Strength*, ed. Christine Miller and Patricia Chuchryk (Winnipeg: University of Manitoba Press, 1996). Reprinted with permission.

Set in Carter & Cone Galliard types by Bob Reitz. Book designed by Richard Eckersley. Printed and bound by Edwards Brothers, Inc.

Library of Congress Cataloging-in-Publication Data
Native athletes in sport and society: a reader / edited by C. Richard King.   p. cm.
Includes bibliographical references and index.
ISBN-13: 978-0-8032-2753-8 (cloth: alkaline paper)
ISBN-10: 0-8032-2753-1 (cloth: alkaline paper)
ISBN-13: 978-0-8032-7828-8 (paperback: alk. paper)
ISBN-10: 0-8032-7828-4 (paperback: alkaline paper)
1. Indian athletes – United States – History.
2. Indians of North America – Sports – History.
3. Indians of North America – Social conditions.
I. King, C. Richard, 1968–
GV709.55.N38 2005   796'.089'97–dc22   2005015163

CONTENTS

ILLUSTRATIONS

ACKNOWLEDGMENTS

Although often attributed to one writer, all books emerge through collaborative work. Nowhere is this more true than in an edited volume; collective effort makes collections possible. Such is this case with this book. Many individuals have contributed to its success.

Most obviously, the participants have made an incredible difference. Patient and passionate, they transformed an intriguing idea into a powerful discussion of an often forgotten subject. A number of other colleagues enhanced this work as well, suggesting text, contributors, or alternative ways of thinking about the project. Over the years this project has percolated, I have benefited from conversations and collaborations with David Leonard, Matt Esposito, Chuck Springwood, Todd Fuller, Joseph Schneider, Laurel Davis, Rory Ong, Tony Clark, Jeff Powers-Beck, John Streamas, Joseph Oxendine, Joe Giovanetti, Eric Anderson, Royse Parr, Dan Ninham, Cheryl Cole, Janet Wirth-Cauchon, Cornell Pewewardy, David Hurst Thomas, and Allan Hanson.

Behind the scenes, librarians at Drake University went out of their way to assist me in locating obscure articles, frequently securing them through interlibrary loan within days of my request. At both Drake University and Washington State University, I likewise have benefited from the labor and attention of several staff members. I was lucky to have the support of Sofia Turnbull, Nancy Smith, Silva Bedoyan Everton, and Jane Fredrickson.

As always, everyone at the University of Nebraska Press was fantastic. Gary Dunham originally encouraged me to pursue this project and guided it from inception to completion with his usual care and professionalism. All authors should be fortunate to work with someone with his skills and intellect.

Finally, this work would have been unthinkable without the love and support of my family. My children, Ellory and Abigail, encouraged—at times forced—me to pause from my editorial burdens, reminding of what really matters in life: mud pies and monkey bars, homemade pizza and Go Fish, high-flying clouds and deep questions. My soul mate and better half, Marcie, although not a sports fan, contributed more than she will ever know to this work. Her perspective, laughter, and presence always comforted and inspired me.

Identities, Opportunities, Inequities
An Introduction

In 1915 Lakota physician and author Charles Eastman surveyed the Native American condition in *The Indian To-day*. In his account of the contributions of indigenous peoples to American society, he stressed the importance of athletes and athletics, reviewing them alongside those who pursued noteworthy intellectual endeavors or creative projects, or who achieved entrepreneurial success. "In the athletic world this little race has no peer, as is sufficiently proven by their remarkable record in football, baseball, and track athletics. . . . From the fleet Deerfoot to this day we boast the noted names of Longboat, Sockalexis, Bemus Pierce, Frank Hudson, Tewanima, Metoxen, Meyers, Bender, and Jim Thorpe." Sport, for Eastman (and many of his progressive peers), was more than an amusement or diversion; he understood it as a pathway toward assimilation and equality. With this in mind, he actively championed it. As he recalled,

I asked that good friend of the Indian, Gen. R. H. Pratt, why he did not introduce football is his school. "Why," said he, "if I did that, half the press of the country would attack me for developing the original war instincts and savagery of the Indian! The public would be afraid to come to our games!"

"Major," I said, "that is exactly why I want you to do it. We will prove that the Indian is a gentleman and a sportsman; he will not complain; he will do nothing unfair or underhanded; he will play the game according to the rules, and will not swear—at least not in public!"

The Indian athlete, then, was a figure charged with immense responsibility: through his actions and achievements he could improve the image and opportunities of indigenous peoples. Many of Eastman's

Euro-American contemporaries shared neither his assessment of Indians and their capacities nor his faith in sport. In fact, in contrast with Eastman's progressive sentiments, athletic competitions afforded many journalists, players, and spectators occasions to reiterate, elaborate, and refine encrusted stereotypes about Native Americans, the conquest of North America, and the future of race relations in the United States.[1]

Nearly a half century after Charles Eastman championed the possibilities of sport, John Tortes "Chief" Meyers, Mission/Cahuilla catcher for the New York Giants and Brooklyn Dodgers, reflected on his life and career: regret about never finishing his degree at Dartmouth College; his friendship with Jim Thorpe and Charles "Chief" Bender; his recollections of the 1911 and 1912 World Series; and his feelings about noteworthy personalities like Giants manager John McGraw and umpire Bill Klem. Throughout, being an Indian played a pivotal role in his place in sport and society: "I don't like to say this, but in those days, when I was young, I was considered a foreigner. I didn't belong. I was an Indian."[2] Later in life he continued to feel marginalized and dehumanized:

In those days, you know, the Indian was in the position of a minority group. Still is, for that matter. Nowadays, you can't ridicule an Irishman on the television, you can't ridicule a Jew, and you can't ridicule a Negro. But they can kill us all the time—make everything out of us they want. Every night you see them on the television—killing us Indians. That's all they do.

That's one reason I don't look at anything but a ball game or the news on the television. I like the ball games and the news, but after the news, then comes the killing. Those things I don't like to talk about. I see them . . . I know them . . . but I don't like to talk about them.[3]

In contrast with the pride and possibility expressed by Eastman, Meyers speaks of pain and exclusion. Racism belittled and violated him as it put him in his place (foreigner, other, an enemy to be killed in television Westerns), undermining his claims to complete cultural citizenship.

At roughly the same moment Meyers reflected on sport and society, Onondaga Oren Lyons played lacrosse at Syracuse University. He was from a family of lacrosse players and a Native nation that continued to play the indigenous game.

I used to sit by the lamplight and watch [my father] fix his pads and his stick—with care, great care, and I could see the satisfaction it gave him. And I would be allowed to fuss with his things, and then run around with his pads on, and watch him get ready for a game. And then I would go with him to the game. . . . And there would be a winner and a loser, but that did not seem to be so much a point of the game as the celebration, the sense of community, the being together with pride.[4]

Lyons had more than fond memories; he also possessed great skills as a goalkeeper. He excelled at lacrosse and was named an All-American in 1958. After graduating from Syracuse, Lyons would become an activist for indigenous rights, a spiritual leader, a faculty member at the University of Buffalo, and the second Native American to be elected to the Lacrosse Hall of Fame. In the early 1980s his commitments to spirituality, sovereignty, and sport coalesced with the formation of the Iroquois Nationals Lacrosse Team. Established to revitalize indigenous heritage and assert autonomy, it has participated in international competitions for nearly twenty years. Echoing the words of Eastman and Meyers, Lyons summarized the import of the team: "This team is so important because it's a place where we can prove ourselves without all those [non-Indian] rules jammed at us. . . . When they say you've got to be an American college boy to be an all-American at lacrosse that's a subtle way of controlling and directing us."[5]

Eastman, Meyers, and Lyons grant us three brief glimpses into the importance of American Indian athletes. Far from superfluous or disconnected from the Native American experience, athletes clearly matter. Eastman, Meyers, and Lyons speak of sports and the peoples that play them with intimacy, affection, and intense interest. They understand, moreover, that the presence of indigenous athletes always poses questions about race and difference. Anti-Indian stereotypes shape the image, actions, and interpretations of indigenous athletes. At the same time, in this racialized context, athletes and athletics embody, enact, and encourage ethnic pride. In addition, athletes and athletics held great promise for Eastman, Meyers, and Lyons. It gave them a chance to play a game they loved, to have fun, to leave the reservation, and even to travel the world. It granted an emergent pan-Indian community the opportunity to challenge stereotypes and demand equality. It afforded the assertion of sovereignty in post–civil rights America. Finally, whether concerned with assimilation or sovereignty, sport facilitated the (re)creation of social worlds, marked by hope and structured by race, situated betwixt and between Indian Country and Euro-America, inflected by tradition and modernity.

Indigenous peoples have played a fundamental and largely underappreciated role in North American athletics. Indeed, American Indians have contributed popular games and contests, excelled as players, and distinguished themselves as coaches. As a social domain, sports have not only encouraged the assimilation of Native individuals but facilitated the preservation of cultural traditions and the reformulation of cultural identities as well. Unfortunately most sports fans today are more likely to think of Indians as mascots than as athletes. And while academics and activists have rightly questioned the centrality of Indian imagery in American sport, with few exceptions they have done little to recuperate the history and significance of Native participation in North American athletics. *Native Athletes in Sport and Society* seeks to redress this pattern of neglect.

Gathering together eleven essays, this collection formulates a broad perspective on the history and significance of indigenous athletes in North America, exploring their lives and careers and recording their accomplishments on the playing field as well as their endeavors outside of sport. At the same time, it interrogates the sociocultural contexts in which they lived and played, detailing the articulations of power and possibility, difference and identity, and representation and remembrance that have shaped the means and meanings of American Indians playing sport in (Native) North America.

Native Athletes in Sport and Society engages these topics within a diverse range of athletic, cultural, and historical contexts. The essays examine the American Indian experience in a variety of sports from golf to rodeo but cluster around three modern sports: baseball, basketball, and football. This emphasis does not suggest that Native Americans have only played these sports or that they did not play sports before the advent of modern games. In fact, sports and games were a vibrant part of all Native nations, reflecting and often integrating spiritual beliefs, social relations, and cultural values. Furthermore, since the emergence of sport as a distinct social domain in North America in the early nineteenth century, Native Americans have excelled in a multitude of sports including baseball, basketball, football, hockey, running, boxing, rodeo, and the indigenous sport of lacrosse. Thus, this concentration says much about the unique history of modern sports, particularly of Native Americans in sports, and the current preoccupations of scholars and fans. Undoubtedly, this concentration obscures athletes in traditional contexts; however, it also offers a comparative perspective that affords a fuller understanding.

While several authors, including Gerald Gems, Linda Peavey and Ursula Smith, and Charles Springwood, detail multiethnic contexts, others concentrate on individuals from specific tribal groups, particularly Lakota, Navajo, Penobscot, Sac and Fox, Snohomish, and Winnebago. Together, they offer a broad historical perspective, documenting sporting lives in context from the late nineteenth century through the early twenty-first century. These contextual biographies draw on a number of conceptual frameworks, including social constructionism, neo-Gramscian, feminism, and postcolonialism, but they are united by care and critique, by sympathetic attention to indigenous athletes and critical accounts of social contexts.

The diverse readings and multiple perspectives presented in this book afford rich discussions of six overlapping themes:

1. the play of power and the power of play within the lives and careers of indigenous athletes

2. the contradictions and conditions of possibilities sport has offered American Indians

3. politics and poetics of identity

4. representations and stagings of Indianness in the context of sport

5. continuity and change

6. the lasting significance of indigenous athletes

The goal of *Native Athletes in Sport and Society* is not to single out a closed set of great athletes. Instead, it endeavors to collect individuals, experiences, and instances that represent and illuminate particular problems and broader themes. Consequently, the contributors examine the multiple roles indigenous athletes have played in American sports. They speak of superstars and fallen stars, of journeymen and amateurs, of coaches and other gatekeepers, of activists and tricksters. Moreover, legendary and unknown athletes stand side by side in the collection. Contextual accounts of individuals often celebrated for their greatness and prowess (like Jim Thorpe and Notah Begay) and locally important or even forgotten competitors combine to craft an intricate, forceful portrait of the American Indian sporting experience. This collection does not concentrate on individual athletes only but engages groups of athletes as well (the Oorang Indians of the National Football League, the Shiprock Cardinals, a Navajo women's basketball team, and the 1904 Fort Shaw Indian Boarding School girls basketball team).

Native Athletes in Sport and Society engages with, builds on, and goes beyond the existing literature on Native American athletes and athletics. No single volume or monograph has attended to the history and significance of indigenous athletes in North American sport and society. This is somewhat surprising given the popular interest in American Indian athletes, the importance of athletes and athletics to indigenous peoples, and the massive literature devoted to the experiences and importance of African American athletes.[6] To learn about American Indian athletes one must consult a number of sources that may be dated, scarce, and scattered. A request for readings on Native American athletes posted on H-AmIndian underscores this point. Respondents pointed not to a single classic monograph but to a series of articles, chapters, and books, some of which were as much as a century old and others that were in obscure sources.

Moreover, existing discussions of indigenous athletes tend to either focus narrowly on the athletes out of context, documenting and even celebrating individual lives, or stress social structures and cultural meanings, broadly interpreting athletics without fully attending to athletes. On the one hand, one can find passing mention of Native Americans in larger histories of individual sports, locate appreciations and analyses of a single player's life and career in both popular and scholarly sources, and even identify book-length biographies on legendary figures, particularly Jim Thorpe and Tom Longboat.[7] With few exceptions these do not address sociohistorical process with either adequacy or sophistication. On the other hand, within the anthropological literature, one encounters renderings of indigenous athletics of varying quality and detail that examine the means and meanings of traditional forms of play in Native America.[8] Here, context obscures the individual. *Native Athletes in Sport and Society* brings these perspectives together to offer "contextual biographies" that integrate critical sensibilities with (com)passionate hermeneutics to simultaneously analyze self *and* society.

In taking both culture and the individual seriously in the context of sport, this collection builds on a set of more dynamic approaches to indigenous athletes and athletics that has begun to emerge over the past quarter century. In 1979 Ward Churchill, Norbert Hill, and Mary Jo Barlow briefly reviewed the place of indigenous peoples in American sport—calling attention to the boarding school experience, racism, and identity—as the celebrated noteworthy athletes and all-Indian teams of the twentieth century.[9] Two years later Peter Nabokov reread the history and significance of Indian running, weaving together thick descriptions of past traditions with accounts of the role running has had in the maintenance and revival of indigenous cultures; throughout, he tells the stories of great runners.[10] A couple of years later Charles Ballem lamented the absence of the Native American athlete from sports history, illustrating the need for their presence through an examination of the career of Michael Thomas.[11] Against this background, Joseph Oxendine undertook the ambitious project of writing *American Indian Sports Heritage*. Oxendine not only describes the diversity, function, and meaning of sports in Native America, but he also devotes a large segment of the book to short sketches of renowned American Indian athletes.[12] Victoria Paraschak closed the remarkable decade with a critical assessment of the possibilities of Native sport history.[13]

These works share a respect for indigenous traditions and a concern for social change by providing broad ethnological and/or historical overviews and short biographical entries, resituating American Indians and sport. Still, in many respects, the indigenous athlete remains secondary to grand narratives. In contrast, this book argues for the primacy of indigenous peoples who have played, coached, and changed the games so fundamental to North American sporting cultures. The often appreciative tone characterizing many of the publications from the 1980s overwhelms more critical and complete attention to indigenous athletes and athleticism in context. They do not have the space or often take the time (let alone have the material needed) to flesh out the many and varied forces and processes shaping Native American engagements with American athletics or the complex and contradictory consequences of these engagements. Given the novelty of these works, this is not a surprise (and may have significance only in retrospect).

A second wave of scholarship during the late 1990s engaged the Native American sporting experience, adding greater theoretical sophistication and using a more focused critical lens. One of the hallmarks of this scholarship has been its close readings of lives and games within specific sociohistorical contexts structured by power and meaning and marked by struggles over and stagings of self and society. Attention to boarding schools, Indianness, and gender and its intersections with race, identity, and revitalization have energized the kind and quality of inquiry. Together they emphasize signs and signification, practice and process, culture and identity, power and resistance. The concerns and commitments of this approach energize this volume but do not delimit its discussion of the indigenous sporting experience in North America.[14]

Native Americans have always played sports, and although the games played varied from one region and people to the next, they included lacrosse and toli, shinny and snowsnake, running and wrestling, as well as snowshoe and canoeing. Unfortunately, little is known of the earliest indigenous athletes. Not until the nineteenth century does the Native American athlete begin to emerge, first in and through Euro-American accounts of indigenous societies and then, more important, in association with the rise of modern sport. In the 1830s George Catlin witnessed the play of Tullock-chish-ko (He Who Drinks the Juice of the Stone). He was so impressed that he described him as "the most distinguished ball-player in the Choctaw nation," and painted a full portrait of him in his game attire.[15] Unfortunately, as Oxendine observes, "There is no way of establishing just *how* great a player he was."[16] Other Euro-Americans made similar observations (which are equally difficult to verify) regarding runners like Big Hawk Chief (who reportedly ran a sub-four-minute mile) and of an unnamed Zuni (who ran a twenty-five-mile circuit in two hours).[17]

We do know how great other athletes were, namely those who participated in Euro-American athletic competitions. In the 1840s a number of Native Americans participated in the emerging sport of running. For instance, in 1844 Seneca John Steeprock attained notoriety for his participation in a footrace in Hoboken, New Jersey, that pitted more than thirty runners from a number of ethnic groups against one another. Even at this early date, the media played up Steeprock's Indianness, claiming "It was a trial of the Indian against the Whiteman on the point in which the Red man most boasts his superiority."[18] A decade later another Seneca, Louis "Deerfoot" Bennett (Hot-Tsa-So-Do-No), would begin competing in footraces in the northeast, and in the early 1860s he became a sensation on both sides of the Atlantic for his achievements as a runner.[19]

While the emergence of institutionalized athletic competitions in the United States and Canada opened up novel opportunities for some Native Americans in the first half of the nineteenth century, boarding schools would have a more lasting impact on indigenous participation in sport, public perceptions of American Indian athletes, and the creation of intercultural worlds. Sport fit nicely within the Euro-American program to assimilate indigenous peoples through education, to "kill the Indian and save the man." Consequently, indigenous games, contests, and traditional forms of play, like so much of Native life, were suppressed and replaced by forms deemed proper and civilized by Euro-American reformers. Physical education was a key component of boarding schools and later was supplemented by organized, interscholastic athletic competitions. In these varied forms, educators hoped to instill a competitive spirit, discipline, morality, and character. In time they would come to see sports as a powerful public relations tool as well. Although he was reluctant to do so initially, Richard Pratt, superintendent of Carlisle Industrial School, embraced the promise of sport. In a letter to Methodist bishop Charles C. McCabe in 1897 Pratt remarked, "Football players must be abstemious and moral in order to succeed. If it was in my power to bring every Indian into the game of football, to contend as my boys have contended with the different young men of the colleges, I would do it, and feel that I was doing them an act of the greatest Christian kindness, and elevating them from the hell of their home life and reservation degradation into paradise."[20] Pratt and his peers believed that Natives playing football would elevate public perceptions of Native Americans, easing the process of assimilation as it erode misconceptions and prejudices.

Athletics proved to be something other than a one-way street toward civilization. Indeed, as many scholars have noted, it offered Native Americans important occasions to express and define themselves, to have fun, and to resist the very regimes Euro-Americans sought to impose upon them. "Given the assimilationist aims of the BIA [Bureau of Indian Affairs] educational system," Alice Littlefield notes, "athletic prowess became a symbol of Indian identity and Indian pride."[21] Others, like Charles Eastman, recognized sport as an important means of racial uplift. In 1900 another progressive leader, Carlos Montezuma, championed football for its transformative potential:

What has made the Carlisle football team strong and famous? The answer is by playing strong and superior teams, and by being gentlemen. Carlisle boys would not even to doomsday have made the record they have, had they practiced among themselves exclusively or on a reservation. The necessary experience must come from without—from contact with the strongest teams. . . . The result speaks for itself. Instead of the Indian being endowed with qualifications of a savage nature that were particularly adapted to football, and that football is in itself a brutal game is absurd. The contrary has been proved by the record of the football team and is attested by every opponent Carlisle has had. All teams the Indians have contested with have one accord and without exception pronounced them gentlemen and praised their clean, manly playing.

Truly we are an "all-American" team. . . .

. . . In every contest there throbs in every heart a grand and noble motive — in every eye there glows a resolution—every nerve is strained to the highest with a determination to contradict misconceptions of centuries and to prove their worth to an end different from that generally accorded them—to prove themselves worthy of becoming true and noble citizens—though it must be done by use of the pigskin.

I can say without fear of contradiction that the Carlisle football team has done more to bring the possibilities of the Indian into public notice than have all other efforts combined.[22]

In sport all things were possible: acceptance, equality, improvement, morality, character, and more.

Now as then, not all Native Americans entered sport with assimilation, ethnic pride, or equality in mind. Many indigenous athletes had more practical concerns, more material motivations. In 1910 Charles "Chief" Bender told a Chicago journalist, "The reason I went into baseball as a professional was that when I left school [Dartmouth College], baseball offered me the best opportunity both for money and advancement that I could see. I adopted it because I played baseball better than I could do anything else, because the life and the game appealed to me and because there was so little racial prejudice in the game."[23]

Bender's assessment aside, racism and anti-Indianism have been central to dominant interpretations of Native American athletes, no less than the opportunities granted them. Churchill, Barlow, and Hill have argued that sports did not enhance public perceptions of Native Americans but merely reconfigured prevailing stereotypes.

The Native American within non-Indian mythology is (and has always been) an overwhelmingly physical creature . . . sport was and is an expedient means of processing this physicality into a "socially acceptable" package without disrupting the mythology; Indians tracked as "Indians" into the mainstream. There could be but one result of such manipulation: dehumanization of the Native Americans directly involved and, by extension, dehumanization of the nonparticipating Native Americans who the athletes represented in the public consciousness. Thus the myth of the American savage was updated, but essentially unchanged.[24]

The media, initially print journalism and later radio and television, have perpetuated an array of damaging racial stereotypes and anti-Indian stories, including exaggerated attention to physicality, projections of savagery, the ever-present nickname Chief, narratives centered on death, deprivation, and desolation, and well-worn clichés about drinking, excesses, laziness, lack of discipline, and unwillingness to train.[25] These images in turn shaped public perceptions. According to Cherokee baseball player Rudy York, "All an Indian's got to do is be seen drinking a beer and he's drunk. Any time an Indian puts on a baseball uniform he becomes about six times as much of a character as any other player."[26] Moreover, fans often shouted racial epithets, did war whoops, and engaged in other racist antics. At the same time, they increasingly incorporated Indian imagery into sports, choosing team names, logos, and mascots that played off of popular (mis)understandings of Indians and Indianness.[27]

During the early twentieth century games became intercultural conflicts and racial dramas, replaying and reworking historical struggles. Beginning at least with runner John Steeprock, this meant that competitions involving Indian athletes or all-Indian teams fostered narratives filled with racial tension and deliberations on racial superiority, Manifest Destiny, and civilization. It also encouraged Native Americans to conform to popular stereotypes on and off the field and enact scenes familiar from world's fairs and Wild West shows. The Oorang Indians of the National Football League (discussed in detail by Springwood) offer a telling example of this pattern. At the same time, as Bloom notes, athletics opened a space in which Native Americans could extract symbolic revenge. Within boarding schools, "competing against other tribes . . . for the same position on a team . . . you beat out people from, from, um, Standing Rock or Turtle Mountain or . . . trying to get the same position you're after . . . to play and beat white teams was even a higher achievement."[28]

Indigenous athletes have always had great meaning for Native Americans as well. During the course of his research into the life of Mose YellowHorse, Todd Fuller learned of the pleasures of memory and the importance of play in one Native nation:

Over the course of more than a decade . . . I have encountered numerous people, both young and old, who smiled when they shared their YellowHorse stories with me. Given this, I realized that I was extremely fortunate to be learning about a man who seemed to make so many people happy. And as I gathered newspaper stories [and] box scores . . . as I listened to and read stories about his professional and personal feats, I realized that YellowHorse kept his dignity intact as he crossed boundaries to play in major league baseball—the most sacred of (white) American games.[29]

Over the course of the twentieth century, then, indigenous athletes have fostered ethnic identity and pride, served as role models, and evoked great joy and happiness.

Increasingly after 1930, Native American athletes began to fade from American public culture. Oxendine points to six features that contributed to the diminishing presence of indigenous athletes:

1. the closing of the Carlisle school
2. the scarcity of other Indian institutions of higher education
3. the poor quality of reservation and local schools
4. a resistance on the part of many Indians to be assimilated into non-Indian society and non-Indian sports
5. passage of laws that prevented Indians from entering all-white colleges
6. a multitude of social conditions both on and off the reservation[30]

Philip Deloria adds to this list shifts within federal policy and associated public perceptions of American Indians. In particular he underscores the importance of World War II and the termination of efforts to abrogate rights, responsibilities, and relationships between the federal government and recognized tribes and to foster civic equality.[31] Moreover, the emergence of the civil rights movement and the narrowing of race relations to questions of black and white eclipsed the "Indian problem" and its significance for most Americans.

Today Native American athletes are less visible than they were a century ago, but they continue to make noteworthy contributions to sports at all levels. Hidden from public view and too often outside of popular discourse, Native Americans have continued to reinvent sport and society. On the one hand they continue to play an array of traditional games, including lacrosse (Iroquois Nationals and Ojibwe Nationals), shinny (there are leagues among the Tohono O'odham), and snowsnake (played among the Cree). On the other hand Native Americans have incorporated Euro-American models and events, creating organization like Wings Across America and the Native American Sports Council, and establishing novel competitions like the Northern Games and the World Eskimo Olympics.

For more than a century, then, as Deloria suggests, to many Native Americans sports have "represented a complex mix of mimetic performance, metaphoric revenge, cultural acceptance, pan-tribal unity, financial windfall, and educational opportunity, but it was not the stuff of life and death."[32] In what follows, the contributors to *Native Athletes in Sport and Society* embrace the multiple meanings, complex relations, and contradictory qualities of athletes and athletics seriously as they explore the lives and careers of indigenous athletes.

In many ways Native American athletes remain invisible. Persistent racial stereotypes and entrenched social structures continue to marginalize indigenous peoples within and beyond the world of sports. As a consequence, the public does not know about, understand, or value them; coaches often refuse to recognize or recruit them; and the mainstream media rarely cover them. Even scholars have neglected American Indian athletes and athletics, perhaps because sports are often thought to be frivolous, disconnected from more important issues like policy, economics, land use, spirituality, and treaty rights, or because sport has been defined as Euro-American domain, or because many researchers and authors are not aware of the rich heritage and lasting contributions of indigenous peoples and communities.

Even when Native American athletes become the subject of public discussion, they too often get lost in Euro-American preoccupations and values. A recent *New York Times* article nicely illustrates this pervasive pattern and its import. In June 2001 Selena Roberts reported on Native American athletes, focusing primarily on the obstacles that prevent them from excelling in elite college and professional sports: prejudice and misunderstanding, lack of opportunity, coaches who are unwilling to recruit athletes from reservations, the isolation of reservation communities, athletes' attachment to family and community, the suppression of individualism, jealousy and conflict within indigenous communities, and inability to adjust to white institutions and expectations. As a result, "Only 310 American Indians were among the 70,856 college athletes in Division I who received athletic aid in the 1998–1999 school year. . . . While American Indians make up about 1 percent of the country's population, according to the 2000 census, they account for only four-tenths of a percent of the scholarship athletes at the major college level." Roberts notes that with the exception of Jim Thorpe, Billy Mills, and Notah Begay, "Native American athletes have not made the leap to the highest level of American sport."[33]

Roberts is right to direct attention to the negligible presence of Native Americans in sports. Indeed, the virtual absence of American Indian athletes and the overabundance of American Indian imagery (mascots, logos, and team names) in sports highlights the signs and structures animating race relations in the United States. However, her reporting obscures rather than clarifies the extent of Native American athletes' success in sports. Like many journalists and much of the public, Roberts has a limited knowledge of the many Native Americans who have participated and excelled in sports at the intercollegiate, professional, and international levels. Although Roberts identified a mere three Native athletes, there are more than two hundred indigenous athletes who have competed at the highest levels over the past century.[34] Moreover, Roberts seems to suggest that only athletes who become famous or nationally known matter, neglecting in the process the numerous local contexts in which Native Americans play sports and what that participation means to the athletes and their communities. Here, too, as Philip Deloria reminds us, Roberts falls into a familiar pattern: "When considering Indian athletes, it is easy to slide into the 'heroic' mode, focusing on Jim Thorpe and perhaps a few other outstanding individuals—'Chief' Bender, Hopi Olympic medallist Louis Tewanima, or William 'Lone Star' Dietz, who head-coached football teams at Purdue and Louisiana Tech as well as the NFL Boston Redskins. But more obscure gridirons and dugouts all across America were also peppered with Indian athletes and coaches."[35]

Why should the significance of Indian athletes be defined in Euro-American contexts exclusively through mainstream measures of success? Finally, Roberts quietly reiterate the classic lament, "Lo, the poor Indian," as she confines indigenous athletes (and indigenous peoples more generally) within stories of tragedy (missed opportunities, premature deaths, unfulfilled dreams) and descriptions of desolation and disadvantage (the reservation and its social problems). In effect, as John Bloom underscores in a discussion of media accounts of Native Americans and sports, "problems on contemporary reservations are framed not as the outcome of historical events or political interests and power but as cultural deficiencies of Native Americans. . . . Native American cultures are portrayed as mired in a history of declension and death . . . and inept at dealing with modern institutions and social realities."[36] Thus, although Roberts covers an extremely important issue, her coverage simultaneously makes Native Americans visible and invisible, discernible through familiar clichés yet effaced by commonsense categories and dominant definitions.

This book strives to make individuals and experiences that are too often invisible visible. It takes up forgotten subjects, including women, racial spectacle, local sports worlds, all-Indian competitions, struggles over Indianness, and the politics of memory. Striving to correct stereotypes, the contributors all offer fuller, more human interpretations. In part this means that they emphasize elements of the Native American sporting experience rarely acknowledged: the pleasures of play, the thrill of competition, the importance of winning, the capacity to make aspects of Euro-American culture Native, the pervasiveness of anti-Indianism, and the centrality of sport to individual and collective identities. Although composed of a series of complex and sensitive portraits, it swerves away from heroic and celebratory narratives. Moreover, many of the contributors foreground gender; several of the essays record the lives of indigenous women in sport. As such they highlight careers and experiences rarely discussed, remembered, or studied. Doubly eclipsed within sport and society, the lives of Native American women athletes encourage reflections on the manner in which ideas about women and femininity shape the play and interpretation of sport among indigenous people. In their contributions, Vicky Paraschak and Ellen Staurowsky push beyond gender as an axis of analysis to interrogate the ways in which race and gender systematically structure the sporting worlds in which women participate as well as the manner in which a broader public responds to them.

In making the marginal, forgotten, and unseen lives of Native American athletes central, memorable, and vital, *Native Athletes in Sport and Society* pushes beyond the limits of the popular. That is, not only does it counter the lingering hold of anti-Indian racism, but it also responds to and challenges the recent return of the indigenous athlete in the popular imagination. During the past few years three memoirs devoted in whole or in part to athletes in Indian Country have enjoyed considerable success: in *A Season on the Reservation*, Kareem Abdul-Jabbar discusses his tenure as a coach of a reservation basketball team; in his controversial *On the Rez*, Ian Frazier dwells on the life and death of SuAnne Big Crow, a Lakota basketball player; and in *Counting Coup*, Larry Colton explores the place of basketball on the Crow Reservation. All of these works offer intimate portraits of athletes and Indianness.[37] Unfortunately they all share three limitations.

First, they all offer accounts perhaps best described as self-involved, even self-indulgent. That is, they foster rapport with readers and garner authority in and through their agendas and experiences. What they do, encounter, think, and feel is as important—and often more important—than what the supposed subjects of their narratives (Native American athletes) do, encounter, think, and feel.

Second, they all fail to adequately contextualize or ground their narratives. Interior or local perspectives are lacking, arguably because the focus is often on the authors. Attention to and incorporation of indigenous models, values, and understandings would have completely reconfigured these texts. Moreover, they do not adequately situate their stories in broader social or historical contexts.

Third, they fall back on popular clichés and ethnocentric bias to render the indigenous sporting experience tangible and meaningful to a largely white audience. Abdul-Jabbar even invokes a series of troubling stereotypes in his account. For instance, he attributes the play of the team he coached to their ethnic heritage: "The Falcons were carrying on a long tradition of running from things that were chasing them or standing in their way. There were legendary stories from the Apache past of their warriors being pursued by enemies and simply riding their horses to death."[38] He describes his players as if they were historic vestiges of a warrior society: "Sometimes I would glance his way and imagine him sitting astride a painted pony two hundred years earlier, ready to ride off into the mountains and hunt."[39]

The essays that follow refuse such easy generalizations, documenting their connections with earlier visions of Indians in sport while challenging their anti-Indianism. The contributors to this volume seek to understand sport through the perspectives, frameworks, and voices of indigenous peoples. Moreover, they examine lives in context and foreground athletes and their experiences against those of researchers and other authors. Finally, they question and critique pervasive popular (mis)conceptions about Indians and Indianness in athletics and beyond. They refuse the comforts of stereotypic thinking for the sake of a good story, opting instead to unpack the place of prejudice and preconceptions in the lives and careers of indigenous athletes.

Native Athletes in Sport and Society offers a fuller understanding of indigenous athletes that is both critical and compassionate. The contributors examine the conditions and consequences of play, the means and meanings of participation, and the lives and legacies of players. Organized chronologically, beginning in the late nineteenth century, the book explores changing ideas, opportunities, and identities over time, as well as persistent patterns and percepts. To be sure, as in all such collective endeavors, the contributors speak with many voices about an array of subjects; however, as I wish to underscore briefly, their efforts converge around a set of fundamental concerns: identity and objectification, power and resistance, racism and sexism, play and remembrance, achievement and its telling.

Gerald Gems opens the collection with a broad discussion of the structured opportunities and expressions of indigenous athletes. Emphasizing the golden age of sport associated with off-reservation boarding schools, he scrutinizes the ways in which Native Americans worked through and against assimilationist paradigms to re-create and reclaim themselves. Resistance, negotiation, and playfulness, Gems rightly suggests, anchored indigenous efforts to know and be themselves in sporting worlds. Consequently, he seizes upon the trickster as a metaphor to talk about Indian athletes and their actions.

Against this background, Daniel Barr renders a poignant portrait of legendary Cleveland baseball player Louis Sockalexis. Like Gems, he documents the social institutions, particularly the media and the franchise, and the cultural misconceptions, namely racism, that shaped Sockalexis's participation in sport and, in turn, the public's reception of him then and now. He does not, however, seek the trickster but the man obscured by popular myths. After detailing Sockalexis's life and career, as well as the broader sociohistorical context, Barr notes that both the enshrinement of the ballplayer by the Cleveland baseball franchise as the source of the team name and ongoing efforts to undermine the veracity of this claim efface Sockalexis and warp his memory.

Whereas Barr rightly laments the abuse of Sockalexis's legacy by largely Euro-American individuals and institutions, Linda Peavy and Ursula Smith salvage an often forgotten moment of indigenous athletic history, demonstrating how members of the 1904 Fort Shaw girls' basketball team and their descendants have used sport for their own ends. Returning to boarding schools, and broader projects and racial politics of assimilation, they follow the young indigenous women as they travel to the 1904 world's fair in St. Louis, where they ultimately won the world championship. Integrating primary sources and the recollections of descendants, they weave a nuanced tapestry that details the oppressive structures of everyday life in which the young women learned and played while giving life to the indigenous players as fully human social agents who find in a sport a means to define themselves and succeed against great odds.

In his account of the life and career of baseball player George Howard Johnson, Jeffrey Powers-Beck takes up many of the same themes, exploring the paradoxical opportunities available to Native Americans by sport during the first quarter of the twentieth century. Powers-Beck argues that in baseball Johnson found a medium in which to make his life better and through which to assert his identity as an American Indian. Even as he sought to claim a measure of dignity, baseball also reflected the formulaic understandings of Indianness and the dead ends of modernity.

Shifting the conversation fully from opportunity to identity, William Bauer thinks about how individuals and institutions interpreted the racial heritage of Tommy Yarr. A standout center at Notre Dame University, Yarr was an Irish Indian—a mixed-blood, biracial and bicultural. Bauer teases out the categorization and racialization of Yarr: initially marked as biracial, he has been remembered almost exclusively as Indian. Bauer concludes that the fluid interpretations of Yarr's ancestry and identity reflect the changing shape of race and racial stratification in the United States.

Building on the previous discussions of the spectacle of Indianness in the early twentieth century, Charles Fruehling Springwood offers a history of the Oorang Indians. An all-Indian team and early National Football League franchise, the Oorang Indians featured athletic greats like Peter Calac, Joe Guyon, and Jim Thorpe. He focuses not only on the halftime performances and media coverage that accentuated prevailing stereotypes about Indians but also on the ways in which the players themselves manipulated and challenged them. In looking at the multiple intersections of culture and power, he clarifies how sport fostered the creation of opportunities and identities for both Euro-Americans and Native Americans.

Ann Cummins collaborates with two former members of the Shiprock Cardinals, Cecilia Anderson and Georgia Briggs, to record the history and significance of the women's baseball team. They tell a multivoiced story rooted in an oral retelling. Their account works against the synthetic desires of anthropological or historical analysis. Instead the authors provide a fragment from a much larger story that gives life to sport as a background for the formation of relationships, for travels and dreams, for winning and playing. In the process they challenge ideas about how and why indigenous people play modern sport, emphasizing the complex institutional context and intimate interpersonal motivations.

Vicky Paraschak centers her analysis on the articulations of race and gender. She is particularly interested in understanding the marginalization of Native American women athletes. Concentrating on the Six Nations Reserve in Ontario between 1968 and 1980, she argues that while indigenous women actively participated in a variety of sports and received local media coverage, biases in national media in bestowing athletic awards, and in scholarship have erased the presence and significance of Native American women in sports.

Like Paraschak, Ellen Staurowsky explores the tensions between local and national sporting worlds, emphasizing the centrality of race and gender to how individuals and institutions interpret the participation of women and girls in sports. She works through these issues by recounting the life of Lakota basketball player SuAnne Big Crow, a high school standout who died at a young age. Staurowsky ably demonstrates the influence of racialized and sexualized social hierarchies on Big Crow's participation in sport and, in turn, how she was understood. Staurowsky argues that the collective memory of Big Crow as a hero by the Lakota affirms their history and culture, precisely as it rejects the values of mainstream society.

C. Richard King explores the significance of Notah Begay. He is particularly interested in determining how audiences and authors make the Navajo golfer meaningful. He attends to Begay's successes and failures, his celebrity, and his efforts to be a role model to clarify expressions of identity, difference, and character in post–civil rights America.

Detailing Grace Thorpe's efforts to have her father, Jim Thorpe, named the greatest athlete of the twentieth century, John Bloom returns to the themes of racial hierarchy, identity, and collective memory. Her campaign, Bloom argues, has little to do with vanity or ranking talent. Instead, it has everything to do with what it means to be Indian in the contemporary United States, the legacies of American imperialism, challenging misrepresentations, and the resurgence of indigenous political resistance over the past half century. Thorpe's campaign may be the penultimate expression of the entanglements of power, Indianness, and repossession found throughout the volume.

A brief epilogue by C. Richard King closes the volume. It simultaneously summarizes the volume and outlines promising new avenues for scholarship.

Notes

1. Charles Eastman, *The Indian To-day: The Past and Future of the First American* (Garden City NY: Doubleday, 1915), 129–30.

2. Lawrence S. Ritter, *The Glory of Their Times: The Story of the Early Days of Baseball Told by the Men Who Played It*, enlarged ed. (New York: William Morrow, 1984), 172.

3. Ritter, *The Glory of Their Times*, 183–84.

4. Quoted in Thomas Vennum, Jr., *American Indian Lacrosse: Little Brother of War* (Washington DC: Smithsonian Institution Press, 1994), 110.

5. Vennum, *American Indian Lacrosse*, 294.

6. On popular interest in Indian athletes, see Michael Oriard, *Reading Football: How the Popular Press Created an American Spectacle* (Chapel Hill: University of North Carolina Press, 1993), 229–47; Jeff Powers-Beck, "Chief: The Indi-gration of Baseball, 1897–1945," *American Indian Quarterly* 25:4 (2001): 508–38. On the importance of athletes, see Philip Deloria, "'I Am of the Body': Thoughts on My Grandfather, Culture, and Sports," *South Atlantic Quarterly* 95:2 (1996): 321–38. On African American athletes, see, for example, Arthur Ashe, *A Hard Road to Glory: A History of the African American Athlete* (New York: Warner Books, 1988); Ocania Chalk, *Pioneers of Black Sport: The Early Days of the Black Professional Athlete in Baseball, Basketball, Boxing, and Football* (New York: Dodd and Mead, 1975); and David K. Wiggins, *Glory Bound: Black Athletes in White America* (Syracuse NY: Syracuse University Press, 1997).

7. See, for example, Bill Gilbert, "Big Hawk Chief, a Pawnee Runner," *American West* 21:4 (1984): 36–38; William Jakub, "Moses YellowHorse: The Tragic Career of a Pittsburgh Pirate," *Pittsburgh History* 79 (1995/1996): 186–89; Max J. Nichols, "Super Chief, Humble Man: The Life of Allie P. Reynolds," *Chronicles of Oklahoma* 73:1 (1995): 4–31. Book-length studies include Bruce Kidd, *Tom*

Longboat (Don Mills, Ontario: Fitzhenry and Whiteside, 1980); and Robert W. Wheeler, *Jim Thorpe: World's Greatest Athlete* (Norman: University of Oklahoma Press, 1979).

8. See, for example, Alyce Taylor Cheska, "Gender Variations in Game Attraction Factors of Native American Youth," in *Studies in the Sociology of Sport*, ed. Aidan O. Dunleavy, Andrew W. Miracle, and C. Roger Rees (Ft. Worth: TCU Press), 29–49; J. R. Fox, "Pueblo Baseball: A New Use for Old Witchcraft," *American Journal of Folklore* 74 (1961): 9–16; James Mooney, "Cherokee Ball Play," *American Anthropologist* 3:2 (1890): 105–32; Morris Edward Opler, "The Jicarilla Apache Ceremonial Relay Race," *American Anthropologist* 46 (1944): 75–97.

9. Ward Churchill, Norbert Hill, and Mary Jo Barlow, "An Historical Overview of Twentieth-Century Native American Athletics," *The Indian Historian* 12:4 (1979): 22–32.

10. Peter Nabokov, *Indian Running: Native American History and Tradition* (Santa Fe: Ancient City Press, 1981).

11. Charles Ballem, "Missing from the Canadian Sport Scene: Native Athletes," *Canadian Journal of History of Sport* 14:2 (1983): 33–43.

12. Joseph Oxendine, *American Indian Sports Heritage*, 2nd ed. (Lincoln: University of Nebraska Press, 1995).

13. Victoria Paraschak, "Native Sport History: Pitfalls and Promise," *Canadian Journal of History of Sport* 20:1 (1989): 57–68.

14. See John Bloom, *To Show What an Indian Can Do: Athletics and Indian Boarding Schools* (Minneapolis: University of Minnesota Press, 2001); Deloria, "'I Am of the Body'"; Gerald R. Gems, "The Construction, Negotiation, and Transformation of Racial Identity in American Football: A Study of Native and African Americans," *American Indian Culture and Research Journal* 22:2 (1998): 131–50; C. Richard King and Charles F. Springwood, "Playing Indian, Power, and Racial Identity in American Sport: Gerald R. Gems's 'The Construction, Negotiation, and Transformation of Racial Identity in American Football,'" *American Indian Culture and Research Journal* 23:2 (1999): 127–32; Victoria Paraschak, "Variations in Race Relations: Sporting Events for Native Peoples in Canada," *Sociology of Sport Journal* 14 (1997): 1–21.

15. George Catlin, *North American Indians* (1841; reprint, Edinburgh: John Grant, 1944), 2:142.

16. Oxendine, *American Indian Sports Heritage*, 240, emphasis original.

17. Gilbert, "Big Hawk Chief."

18. Oxendine, *American Indian Sports Heritage*, 162.

19. Oxendine, *American Indian Sports Heritage*, 163.

20. Quoted in Bloom, *To Show What an Indian Can Do*, 1.

21. Alice Littlefield, "The BIA Boarding School: Theories of Resistance and Social Reproduction," *Humanity and Society* 13:4 (1989): 438.

22. Carlos Montezuma, "Football as an Indian Educator," *The Red Man*, January 1900, p. 8.

23. Quoted in Steven A. Riess, "Race and Ethnicity in American Baseball: 1900–1919," *Journal of Ethnic Studies* 4:4 (1977): 48.

24. Churchill, Hill, and Barlow, "Historical Overview of 20th Century Native American Athletics," 31.

25. See Bloom, *To Show What an Indian Can Do*; Deloria, "'I Am of the Body,'"; Oriard, *Reading Football*; Powers-Beck, "Chief."

26. Rudy York, "A Letter to My Son," in *The Fireside Book of Baseball*, ed. Charles Einstein (New York: Simon and Schuster, 1956), 385.

27. See Laurel Davis, "Protest against the Use of Native American Mascots: A Challenge to Traditional, American Identity," *Journal of Sport and Social Issues* 17:1 (1993): 9–22; C. Richard King and Charles F. Springwood, eds., *Team Spirits: The Native American Mascot Controversy* (Lincoln: University of Nebraska Press, 2001); Cornel D. Pewewardy, "Native American Mascots and Imagery: The Struggle of Unlearning Indian Stereotypes," *Journal of Navaho Education* 9:1 (1991): 19–23; and Ellen J. Staurowsky, "An Act of Honor or Exploitation? The Cleveland Indians' Use of the Louis Francis Sockalexis Story," *Sociology of Sport Journal* 15:4 (1998): 299–316.

28. Bloom, *To Show What an Indian Can Do*, 54.

29. Todd Fuller, *60 Feet, 6 Inches, and Other Distances from Home: The (Baseball) Life of Mose YellowHorse* (Duluth: Holy Cow Press, 2002), 20.

30. Oxendine, *American Indian Sports Heritage*, xxi.

31. Deloria, "'I Am of the Body.'"

32. Deloria, "'I Am of the Body,'" 334.

33. Selena Roberts, "Off-Field Hurdles Stymie Indian Athletes," *New York Times*, 17 June 2001, p. 1.

34. Oxendine, *American Indian Sports Heritage*; C. Richard King, *Native Americans in Sport*, 2 vols. (Armonk NY: M. E. Sharpe, 2004).

35. Deloria, "'I Am of the Body,'" 330.

36. Bloom, *To Show What an Indian Can Do*, 126.

37. Kareem Abdul-Jabbar, *A Season on the Reservation: My Sojourn with the White Mountain Apache* (New York: William Morrow, 2000); Larry Colton, *Counting Coup: A True Story of Basketball and Honor on the Little Big Horn* (New York: Warner Books, 2000); and Ian Frazier, *On the Rez* (New York: Farrar, Straus, and Giroux, 2000).

38. Abdul-Jabbar, *A Season on the Reservation*, 41.

39. Abdul-Jabbar, *A Season on the Reservation*, 66.

Native Athletes
in Sport &
Society

1. Negotiating a Native American Identity through Sport

Assimilation, Adaptation, and the Role of the Trickster

No one lost that night. A statement was made. "We're Indians. Respect us. Respect us for who we are."—Stuart Desjarlait, 1995

In the quote above Stuart Desjarlait, the brother of the Red Lake High School basketball coach, is referring to the team's 117–113 overtime loss in the semifinals of the Minnesota state tournament. It marked the first time that a team composed entirely of Native Americans reached that level in interscholastic competition, and they drew thousands of followers to the gymnasium from all over the Midwest. The arena harbored more than an athletic event, and Desjarlait's words signified one victory in a centuries-long struggle. Despite the loss, the team's heroic efforts won the respect of their all-white opponents and their fans. The crowd gave the Red Lake team a standing ovation, while the victors embraced the Red Lake players, finally recognizing their value not only as athletes but also as human beings.[1]

Native Americans have long used sport as a means to achieve a sense of pride, self-esteem, and respect, but not always in ways easily distinguished by whites. They had long endured humiliation at the hands of whites, including conquest, subjugation, and virtual extinction. By the late nineteenth century, racialization and its justification had assumed the cloak of science as social Darwinism. Europeans and North Americans thus established a racial hierarchy based on physical characteristics including skin color, perceived mental abilities, and ascribed levels of modernity and civilization. The white media portrayed the Native population as brutal savages bereft of worth, often demonizing them as inferior, primitive versions of cultivated Anglos.[2]

Confronting such faulty characterizations, Native peoples tried to retain their pride, self-esteem, and cultural values, which they believed were morally superior to those of the greedy and aggressive white society. Native Americans often rewrote such depictions in their own minds, preferring an alternative perception of race and culture. The Pueblo tale titled "The Well-Baked Man," for example, explains racial differences via the trickster Coyote, who removes white men from God's oven before they become fully baked, creating an inferior product.[3]

The trickster proved to be not only a means of rationalization for Native Americans but a pragmatic coping device to gain self-aggrandizement by reckoning with the dominant culture in ways more important and meaningful than were apparent to whites' eyes. As white society intruded and imposed itself on the Native population, the trickster allowed for more subtle resistance and the renegotiation of power relationships as identities were being reconstructed.

The Anglos commonly employed force or coercion to achieve their aims. Under the guise of the more benevolent perspective of the social gospel, conquerors took on the "white man's burden" of educating, Christianizing, and civilizing the conquered. In the United States the process of cultural assimilation began with the forced relocation of tribes to allotted lands or reservations, the imposition of agricultural or vocational lifestyles at the expense of nomadic or traditional ones, and institutionalized education. The latter took on great significance for Native American children with the founding of the Carlisle Industrial School for Indians in 1879. A residential school in Pennsylvania, Carlisle housed Native Americans from seventy different tribes from across the country under government surveillance and tutelage. The perceived success of its assimilation efforts spawned another twenty-five government schools over the next two decades.[4]

Such schools posed particular problems for students bereft of their familiar environment, culture, and tribal and family support. Grouped and classified homogeneously as "Indians," they struggled to maintain their tribal identities. For some the collision of cultures on the frontier had produced mixed identities that intermingled race, religion, and ethnicity. Carlisle's most famous resident, Jim Thorpe, serves as an example. Born in 1887 on Native American land in Oklahoma to an Irish American father and a Sac and Fox mother, Thorpe was baptized a Catholic. On numerous occasions Thorpe fled each of the three residential schools to which he had been sent for the solace and more traditional lifestyle that he coveted in Oklahoma.[5]

Though a "half-breed" significantly influenced by his father, Thorpe chose an Indian identity. Thorpe relinquished his Indian name, Wa-tho-huck (Bright Path), at the mission school, but he relished the rumor of his mythical ancestral relationship to Black Hawk, the great Sac warrior who retaliated against repeated white incursions on Native land in the Black Hawk War of 1832. Like his hero, Thorpe lost his battle with whites and never gained a full measure of self-determination.

Native Americans had few choices in the late nineteenth century. They could accept white culture, adopting its language, clothing, lifestyles, norms, and values as the Cherokee nation did, only to be betrayed and have their lands taken. An estimated four thousand Cherokees, one-fourth of the tribe, died on the eight-hundred-mile forced march to Oklahoma in 1838. Others rejected white impositions, retaining a semblance of traditional lifestyles on allotted spaces, suffering governmental impositions, and mourning the gradual and inevitable loss of Native culture. Most—especially those like Thorpe who were forced to attend government schools—eventually chose to adapt white culture to their own values. Such a choice required living in two worlds and often being subjected emotionally and intellectually to an ascribed inferiority and the "superiority" of the dominant white culture. Light-skinned Anglo phenotypes might even choose to masquerade as white, living a surreptitious life.[6]

Native American athletes in particular lived within two worlds, bridging both cultures and adopting or adapting the dominant norms when necessary or beneficial. Because commercialized sporting events most often took place in urban settings, athletes experienced a broader exposure to the white world than did those who remained on reservations or were restricted to school campuses. They learned the white ways, logically and practically applying Anglo practices when necessary to gain a measure of acceptance and adapting others to promote residual and traditional Native values.

The athletic field proved particularly useful as a contested space in the collision of cultures. Most Native Americans were familiar with running and territorial games from their indigenous cultures and easily adapted to the "American" sports of track and field, baseball, football, and basketball, sports designed to foster teamwork, cooperation, and self-sacrifice. Such activities and values held some transfer with Natives' own principles and practices. Moreover, Native games had also served as surrogates or training for warfare, and the "Americanized" Native athletes found in sports the means to effect retaliatory measures when the U.S. government banned Native pastimes. For example, the Sauk and Fox tribe favored games that required speed, body contact, strength, and daring, and Thorpe used all of these to punish would-be tacklers on the football field. Such adaptations helped maintain some traditional values as well as the rearticulation of power relationships by both overt and subtle means.[7]

Athletes also found practical benefits in sport not usually accorded to nonathletes. Intent on showing the success of his assimilation efforts, Richard Henry Pratt, superintendent of the Carlisle school, often allowed athletic events and their requisite travel to supersede schoolwork. Athletes found such trips a welcome respite from the strict regimen of institutional life. Football players at Carlisle traveled first class, and on campus they had their own residence hall complete with a pool table and music box. Athletes enjoyed better food at their own training table and had the privilege of ordering suits at the local haberdashery, paid for from the athletic fund. Athletic director and football coach Glenn "Pop" Warner even subsidized his best athletes with cash. As Carlisle athletes gained national exposure they found additional lucrative offers during the summer months as professional baseball players on semi-pro and town teams. Normally, Carlisle students participated in the summer "outing" program that indentured them to farm families or craftsmen. While the school garnered $30,000 a year from the summer work and the manual training shops earned $100,000 annually, the students received only $10 a month for their work, and some reported being paid much less. The school administration rationalized the system as "a chance [for the students] to earn their keep . . . and [it] afforded them the advantage of white home life."[8] A white teacher

4

at the school claimed that it "permitted them to absorb civilization by actually living with it."[9]

By 1907 the athletic fund at Carlisle had registered more than $50,000 in profits, and athletes on urban ventures were entertained accordingly. Coach Warner paid out $9,283 in such expenses. He also paid tutoring fees for one athlete who wished to enter nearby Dickinson Law School and upgraded the facilities for all students lest the athletes' privileges breed resentment. But Warner's charges learned white ways and the commercial benefits too well, and they turned the tables on their teacher. Louis Leroy, a talented pitcher on the baseball team, ran away to join a professional team. Warner discovered him masquerading as an Italian and returned him to Carlisle, but Leroy persisted and played for the New York entry in the American League in 1905 and 1906. So many athletes fled the school for the more lucrative professional leagues that Warner decided to drop the baseball program in 1910, fearing that he would be unable to field the more famous and profitable football team.[10]

Native American athletes recognized the power of their bodies and the value of their physical skills and bargained accordingly. Normally a driven, unrelenting, and abusive coach, Warner had to make some concessions. Using their own coaches when Warner temporarily left the school, the 1906 football team drew large crowds en route to a 9–2 season that included a defeat of the University of Minnesota, the western champs at Minneapolis, and a No. 5 national ranking. Carlisle linemen chose to use their Indian names in 1907, a measure of their Native American pride and perhaps a marketing ploy that highlighted their status as "others" and increased gate receipts. The University of Chicago, which had foregone a game with Carlisle in 1900 because a loss might "jeopardize chances for (the) western championship," opted for commercial gain in 1907 with an offer of $17,000 to play Carlisle. Chicago paid on the field as well, losing 18–4. That year Carlisle also defeated perennial power Harvard University before a crowd of 30,000 and garnered a 10–1 record.[11]

Native American games had sometimes served as surrogate forms of war, relieving cultural stress within and among tribes. Athletes forced to operate within a white world soon adapted the psychology to their own circumstances. Pop Warner admitted that, contrary to the Carlisle spirit, players viewed athletic contests as racial confrontations, and he incited their racial pride and vengeance. Newspapers portrayed football games as frontier conflicts. In 1914 one Haskell Indian Institute player wrote home that he was at "hard practice for war . . . mobilizing our troops . . . trained and equipped for the coming campaign."[12]

When Carlisle appeared at Dickinson for a 1905 contest, the hosts' pregame festivities included a cowboy scalping a mock Indian. Carlisle retaliated with its own Dickinson dummy in a football uniform, filling its chest with an arrow after each score in a 36–0 rout. The Native Americans took especial pleasure in defeating Army, the symbol of the governmental military might that had subdued and killed their ancestral brethren. A Carlisle historian asserted that "Redskins play football as if they are possessed" when encountering Army teams; indeed, the Native Americans lost only once to the West Point team, and that was in 1917 when the football team no longer enjoyed prominence and federal authorities were about to close the school.[13]

Before a game in 1912 against Army, Warner allegedly told his players, "These are the Long Knives. You are Indians. Tonight we will know whether or not you are warriors." Carlisle won 22–6. Retaliation tasted even sweeter when the whites were beaten at their own game. The "warriors" represented at least ten different tribes, and they led the nation in scoring with 504 points. Jim Thorpe scored twenty-five touchdowns and won election to the All-American team as Carlisle finished the season with a 12–1–1 record.[14]

Carlisle football players, like their baseball counterparts, found ready employment on the burgeoning professional circuit and as coaches. Green Bay reportedly paid Tom Skenandore of the Oneida tribe for his services as early as 1896. By 1902 at least two current and two former Carlisle players, including assistant coach Bemus Pierce, a Seneca Indian, earned additional income as pros. Many more learned to negotiate such opportunities and benefits in the white world. Those who left to participate on the renegade professional circuits in baseball and football must have felt a sense of fidelity with ancestors who resisted the restrictions of reservation life.[15]

Some gained greater acceptance as coaches and managed a greater level of dignity by assimilating to white standards and professions. Frank Mt. Pleasant, a Carlisle quarterback and Olympic athlete, later won high honors at Dickinson College and coached at Franklin and Marshall. He also served as an officer in France during World War I. Bemus Pierce, Carlisle's greatest lineman and three-time team captain, coached at his alma mater, as well as the University of Buffalo, Kenyon College, and Haskell Indian Institute before turning to farming in his native New York. He resumed sports responsibilities as athletic director of the Sherman Indian Institute in Riverside, California. Ed Rogers, a Carlisle end and interim coach, attended the University of Minnesota and became a lawyer. Jimmy Johnson of the Stockbridge tribe went on to Northwestern University and practiced as an oral surgeon in Puerto Rico. Albert Exendine coached football for twenty-seven years at Carlisle, Otterbein, Occidental, Georgetown, and Oklahoma A&M while attending law school in the off-season. He eventually left coaching to practice law for the Bureau of Indian Affairs. William Lone Star Dietz, an Oglala Sioux, paid his way through Friends University in Kansas by playing semi-pro baseball and football. He later attended and played for Carlisle, where he became an assistant to the art teacher and Coach Warner. As head coach at Washington State, Dietz led his team to an undefeated season and a victory in the 1916 Rose Bowl. Dietz also taught in the school's fine arts department. He coached several collegiate teams before accepting the head coach position with the professional Boston Braves (later Washington Redskins) in 1933. He returned to college coaching and a career as an artist in 1935. Gus Welch also attended law school and coached at Washington State after serving as a cavalry captain in World War I. Such men had clearly learned to use the dominant white system to their advantage.[16]

While some felt relatively comfortable with assimilation, others found meaning in adaptation and, at times, resistance. For them the role of trickster assumed greater importance. Forced to live with an ascribed, often demeaning status, the trickster provided Native Americans with small but important victories and the means to retain pride and self-esteem.

A familiar figure in the oral culture of Native Americans, the trickster often appeared in the coyote tales or in the fable of the tortoise and the hare. Sometimes devious, comical, or foolish, the trickster often subverted and manipulated the ascribed roles in a power relationship through wit, guile, or deception. In the process the trickster might foil or mock authority, even cast the superior as the butt of a joke or a fool, thus reversing, at least temporarily, the dominant-subordinate roles and providing a measure of relief and psychological escape from oppression. The trickster not only entertained but enlightened others, educating them in a practical means to manage anger, frustration, and suppression. Through humor and invoking the role of the trickster, subordinate groups might mute the effects of their subordination.[17]

Native Americans possessed and valued a keen sense of humor. In a 1896 football game against Penn, Carlisle players knocked down the opponents' William Bull, whom they then deemed "Sitting Bull," in reference to the Sioux chief. After each Harvard game the Indian athletes made fun of the Harvard blue bloods by parodying their Cambridge accents, "even those [Carlisle players] with very little English attempting the broad A."[18]

Charles Bender, a Chippewa, grew up on a reservation and attended Carlisle before attaining Hall of Fame status as a Major League pitcher. Inevitably dubbed "Chief" by Anglo fans and sportswriters, Bender upheld his Native American identity, signing autographs with his proper name. When hostile fans greeted him with imitation war cries before games Bender simply moved nearer to the seats and addressed them as "foreigners," reminding them of their latecomer status.[19]

Native Americans often employed trickery in their contests with whites. Although white writers attributed Carlisle's success to Warner's coaching genius, trickery had long been a staple of Native games. In 1903 Carlisle humiliated mighty Harvard before 15,000 football fans. Quarterback and kick returner Jimmy Johnson faked fair catches before making long returns; but the Indians saved their best trick for the second half. Receiving the kickoff, the Carlisle players crowded around the receiver, who placed the ball under the back of a guard's jersey, secured by an elastic band produced by the industrial arts class. He scampered for a 103-yard score as the befuddled Harvard players chased Johnson.[20]

In 1907 Carlisle defeated the University of Chicago before 28,000 with Albert Exendine scoring the lone touchdown on the newly legalized forward pass. Exendine scored by running around the Chicago team bench and then catching Pete Hauser's throw, circumventing the rule that disallowed a completion, but not a player, out of bounds. That same season Carlisle, an underdog, defeated an unsuspecting Penn team

26–6 before more than 22,000 spectators in Philadelphia with passes, quick kicks, and a fumble that may have been a planned play. Carlisle's dominance (402 yards gained to Penn's 76, and 22 first downs to 3) in front of a white audience forced their alleged superiors to concede respect. The *Denver Express* allowed that "Man for man, pound for pound, he has no superior. Through all the years of 'molly-coddling' and paternalism on the part of the 'dominant race' the hereditary trait in the Indians still manifests itself. He can give and take with the best of them in the severest strain the white man can put on the athletic field."[21]

When Carlisle defeated Harvard in 1907, students snakedanced through the town in a victory parade. Native American boys wore nightshirts and pillowcases over their heads, similar to the nativist Ku Klux Klan's garb, and carried the "remains" of Harvard bedecked in a crimson sweater on a stretcher. Such public display in a victory celebration mocked pretensions of superiority and reaffirmed indigenous pride and self-esteem.[22]

Carlisle players often employed trickery in their games against Syracuse, where Native Americans from Canada and New York reservations came to watch. They "played possum" by feigning injuries in the pregame warm-up, appearing bandaged and weak. Syracuse, which had defeated a powerful Yale team a week earlier, expected an easy win but went down in defeat. In 1906 they even sewed imitation footballs on their jersey fronts to confuse the Syracuse players before the practice was deemed illegal. In a 1911 game Syracuse players smashed the nose of the Carlisle guard and were amazed to witness his return under a mask of tape in the second half, through which he meted out revenge. Only after the game did they recognize Emil Hauser, also known as Wauseka and Carlisle's assistant coach, who served as the impostor to exact retribution. When Carlisle played the University of Minnesota in 1907, Native Americans from the Dakota and Wisconsin reservations traveled to the game. They witnessed a Minnesota defeat by virtue of a trick play, the tackle eligible, in which a lineman catches a pass.[23]

Carlisle players had learned strategies from their athletic predecessors, as fathers had taught sons in their traditional culture. In 1899 Columbia's Harold Weeks had gained fame by hurdling over opposing lines, "but when the Carlisle line began to rise up and meet his face with the heels of their hands the famous dives became few and far between."[24]

After defeating Penn, a Carlisle student wrote home that "they were pretty good . . . and heap much bigger but we beat him anyhow. . . . We too slick for him. Maybe white man better with cannon and guns but Indians just as good in brains to think with."[25] Sport thus provided a means to attack the tenets of social Darwinism and colonial ideology.

White scientists, educators, journalists, and others who fashioned the popular culture promoted stereotypical perceptions of the inferior Native American. Sitting Bull, the famed Sioux chief, had realized the distortions in white images as early as 1881 during photograph sessions after his surrender. He astutely retained the power to market himself and his own representation. Refusing to situate himself in martial poses, he also found ways to manipulate his celebrity status. He used exhibitions as a means to escape the dreary reservation and make money. When translators at one such display misrepresented his words to capitalize on the Custer affair at Little Big Horn, of which he had not spoken, he took further steps to safeguard his image. In order to appear in Buffalo Bill Cody's Wild West Show, he exacted an exorbitant salary, remuneration for his entourage, his choice of an interpreter, nonparticipation in the Indian shoot-outs, and the right to sell his photos and autographs. Like the proverbial trickster, Sitting Bull had reversed power relationships with whites to his own advantage.[26]

Still, newspapers continued to feature anatomical comparisons between the Carlisle football players and their white opponents. Cartoons pictured them as savages and wild men. The world's fair of 1904, held in St. Louis, organized "Anthropology Days" to exhibit the racial and cultural differences between the "civilized" and "more primitive" peoples. Athletic events staged between various tribes or nations intended to show the superiority of whites' physical capabilities.[27]

Carlisle students protested such images in their school newspaper. They criticized the untrue and libelous brands of moving pictures of Indian life and romance which are shown throughout the country, and are supposed by the uninitiated public to be true to life. . . . The majority of these pictures are not only without foundation in fact, but do not even have Indians to pose for them . . . white men or Mexicans usually pose as Indians, with blackened faces, wigs and Indian costumes; their actions and gestures are absurdly grotesque, and exaggerated. These make-believes do not run, talk, or walk like Indians, and their whole make-up brands them as "fakers."[28]

Lacking any power to change minds beyond their own campus, Carlisle athletes fought the stereotypes on and off the field at their own school. At the football team banquet of 1897, A. J. Standring, assistant superintendent at Carlisle, congratulated the team on its victories but suggested that the wins were gained by white coaching and management. Team captain Bemus Pierce arose to offer a rebuttal to the charge and later called for Indian coaches for Indian teams. The following year bandmaster Dennis Wheelock of the Oneida tribe proclaimed the greediness and selfishness of whites. He stated, "The only way I see how he (the Indian) may reoccupy the lands that once were his, is through football, and as football takes brains, takes energy, proves whether civilization can be understood by the Indian or not, we are willing to perpetuate it."[29]

As a territorial game football became the means to win back lands, at least in a symbolic fashion. When Carlisle played Dartmouth in 1914, one of the many schools that had appropriated the "Indian" nickname, the true bearers of the appellation proved merciless in a 24–10 drubbing. When Peter Hauser got kneed by an opponent, he retaliated verbally with the question, "Who's the savage now?"[30]

Consistent with the role and strategies of the trickster, Native athletes even upheld or promoted negative or incorrect images if such practices provided personal benefit. In 1921 Jim Thorpe agreed to organize a team composed entirely of Native Americans to play in the National Football League as an advertising idea for Walter Lingo, owner of the Oorang Kennels in Ohio, a breeder and seller of hunting dogs. (See Charles Springwood's essay in this volume.) Thorpe recruited many old friends from Carlisle, and the players represented at least ten different tribes. Players used their Native American names, performed pregame Indian dances with drums, and exhibited their skills with tomahawks. One player even wrestled a bear. Nevertheless, the team seemed inept on the field, often losing by astronomical scores despite the presence of several former All-Americans. Thorpe played infrequently if at all, and the team won only four games in its two-year existence. The players gladly accepted Lingo's money and had a good time spending it. Leon

Boutwell of the Chippewa tribe, the team's quarterback, later offered an explanation.

"White people had this misconception about Indians. They thought we were all wild men, even though almost all of us had been to college and were generally more civilized than they were. Well, it was a dandy excuse to raise hell and get away with it when the mood struck us. Since we were Indians, we could get away with things the white men couldn't. Don't think we didn't take advantage of it."[31]

Thorpe later utilized the stereotype in the 1930s when, in need of money, he agreed to act as Chief Black Crow in the movie *Battling with Buffalo Bill*. Lone Star Dietz also employed the stereotype when necessary. Although he had earlier remarked that "the white artist always treated his Indian subjects in a stereotyped way, placing them on canvas with a haughty but awkward pose," Dietz accepted the offer of George Preston Marshall, the racist owner of the Boston Braves pro football team, to become head coach in 1933. Soon after the team changed its name to the Redskins. Today they perpetrate the masquerade, complete with a headdressed mascot and logo in the nation's capital. Lacking the current political power of Native resistance efforts, Thorpe and Dietz simply appropriated the negative images for their own benefit, not unlike the trickster.[32]

Sport—the physicality of football in particular—often empowered Native American athletes, enabling them to reverse the dominant-subordinate roles by beating whites at their own game. Although a small school, Carlisle managed to beat larger, more prestigious academic institutions, including Harvard, the symbolic bastion of white supremacy. From 1900 to 1907 Carlisle never gave up a touchdown to a visiting team. An even better measure of the value placed on such encounters might be the level of student support for the team. Just as Native Americans traveled many miles from reservations to watch Carlisle defeat bigger, supposedly stronger white teams, the school's female students spent their own money to accompany the team to its road games.[33]

Native American prowess on the field belied the tenets of social Darwinism, and within the confines of the athletic arena athletes found the freedom to disprove the prevailing racial stereotypes. Heroic figures emerged as role models for Native American youth. In a rough game against Brown, an opponent slugged Hawley Pierce. Older brother and team captain Bemus Pierce called a timeout. He took Hawley on an inspection tour of the Brown team and asked him to identify the offender. Mindful of Superintendent Pratt's required pledge that Carlisle players never fight during a game, Bemus announced that he would "take care of him after the game." Brown's infractions subsequently ceased. In a game against Wisconsin, a burly opponent repeatedly slugged the smaller Carlisle players until Pierce leveled him with a forearm smash and then informed the perpetrator of the new "tackling" technique.[34]

Jim Thorpe's intimidation of opponents carried legendary status. He not only taunted white opponents after long runs, but opponents believed that his shoulder pads hid iron plates, and his feared and jarring tackles caused many opponents to fumble the ball. Thorpe proved as devastating on the professional football circuit. George Halas, owner-player of the Chicago Bears, claimed that when Thorpe "threw himself against a runner, it was better to be hit by a falling tree."[35]

Other athletes responded similarly within the rules of the game. Louis Sockalexis, a full-blooded Penobscot, played baseball for the Cleveland Spiders of the National League. (See Daniel Barr's essay in this volume.) In his first game New York fans greeted him with demeaning war cries when he came to bat. He retaliated with a home run.[36] John "Chief" Meyers, a Cahuilla Indian from California, related a similar story. Although he played professional baseball as a catcher from 1906 to 1917, he "was considered a foreigner. I didn't belong. I was an Indian." In his first game his own pitcher disregarded his signals for pitches, and the opposing pitcher threw at his head. He answered with a three-run homer that won the game. In later years Meyers resorted to the trickster strategy, misrepresenting his true age in order to prolong his career.[37]

As Native Americans learned white ways, they gained both knowledge and power. Students at Carlisle, led by Gus Welch, a football star, initiated a congressional investigation in 1914 that eventually closed the institution. The athletes resented Coach Warner's authoritarian and abusive demeanor that offended their Native American values, and all students seethed over the widespread financial mismanagement and embezzlement of funds. Welch eventually returned to his Native lifestyle and sued the government for underpaying him when it claimed his land for a highway project. Although he lost the case, Welch instructed the court that "The white man has been taking land from the Indian so long that it has become a habit with him. There's nothing an Indian man can do about changing the white man's habits."[38] But, like the trickster, Welch and the other Carlisle students turned the power of the government against itself. The school that had done do much to change Native America closed its doors in 1918.

Forced to live in a larger white world that they could not change, Native Americans reacted in ways that suited their individual situations. Louis Tewanima, allegedly "taken prisoner" and sent to government schools, emerged as a great runner, representing the United States at the 1908 and 1912 Olympics. Tewanima then rejected the white world to return to his Hopi roots, where he fittingly became a priest of the antelope clan.[39]

Tom Longboat, the great runner of the Canadian Onondagas, traveled between both worlds. He resisted white trainers and managers and conducted his own workouts. He won the 1907 Boston Marathon and ran in the 1908 Olympics; but his 1909 race against the Englishman Alfie Shrubb for the professional marathon championship may be most memorable. Held at Madison Square Garden in New York, Longboat took recourse in the role of the trickster. He feigned tiredness, lagging behind for fifteen miles as Shrubb pushed himself to extend a long lead. Longboat then increased his pace, gradually running down the fatigued white man. Longboat even waved to his supporters as he ran, and the exhausted Shrubb tumbled off the track more than a mile short of the finish, leaving Longboat an easy win. The champion defeated many whites throughout his career but never outpaced his friends when accompanied on the reservation, where he preferred to spend his time.[40]

Other Native American athletes felt alienated in the white world. Sockalexis fell victim to alcohol, to which he was allegedly introduced by teammates. John Levi, a multisport athlete and 1923 football All-American at Haskell Indian Institute, whom Jim Thorpe considered even better than himself, quit the New York Yankees to coach his more familiar alma mater.[41] In 1926 Mayes McLain, a Haskell running back, led the nation in scoring with 253 points, but the National Collegiate Athletic Association failed to recognize his record. Haskell had attempted to "attain a position among the football teams of the west similar to that occupied by the Carlisle team among those of the east" as early as 1900.[42]

Native Americans demonstrated their pride in the Haskell team by raising all of the $185,000 required to build a 10,500-seat stadium on the Kansas campus in 1926. More than seventy tribes registered for the homecoming dedication, perhaps the first display of the pan-Indian movement that elicited a greater measure of activism in the 1970s. The festival included powwows, a buffalo barbecue, dances, plays, and the football game, in which Haskell defeated Bucknell by a score of 36–0. "All Indians joined together against a common foe" for the 1926 season, as the Native American squad went undefeated.[43] The contest of unbeatens between Haskell and Boston College resulted in a 21–21 tie in Boston. Unlike the tricksters of Carlisle, Haskell played straight football, and the *Boston Globe* admitted that they were "more powerful" than their white counterparts but judged the Bostonians to be "smarter." When Haskell defeated a previously unbeaten Xavier team, the *Cincinnati Enquirer* termed it "the modernized version of warfare of the Indian empire of the past."[44] Although Haskell sported a 12–0-1 record in 1926, the best teams failed to include Haskell on their schedules, and the Missouri Valley Conference denied its application for membership. Rejected by the white football powers who ensured that there would be no more Carlisles, Haskell faded into football obscurity.

Even Native American athletes who learned to use the system to their advantage felt disappointment and heartache. Thorpe had written to his brother Frank in September 1912, "We have our first game next Saturday. . . . I have the chance to make a bunch of dough after leaving this school. . . . God it's hard to go back again but it is for my own good, so I will make the best of things."[45] He did, and led the nation in scoring that year. Despite his proficiency in baseball, he and other Native American football players soon earned as much as $250 per game for pro football teams. When team owners decided to organize the American Professional Football Association in 1920, later renamed the National Football League, they chose Thorpe as the nominal president at a salary of $2,500. However, once age had eroded Thorpe's skills, he was relegated to day labor jobs and bit movie parts. He still managed to retain his pride in the latter roles by forcing movie executives to employ other Indians for Native American roles rather than the "fakirs" of previous years.[46] As Thorpe grew older, skeptics tried to provoke him. On one occasion, a professional wrestler bested Thorpe, then bragged that he had thrown the world's greatest athlete. Thorpe repaid him with a forearm smash that left the grappler unconscious.[47] The stress and tension of living in two worlds resulted in three marriages, alcoholism, and barely eking out a living. Thorpe finally succumbed to a heart attack in 1953. (See John Bloom's essay in this volume.)

By the mid-1950s other Native American athletes had learned to better adapt white sport forms to their own needs and values. When missionaries and teachers introduced baseball to the essentially noncompetitive Pueblo culture, the Pueblos found a new way to practice their old witchcraft, which the whites wanted to exterminate. Casting spells on opposing teams and players invoked age-old customs, preserved traditions, reduced social tensions, and accounted for successes or failures. Similarly, when the Mississippi legislature banned Choctaw stickball games, the tribe found an adequate substitute in softball, where traditional magic protected one's team from opposing witches and helped underdogs gain victories. In more recent years, Choctaw female softball players have gained great recognition, status, and leadership opportunities due to their athletic abilities. Both Navajos and Utes have also adapted basketball to their particular cultural values, emphasizing fun more so than winning, and maintaining clan loyalty by passing the ball to kin during games.[48]

Just as Albert Exendine had taught Jim Thorpe, and Thorpe educated Gus Welch, Welch instructed younger children how to play and how to maintain their own civilization despite white ravages. Welch informed them, "Now that we are no longer people of the chase, poor physical condition is the curse of the Indian. A game of some kind is our one chance against tuberculosis."[49] His words presaged current reservation conditions. Perhaps sport, in its multiple meanings, can offer hope.

Like the athletes who have preceded them, today's players have found a voice and a means of empowerment in sport. For those who chose or were forced to live in two worlds, sport provided a means to negotiate white society and multiple identities. It allowed for a degree of assimilation or, for some, a decision to reject dominant impositions in favor of traditional lifestyles and a Native American identity. In either case, Native American athletes managed to challenge the social Darwinian myth of white superiority, often claiming a measure of revenge and retaliation on the contested spaces of sport. Tricksters enlightened and entertained others in one means of coping with their altered states, and heroes provided the means to retain a sense of dignity and self-esteem.

Notes

1. Frank Clancy, "Warriors," *USA Weekend*, 12–14 February 1999, pp. 4–6.

2. Jack D. Forbes, "The Manipulation of Race, Caste, and Identity: Classifying Afro-Americans, Native Americans and Red-Black People," *Journal of Ethnic Studies* 17:4 (1990): 1–51; see Thomas Pakenham, *The Scramble for Africa, 1876–1912* (New York: Random House, 1991), as one example of European greed. On nineteenth-century research, see William H. Tucker, *The Science and Politics of Racial Research* (Urbana: University of Illinois Press, 1994), 9–36; and Stephen Jay Gould, *The Mismeasure of Man* (1981; reprint, New York: W. W. Norton, 1996), 63, 87–101, 402–12. See King and Springwood, eds., *Team Spirits*, for current reactions to such representation.

3. Patricia Nelson Limerick, *The Legacy of Conquest: The Unbroken Past of the American West* (New York: W. W. Norton, 1987), 221.

4. Jack Newcombe, *The Best of the Athletic Boys: The White Man's Impact on Jim Thorpe* (Garden City NY: Doubleday, 1975), 32–45; Glenn S. Warner, "The Indian Massacres," *Collier's*, 17 October 1931, pp. 7–8, 61–62; Frederick C. Hoxie, *A Final Promise: The Campaign to Assimilate the Indians, 1880–1920* (New York: Cambridge University Press, 1989); Oxendine, *American Indian Sports Heritage*, 173–74. Nineteen of the schools still existed in 1964. Some remain today, while others have been supplanted by tribal schools on reservations.

5. Newcombe, *The Best of the Athletic Boys*, 5, 32, 38–45, 57, 95, 137. Thorpe attended a local mission school and Haskell Indian Institute in Kansas before being sent to distant Carlisle. See Edward Countryman, *Americans: A Collision of Histories* (New York: Hill and Wang, 1996), on the intermingling of American identity.

6. Newcombe, *The Best of the Athletic Boys*, 7–8; Eric Foner and John A. Garraty, eds., *Reader's Companion to American History* (Boston: Houghton Mifflin, 1991), 1081. No tribal records or census rolls provide verification of the Black Hawk ancestry, although both of Thorpe's parents were members of the Thunder clan through Thorpe's paternal grandfather, who lived and married among the tribe. See Quintin Hoare and Geoffrey N. Smith, eds., *Selections from the Prison Notebooks* (New York: International, 1971), on Antonio Gram-

sci's hegemony theory and the process of domination and negotiation of social power. Forbes, "The Manipulation of Race, Caste, and Identity," 35; and Edward W. Said, *Culture and Imperialism* (New York: Alfred A. Knopf, 1994), are instructive of the power and nuances of colonial ideology.

7. Oxendine, *American Indian Sports Heritage*, xix, 3–33; Kendall Blanchard, *The Anthropology of Sport* (Westport CT: Bergin and Garvey, 1995); Newcombe, *The Best of the Athletic Boys*, 11, 40; George Kirsch, Othello Harris, and Claire E. Nolte, eds., *Encyclopedia of Ethnicity and Sports in the United States* (Westport CT: Greenwood, 2000), 329–35.

8. Oxendine, *American Indian Sports Heritage*, 188, 211; Newcombe, *The Best of the Athletic Boys*, 107–8, 111, 115, 121, 139; Glenn S. Warner, "Heap Big Run—Most—Fast," *Collier's*, 24 October 1931, pp. 18–19, 46.

9. John S. Steckbeck, *Fabulous Redmen: The Carlisle Indians and Their Famous Football Teams* (Harrisburg PA: J. Horace McFarland, 1951), 6.

10. Newcombe, *The Best of the Athletic Boys*, 119–21, 139, 140, 147, 156, 169.

11. Steckbeck, *Fabulous Redmen*, 62, 66; Newcombe, *The Best of the Athletic Boys*, 110; Glenn S. Warner to A. A. Stagg, 5 March 1900, and Stagg to Warner, 10 March 1900, Amos Alonzo Stagg Papers, box 41, folder 9, Special Collections, University of Chicago; Warner, "Indian Massacres," 62. Warner coached Carlisle from 1899 to 1903 and returned to coach from 1907 to 1914.

12. Blanchard, *The Anthropology of Sport*, 243–44; David Wallace Adams, *Education for Extinction: American Indians and the Boarding School Experience, 1875–1928* (Lawrence: University Press of Kansas, 1995), 186–89.

13. Steckbeck, *Fabulous Redmen*, 54–55, 95.

14. Alexander M. Weyand, *The Saga of American Football* (New York: Macmillan, 1955), 101; Steckbeck, *Fabulous Redmen*, 95–96.

15. Marc S. Maltby, *The Origins and Early Development of Professional Football* (New York: Garland, 1997), 60, 71–77, 90–92; Robert W. Peterson, *Pigskin: The Early Years of Pro Football* (New York: Oxford University Press, 1997), 38–39.

16. Warner, "Heap Big Run," 46; Newcombe, *The Best of the Athletic Boys*, 152–53, 200, 243; David L. Porter, ed., *Biographical Dictionary of American Sports: Football* (Westport CT: Greenwood, 1987), 469–70; Porter, *Biographical Dictionary of American Sports: 1989–1992 Supplement for Baseball, Football, Basketball, and Other Sports* (Westport CT: Greenwood, 1992), 396–97; John C. Hibner, "Lone Star Dietz," *College Football Historical Society* 1:5 (August 1988): 1–4; John Charles Hibner, *The Rose Bowl, 1902–1929* (Jefferson NC: McFarland, 1993), 13–21, 46–62. The art teacher at Carlisle, Angel DeCora, became Dietz's wife. She previously worked as an illustrator and writer for *Harper's Weekly*. A member of the Winnebago tribe, DeCora was considered to be one of the best educated

Native Americans in the country at that time. Dietz also coached the Mare Island Marines in the 1919 Rose Bowl.

17. See Catherine Peck, *A Treasury of North American Folk Tales* (New York: Book of the Month Club, 1998), 203–53, on the roles of tricksters. See Oxendine, *American Indian Sports Heritage*, 76–77, on tribal fables. See Lawrence W. Levine, *Black Culture and Black Consciousness: Afro-American Folk Thought from Slavery to Freedom* (New York: Oxford University Press, 1977), 83, 102–21, 125–31; and John W. Roberts, *From Trickster to Badman: The Black Folk Hero in Slavery and Freedom* (Philadelphia: University of Pennsylvania Press, 1989), 18–44, on African Americans' use of the trickster as a coping mechanism.

18. Blanchard, *The Anthropology of Sport*, 157; Adams, *Education for Extinction*, 88; Warner, "Heap Big Run," 19.

19. Mike Shatzkin, ed., *The Ballplayers* (New York: Arbor House, 1990), 68; Harry Grayson, *They Played the Game: The Story of Baseball Greats* (New York: A. S. Barnes, 1945); Forbes, "The Manipulation of Race, Caste, and Identity," 28.

20. Oxendine, *American Indian Sports Heritage*, 76–78, 190, 247; Newcombe, *The Best of the Athletic Boys*, 86–89.

21. Steckbeck, *Fabulous Redmen*, 110; Newcombe, *The Best of the Athletic Boys,* 115–17, 119.

22. Newcombe, *The Best of the Athletic Boys,* 117–18. Exendine, star of the 1907 team, had also played a clown in the school play. He tutored Jim Thorpe, who suffered as the victim of team pranks in his first season on the football team. Thorpe learned to employ the trickster strategy in his own relationships with whites thereafter.

23. Newcombe, *The Best of the Athletic Boys*, 113, 119; Steckbeck, *Fabulous Redmen*, 65, 107; Oxendine, *American Indian Sports Heritage*, 190.

24. Oxendine, *American Indian Sports Heritage*, 20–22; Warner, "The Indian Massacres," 61.

25. Warner, "Heap Big Run," 46.

26. See Joy S. Kasson, *Buffalo Bill's Wild West: Celebrity, Memory, and Popular History* (New York: Hill and Wang, 2000), 169–83, on Sitting Bull. Luther Standing Bear, a Lakota Sioux and Carlisle student, alerted the chief to the translators' subterfuge.

27. Oriard, *Reading Football*, 189–276; *The Greatest of Exhibitions: Official Views of the Louisiana Purchase Exposition* (St. Louis: Sam'l F. Myerson, 1904), 36, 190, 192, 283, 285.

28. *The Red Man*, December 1911, cited in Newcombe, *The Best of the Athletic Boys*, 175.

29. Adams, *Education for Extinction*, 189–90; Newcombe, *The Best of the Athletic Boys*, 80–81.

30. Newcombe, *The Best of the Athletic Boys*, 217; Warner, "Heap Big Run," 19.

31. Bob Braunwart, Bob Carroll, and Joe Horrigan, "Oorang Indians, 1922–1923," *Coffin Corner* 3:1 (January 1981): 1–8. See Kasson, *Buffalo Bill's Wild West*, 183–95, for previous and similar use of imagery by Native Americans for their own advantage.

32. Newcombe, *The Best of the Athletic Boys*, 9, photos opposite pp. 135 and 244; Hibner, "Lone Star Dietz," 1–4. See Suzan Shown Harjo, "Fighting Name-Calling: Challenging the Redskins in Court," in *Team Spirits*, ed. King and Springwood, 189–207, on current developments.

33. Newcombe, *The Best of the Athletic Boys*, 112, 114.

34. Newcombe, *The Best of the Athletic Boys*, 80–81.

35. Newcombe, *The Best of the Athletic Boys*, 230; George Halas with Gwen Morgan and Arthur Veysey, *Halas by Halas* (New York: McGraw Hill, 1979), 51. Halas recounts Thorpe's intimidating hits on pp. 51–52.

36. Grayson, *They Played the Game*, 67–68.

37. Lawrence S. Ritter, *The Glory of Their Times: The Story of the Early Days of Baseball Told by the Men Who Played It* (New York: Vintage, 1985), 170–84.

38. Newcombe, *The Best of the Athletic Boys*, 155, 198, 241–43; Adams, *Education for Extinction*, 321–26; Oxendine, *American Indian Sports Heritage*, 19, 184–93.

39. Newcombe, *The Best of the Athletic Boys*, 125–26, 185, 189, 244.

40. Brenda Zeman, *To Run with Longboat* (Edmonton: GMS2 Ventures, 1988), 3–20.

41. Kirsch, Harris, and Nolte, *Encyclopedia of Ethnicity and Sports in the United States*, 437–38; David L. Porter, ed., *Biographical Dictionary of American Sports: Baseball* (Westport CT: Greenwood, 1987), 522–23; Grayson, *They Played the Game*, 67–68; Oxendine, *American Indian Sports Heritage*, 198–99.

42. Oxendine, *American Indian Sports Heritage*, 198; Ray Schmidt, "Princes of the Prairie," *College Football Historical Society*, 2:2 (February 1989): 1–8; William Peterson to Amos Alonzo Stagg, 6 December 1900, Stagg Papers, box 41, folder 9, University of Chicago, Special Collections.

43. Oxendine, *American Indian Sports Heritage*, 200, 201.

44. Schmidt, "Princes of the Prairie," 5, 6, 8.

45. Cited in Newcombe, *The Best of the Athletic Boys*, 193.

46. Newcombe, *The Best of the Athletic Boys*, 218, 235–36; Professional Football Researchers Association, *Bulldogs on Sunday* (PFRA, n.d.), 1–16; Arch Ward, "The Red Terror," undated newspaper reprint, *College Football Historical Society* 8:3

(May 1995): 14. See Ian Frazier, "On the Rez," *Atlantic Monthly*, December 1999, 59, for a brief history of Native American film roles.

47. Newcombe, *The Best of the Athletic Boys*, 245–47.

48. J. R. Fox, "Pueblo Baseball: A New Use for Old Witchcraft," *Journal of American Folklore* 74 (1961): 9–16; Blanchard, *The Anthropology of Sport*, 18, 43–44, 54–55, 70, 175–78, 199, 222–23; Maria T. Allison and Gunther Luschen, "A Comparative Analysis of Navaho Indian and Anglo Basketball Sports Systems," *International Review of Sport Sociology* 14 (1979): 75–86.

49. Warner, "Heap Big Run," 19.

2. "Looking Backward"
The Life and Legend of Louis Francis Sockalexis

In 1897 Louis Francis Sockalexis, a Penobscot from Maine, became the first fully recognized American Indian to play professional baseball. Although Sockalexis played portions of only three seasons (1897–99) with the National League's old Cleveland Spiders team, his life and legacy remain at the center of an ongoing controversy surrounding the mythic foundations of the Cleveland baseball team's nickname: "Indians." Since the formal adoption of the nomenclature in 1915, popular traditions have held that Sockalexis was the inspiration for the name. According to legend, Clevelanders recalled the athletic exploits of Sockalexis so fondly that they proposed the name "Indians" to honor their hero's accomplishments. Contemporary critics have debunked much of this triumphant tale, arguing that the name change had more to do with exploitation and financial gain than recognition of Sockalexis as a ballplayer. [1] Yet the ongoing debate over the origins of the Indians name has blurred the commentary that Sockalexis's playing career offers concerning Native efforts to assimilate into mainstream American society during the late nineteenth century. Moreover, the man behind the myth remains elusive. Because of Sockalexis's centrality in the naming controversy, historians, activists, and commentators have overlooked his outstanding collegiate baseball career and tantalizing professional athletic promise, rarely affording them equal footing with discussions of his racial heritage and marketing value as determinants for the exploitation of his legacy by the Cleveland baseball franchise.

This essay seeks to correct this oversight by unpacking Sockalexis's life and baseball career from the myth and controversy that surround

Louis F. Sockalexis. Courtesy National Baseball Hall of Fame Library, Cooperstown, New York.

his legacy. Sockalexis's accomplishments as a pioneering Indian athlete, as well as his struggle to find accommodation in the abrasive world of late nineteenth-century professional sports, merit equal footing with the controversy surrounding the team nickname. Such biographical exploration is not intended to detract from current discourse over his position in the ongoing controversy but to uncover the individual at the center of so much contention.

The Original Cleveland Indian

Sockalexis was born on 12 October 1871 on the Indian Island Reservation in Maine. [2] His father and grandfather were elected leaders of the Penobscot nation, a small remnant of the once mighty Abenaki Indian Confederacy that originally inhabited much of northern New England. Few Native peoples remained within the state's confines at the time of Sockalexis's birth, but among the survivors of Euro-American settlement none was more persistent or progressive-minded than the Penobscots. The tribe had endured because the early leaders were willing to interact with the white population and to assimilate American culture into their traditional lifestyle. At the time of Sockalexis's birth, however, the reservation was plagued by poverty and unemployment. Opportunities for economic or social advancement were scarce. Most Penobscots carved out a meager existence by providing foodstuffs for the burgeoning logging industry or by hiring themselves out as guides for wealthy New Englanders who vacationed in the scenic Kennebec and Penobscot River country. [3]

Sockalexis spent his adolescent years on the Indian Island Reservation despite federal policies that mandated the removal of Indian children from reservations to government-sponsored boarding schools. Perhaps because of his father's influence or his family's ties to local officials, Sockalexis was not removed from his reservation like thousands of other American Indian children of the era. [4] Instead he received his education locally at a Catholic missionary school in Old Town, a nearby white community. Despite irregular attendance at the school, Sockalexis gained exposure to some of the emerging popular pursuits of the period, including baseball. Following the conclusion of the Civil War, baseball had emerged as a fashionable leisure pastime. By the early 1880s countless amateur and youth leagues had sprung up throughout New England. [5] Sockalexis displayed a strong affinity for the game. Shortly after graduation from the mission school, Sockalexis joined the Knox County amateur baseball league, where he established himself as a talented pitcher and outfielder. The experience was both enjoyable and mildly profitable. Most amateur leagues of the era paid athletes to play, and Sockalexis earned as much as ten dollars per game. He soon emerged as a standout player in the Knox league, dazzling spectators and competitors alike with his strong and accurate throwing arm, fleetness of foot, and powerful left-handed hitting. Romantic accounts even credit his early baseball exploits as the inspiration behind Joe Crowfoot, a fictitious American Indian baseball player who appeared in Maine newspaper reporter Gilbert Patten's *Frank Merriwell at Yale* dime novels.[6]

Sockalexis's baseball prowess drew attention not only from spectators and reporters but also from his fellow players. Michael "Doc" Powers, a catcher on the baseball team at Holy Cross College, took an exceptional interest in the young Penobscot. Powers's family, like that of many New Englanders, spent summers vacationing at Maine's picturesque retreats, or "camps" as they were then known. While his family enjoyed the New England summer, Powers honed his skills in the Maine amateur leagues, including the Knox league where he became a teammate of Sockalexis. Powers was so impressed by Sockalexis during the summer of 1894 that he encouraged Sockalexis to try out for the Holy Cross baseball team that autumn. In September Sockalexis accompanied Powers to the college campus in Worcester, Massachusetts, where he auditioned for manager Jesse Burkett, a star player with the National League's Cleveland Spiders and a future Hall of Fame center fielder. At the time, professional baseball was a seasonal sport that did not pay exceptionally large salaries even to its brightest stars, leading Burkett and other players to supplement their athletic incomes by taking second jobs during the off-season. Many became coaches for collegiate teams, who played their games before and after the Major League season. This arrangement brought Sockalexis into contact with Burkett, who would eventually help open the doors that would allow him to reach the Major Leagues.

Before Louis Sockalexis ever donned a Cleveland baseball jersey, however, he became a collegiate phenom. Burkett was so impressed with Sockalexis's physical skills, especially his ability to hurl a baseball from deep in center field to home plate with considerable force and near perfect accuracy, that he quickly signed the twenty-four-year-old to a scholarship. Over the next two seasons, Sockalexis excelled as both a pitcher and an outfielder for the Crusaders. He compiled impressive batting averages of .444 and .436, pitched three no-hit games, stole six bases in a single game against Brown University, and was credited by a group of Harvard professors with setting a world's record for the longest baseball throw (138 yards). Despite his brief tenure at the college, Sockalexis helped transform Holy Cross into an eastern baseball power, for which he later earned posthumous induction into the college's Athletic Hall of Fame as one of its six charter members.[7]

Following the 1896 Major League season, Burkett took over the baseball program at Notre Dame and brought his prized outfielder with him to Indiana. Sockalexis posted another impressive campaign as Notre Dame's center fielder during the spring of 1897, but Burkett had grander plans for his protégé. Burkett was an exceptional Major League player who had posted batting averages of .409 and .410 for the Cleveland Spiders in 1895 and 1896. Yet the Spiders, despite also having Denton "Cy" Young on their roster, finished second both seasons to the Baltimore Orioles. Burkett was an outstanding center fielder, but his teammates in the Cleveland outfield, Jimmy McAlee and Henry Blake, were statistically below-average players. They hit a combined .269 in nearly 1,700 at bats during 1895–96. Burkett may have cited their unspectacular play to convince Cleveland player-manager Patsy Tabeau to give Sockalexis a tryout in an effort to improve the Spiders' chances of dethroning the Orioles in the National League standings.[8]

Sockalexis arrived in Cleveland early that spring to audition for Tabeau. The manager was so impressed that he signed Sockalexis to a Major League contract and awarded him a starting position in right field next to Burkett. Tabeau was not the only one keenly interested in the talented newcomer. Although it is now believed that Sockalexis was not the first American Indian to play for a professional baseball team, his addition to the Cleveland Spiders created an almost instantaneous local media frenzy. James Toy, a half-Sioux utility infielder who had enjoyed a short and sporadic career with the Cleveland Blues and Brooklyn Gladiators of the American Association during the late 1880s, had not been recognized during his lifetime for his Native heritage. Such was not the case with Sockalexis. Local sportswriters were intrigued by the prospect of a full-blood American Indian playing Major League baseball, and they devoted a great deal of attention to his progress.

During an intrasquad practice game, the media found a lasting outlet for its enthusiasm. When dividing his players into opposing sides, Tabeau labeled the portion of team with Sockalexis as the "Indians," a quip that started a media fascination with the substitute name. During that era the nicknames of sporting teams were informal and flexible, often changing to reflect a popular player or clever marketing scheme. Just four days after Sockalexis joined the team, the *Cleveland Plain Dealer* referred to the baseball team as "Tabeau and his Indians." The new nickname quickly spread throughout the league. A week later the 22 March edition of *The Sporting Life*, a weekly national magazine, printed an article titled "The Indian Ballplayer Now Playing with the Cleveland Club" and conjectured that his prowess would "result in relegating to obscurity the title of 'Spiders' . . . to give place to the more significant name Indians."[9]

Sockalexis's stellar play during the early portion of the season fueled the media's infatuation. After collecting two hits, including a home run, and sparking the team to its first victory of the year, a newspaper headline read "Indians Hang One Little Scalp on Their Belts" and praised Sockalexis for inspiring the victory. When a winning streak ensued behind the hot-hitting Sockalexis and Burkett, the Cleveland media credited Sockalexis with much of the team's success, which more often than not was well-deserved praise. On four separate occasions in late May, Sockalexis provided last-minute, ninth-inning heroics that enabled Cleveland to pull out victories. At mid-season he led the Spiders with a .413 batting average and was the marvel of the baseball world. *The Sporting News* claimed that Sockalexis was "the best advertised player in the business," and a *Cleveland Plain Dealer* article even claimed that he attracted "a visibly larger percentage of women than usual" to ballparks across the league.[10]

While Cleveland was winning, local sportswriters lauded Sockalexis and continued to refer to the team as the Indians. True to the jingoistic journalism of the period, game reports often characterized bats as "war clubs" and victories as "scalps." Although Louis was only a rookie, sportswriters dubbed him "chief of the Indians," especially after games in which he had been instrumental in securing victory. Cartoons dotted the sports pages featuring Sockalexis, the "Big Man Not Afraid of His Job," dressed in a feathered headdress with a baseball bat for a war club, leading his "tribe" as they vanquished their foes. The caption of one such caricature read "Sockalexis—Chief of Sock 'em!" The media's use of such stereotypical representations of American Indian culture appears unenlightened and insensitive by modern standards, but there is little indication that there was any intention to disparage Sockalexis or Native peoples in general. Jingoistic journalism was commonplace during the era in politics, sports, and nearly every other arena of media coverage, as polemics were common in media commentary on American society. Moreover, there was no underlying racist commentary or narrative present in these articles, at least not during the early months when Sockalexis was playing well. Instead, the sportswriters followed in the footsteps of Buffalo Bill's Wild West Show by playing to the American public's fascination with supposedly vanquished Native culture. They sought to capitalize on Sockalexis's success to sell newspapers and tickets by adopting publicly recognizable Native antecedents to compose flashy headlines that brought attention and fanfare to the American Indian baseball player and by extension the entire team. On occasion Sockalexis's promotional image was extended to his teammates, such as occurred after a victory over St. Louis in early May. A giddy newspaper recap exclaimed that the team "jammed the ball around with reckless abandon and playful ferocity that usually characterizes a tribe of Indians doing a scalp dance upon an expiring foe."[11]

Sockalexis's personal reaction to the media attention and fanfare is difficult to gauge. There are few accounts of his experiences in his own words, although media commentary contends that early on Sockalexis handled his celebrity with ease. Taking things in stride was no small accomplishment. The professional sports environment that he experienced as a member of the Cleveland Spiders was very different from that of today. Baseball, in particular, was a rough game, marked by regular episodes of violence and profanity that would easily surpass even the worst episodes of the modern era. Fans held players, especially those from the visiting team, in low regard and often cursed loudly at them or even hurled objects at them. It was not uncommon for fans to leave the stands and run onto the playing field to physically confront the athletes. Such raucous behavior was also exhibited by the players, some of whom did not hesitate to attack fans, umpires, or one another with bats, balls, and fists. The climate on the field was at times so chaotic that some umpires reportedly carried revolvers in case the situation got too far out of hand.[12]

Sockalexis was a target for these sanctioned forms of social abuse because he was both an American Indian and an outstanding player. Whether at home or on the road, he was the object of the crowd's attention. Elmer Bates, a reporter for *The Sporting Life*, noted that "all eyes are on the Indian in every game [and] he is expected not only to play right field like a veteran but to do a little more batting than anyone else." The attention was often neither polite nor positive. According to Bates the taunting was often degrading and "calculated to disconcert the player." The *Cleveland Plain Dealer* reported that the crowd in Louisville "tried to have some fun with Sockalexis' name and imitated the war whoop of various tribes" during the season opener in 1897. Sockalexis appears to have been outwardly unfazed, as the same report indicates that "the handsome Indian smiled good naturedly" at his tormentors. Perhaps it was a facade, but Sockalexis genuinely seems to have been indifferent to the taunts. "If the small and big boys of Brooklyn and other cities find it a pleasure to shout at me, I have no objections," he commented during an interview with the *New York Sun*, "no matter where we play, I go through the same ordeal."[13]

Although he "played good steady ball" and conducted himself with ease on the baseball diamond during the early months of the 1897 season, Sockalexis's life off the field fell into disarray. Even for the media favorite, the urban environment of Cleveland was a dramatic change from the Indian Island Reservation or the small college communities to which he was accustomed. In 1897 Cleveland was a booming city of 400,000 inhabitants, a center for oil refining, and a railway and shipping hub for the burgeoning steel industry. League Park, the brick and steel mausoleum that served as the Spiders' home field, lay in the midst of this railroad and manufacturing district. The park was accessible only by trolley car and subject to foul smells and poor air quality due to its close proximity to the oil refineries. Moreover, the sports environment was very different from that which Sockalexis had known as an amateur. Players were a commodity to be bought or sold at the sole discretion of the team owner, a reflection on the low status of hired labor during the period. Although injuries were common, there was no disabled list or paid injury leave. Players who missed time due to an injury were ridiculed by the media and even by their teammates as lazy or cowardly. Players also were expected to maintain strict Victorian values, at least in eyes of the public, and management often hired private detectives to spy on players suspected of violating team mandates against drinking, gambling, or carousing with unsavory women.[14]

Yet many professional athletes parlayed their notoriety into a wild lifestyle. Drinking and carousing were common pastimes, and Sockalexis embraced the rampant nightlife of the city alongside many of his teammates. Like many professional athletes of the era, he became a borderline alcoholic. Exactly when Sockalexis turned to alcohol is unclear. Newspapers of the time often launched moralistic crusades against alcoholism, and their overzealous prosecution of this objective renders it difficult to decipher the origins and extent of the drinking problems of public figures. It may have gone further with Sockalexis. After reports of his alcoholism appeared early in July 1897, newspaper accounts increasingly portrayed him as a stereotypical drunk Indian, too ignorant and morally bankrupt to fend off vice. In the process his previously heroic image was debunked. Accounts contended that Sockalexis began abusing alcohol at Notre Dame and that he had been expelled from the school after a drunken brawl with a teammate. Sockalexis denied the charge, and there is no evidence for the contention, but the deconstruction of the heroic Sockalexis went on unhindered.[15]

By mid-July 1897 Sockalexis clearly was in trouble. Many of his difficulties stemmed from a severe foot injury he had sustained while running the bases earlier that month. He attempted to play through the injury, but the pain eventually forced him to the sidelines. The Cleveland media immediately questioned his integrity and toughness. Sockalexis had been enduring a difficult stretch in the field, and the media quickly asserted that "a lame foot is the Indian's excuse." The accusation signaled the media's changing opinion of Sockalexis. The local media had been his staunch supporters, but the team's declining fortunes and Sockalexis's run of bad plays in the outfield undermined his promotional value, and the media set out to transform the former hero into a scapegoat. Stereotypes that originally had been employed in a light-hearted manner to attract attention to his exploits quickly became tools for racial debasement. When Sockalexis played poorly, reporters characterized him as a "wooden Indian," a common derogative used to indicate laziness. Other reports insinuated that his athletic failings resulted from a biological inferiority that left Native people incapable of matching the white work ethic, whether it be in sport or in the foundry. Such attacks conveniently ignored the fact that Sockalexis led the Spiders in many offensive categories during the summer of 1897 and instead focused on the immoral or decadent stereotypes that plagued American views of non-white races.[16]

Sockalexis's injuries and escalating problems with alcohol made him an easy target. A *Cleveland Plain Dealer* report of a game on 13 July, during which Sockalexis made two errors in right field, alleged that his difficulties in the field stemmed from his consumption of "too many mint juleps prior to the game." The article failed to mention that Sockalexis had two of Cleveland's seven hits and had scored both of the team's runs in the 8–2 loss to Boston. But reality was less important than perception. In the media's estimation, Sockalexis was "a broken idol" who exemplified the inability of American Indians to achieve the highest ideals of Victorian America. Similar articles accused Sockalexis of spending too many evenings carousing with prostitutes and known criminals, and a 22 July *Plain Dealer* article exclaimed that "management can no longer control Sockalexis." In many regards the media criticism was a thinly concealed condemnation of eastern philanthropists' efforts to educate American Indian children and forcibly assimilate them into mainstream American culture. Cleveland sportswriters seemed determined to make Sockalexis an example of the futility of this effort by deconstructing his once heroic public image into the stereotypes that labeled all Indians as lazy, drunk, and stupid.[17]

Although newspapers of the period often printed stories of fallen public figures that pandered to the Victorian-inspired public fascination with vice and addiction, Sockalexis was naive to such practices. His play worsened during the second half of the 1897 season under the weight of the media scrutiny, and his drinking increased. He missed games, reinjured his foot (allegedly fleeing from police), and became difficult to manage. As his difficulties mounted, anger replaced Sockalexis's once cool demeanor. On one occasion a brawl erupted between Sockalexis and a former teammate after an opposing pitcher repeatedly fired pitches at Sockalexis's head. More than once manager Patsy Tabeau suspended or fined the troubled outfielder. Sockalexis became an ineffective part-time player and eventually was farmed out to the minor leagues in September, despite still ranking third on the team with a .338 batting average.[18]

Despite the setbacks he experienced during his first year in Cleveland, Sockalexis returned to play baseball for the Spiders for the next two seasons. During both years he received little playing time and even less media fanfare. He spent the majority of his time during those last two seasons in the minor leagues or suspended. He played in only twenty-one games and batted a dismal .224 during the 1898 season. Attendance dropped sharply as the season progressed, even though the team finished in fifth place with a respectable 81–68 record. Prior to the 1899 season, team owner Frank Dehass Robison transferred eighteen of the Spider's best players to his other professional team, the St. Louis Perfectos (Cardinals), who enjoyed better fan support. Sockalexis was not deemed worthy of transfer and remained in Cleveland, where he saw action in only seven games during 1899 while sitting the bench on a team that established a professional baseball record for futility by losing 134 games. New manager Lave Cross eventually cut Sockalexis after he missed a team train due to a run-in with police outside a Cleveland bar.[19]

After three short and turbulent seasons, Louis Sockalexis's professional baseball career was over. The man whom New York Giants manager John McGraw once proclaimed the best baseball player he ever saw spent the remainder of his life in obscurity. Some accounts contend that Sockalexis continued to play baseball in the New England minor leagues or coached baseball on the Indian reservations, but there is little evidence to support either assertion. What is known is that Sockalexis left the Indian Island Reservation at some point after the end of his playing days to work as a laborer for a logging company in Vermont. He died there on Christmas Eve 1913 from heart failure.

Sockalexis was not the Native equivalent of Jackie Robinson. The racial segregation of professional baseball was incomplete during his playing career, but his experiences as the first recognized American Indian player in the Major Leagues offer tragic testimony for the difficulties faced by American Indians who tried, and often failed, to successfully integrate into urban America at the end of the nineteenth century. Sockalexis played during an era when Native peoples were encouraged to integrate yet were never afforded equal status in that society and were routinely denigrated if they failed to meet the challenges imposed by forced assimilation. Still, as their traditional lifeways increasingly came under assault from American reformers who allegedly wanted to help Native peoples better their lives, many American Indians left their reservations and traditions behind in an effort to make a place for themselves in the growing cities of the United States. Some achieved success, such as the Mohawk construction workers who helped erect the skyline of New York City, but many Native Americans struggled to adapt to their new environments. Unhappiness and poverty often characterized their existence, and thousands, like Louis Sockalexis, wound up returning to their reservations discontent and disheartened by their experiences in the urban world. Sockalexis himself contended after the 1897 season that it was "some hard luck" and his inability to find an equitable existence in mainstream society that led to the abrupt end of his athletic career. [20]

A Life's Legacy

Despite his uneven experience with professional baseball, Sockalexis's legacy as the first recognized American Indian to play in the Major Leagues continues to occupy a prominent position in modern sports consciousness. His name remains at the center of a controversy surrounding the Cleveland baseball franchise's employment of the nickname "Indians." For decades team officials have contended that the term derived from the team's intention to honor Sockalexis, but that assertion has come under attack in recent years. Activists, academics, and even the media have levied accusations that the team management deliberately hides behind its ties to Sockalexis's Native heritage in order to deflect criticism from their controversial Chief Wahoo mascot, a cartoon stereotype depicting an Indian with a wide grin and dark red complexion. Team media guides and the Indians' *Gameface Magazine* have claimed for many years that fans selected the name to honor Sockalexis, but critics contend that team management has distorted facts and history to save face in light of increasing Native protest against the Wahoo imagery. Recent team publications have responded by minimizing the contention that Sockalexis was the inspiration for the name change, but team officials continue to deny critics' assertions that the team deliberately "uses a fictionalized Indian past for the purpose of silencing the protests of real Indians in the present." [21]

Much of the debate centers on the selection process that took place in January 1915. Then team owner Charlie Somers asked a committee of Cleveland-area sportswriters to suggest a replacement for the nickname "Naps," which honored Napoleon Lajoie, the team's second-baseman, manager, and best player. Lajoie had been traded to Philadelphia in 1914, necessitating a new nickname. Critics argue that the sportswriters' selection of "Indians" for the new name had little to do with Sockalexis and instead represented the desire of the writers and the owner "to overhaul the image of the team." They contend that "there is no evidence the team was named after Sockalexis" and label the popular conception that he inspired the Indians nickname "a form of cultural illiteracy."[22] The basis for this assertion comes largely from the 1915 newspaper articles that announced the name change. These include a *Cleveland Plain Dealer* article that prominently features a cartoon resplendent in its bigotry and racial stereotyping, but it makes no mention of Sockalexis as a factor in the adoption of the new name. However, champions of the Sockalexis connection point to a more substantive *Plain Dealer* article that appeared the following day. The article, titled "Looking Backward," refers to Sockalexis numerous times, fondly recalls that "as a batter, fielder, and base runner, he was a marvel," and directly credits the Penobscot as the inspiration for the new name. The piece acknowledges that "while there will be no real red Indians on the roster, the name will recall fine traditions . . . looking backward to a time when Cleveland had one of the most popular teams of the United States."[23]

The contrasting newspaper reports render it difficult to objectively assess Sockalexis's influence on the renaming of the team. Was he truly an inspiration for the name change or merely a pawn of commercial manipulation? An examination of the various factors that precipitated the name change offers clues that reveal the real forces at work. Following the 1914 season, the Cleveland franchise was heavily in debt. The club had finished last in the American League that season, had the lowest attendance of any team in the league, and Charlie Somers's failing coal business was eroding the financial capital that backed the franchise. Somers desperately wanted to resuscitate the team's failing fortunes and turned to local sportswriters to help him come up with a name that might recapture the fans' imagination. Although a recent *Cleveland Indians Media Guide* contends that "Indians" was suggested by a young fan "as a testament to the game's first American Indian," in truth the sportswriters chose the name. It is conceivable that these writers had a slippery connection to Sockalexis. When he died in 1913 Sockalexis was only forty-two years old; many of the Cleveland sportswriters who originally covered the team while he played in 1897 were likely still alive. The names of the men consulted by Somers in 1915 are not available, but it seems likely that at least some of them were the same reporters that had first adopted and promulgated the "Indians" label during the summer of 1897. As the principal architects of the excitement and attention generated by both Sockalexis and the old call name, these sportswriters perhaps hoped to re-create that atmosphere in an effort to rescue the franchise.[24]

Moreover, the adoption of the popularized "Indians" nickname was also consistent with the accepted practice of recycling old National League nicknames. The Red Sox, White Sox, Athletics, Browns, and Senators were all old National League names that were revived by clubs that joined the new American League after its formation in 1901. The new league, which offered higher salaries and less onerous morality control, quickly attracted the best players and soon surpassed the National League in attendance. A 1903 settlement created the basis for the current Major League system; the National and American Leagues united to form a professional baseball league and agreed to send their respective champions to the World Series. Several National League clubs transferred to the American League, including Cleveland (then known as the Blues), and reached into their past to retrieve popular team nicknames. Cleveland fits the pattern perfectly, as the team not only resurrected the informal but popular Indians nomenclature but also revived the old Spiders nickname for its top minor league affiliate.[25]

The evidence clearly indicates that team officials and Cleveland sportswriters were more interested in creating an exciting new image for the team than in honoring the memory of their pioneer athlete. The widespread appeal of Native imagery during the early twentieth century lends further support to this assertion. The example of the "miracle" Boston Braves, who in 1914 rose from a last-place finish to win the World Series after adopting an Indian sobriquet, was fresh in the mind of the American sports world. Perhaps Cleveland sportswriters hoped the name change might inspire the team's fans to believe their team could have a similar turnaround. In addition, American Indian athletes had recently garnered a great deal of public attention at the 1912 Olympics, where Sockalexis's cousin ran the marathon and Jim Thorpe won gold medals in both the decathlon and pentathlon. Thus the new nickname presented an opportunity for both the owners and the sportswriters to overhaul the image of the team, using the kind of literary drama and excitement made possible by the "Indians" signifier.

Beyond the controversy surrounding the name change, the debate continues to obscure the life and career of Louis Sockalexis. While successfully undermining the Cleveland franchise's foundation of deceit, contemporary critics have inadvertently denied recognition of his accomplishments as a pioneering athlete and failed to apply his life story to the larger relationship between American Indians and the mainstream culture. Instead they too often consider him simply a misappropriated figure whose legend has been unjustly manipulated by the Cleveland baseball organization. Like American Indians in general, Sockalexis has been relegated in modern understanding to the status of victim. Yet he was and is more than just the central figure in an ongoing campaign of deceit and degradation involving stereotypical Native imagery and racial profiling. While there is little doubt that the Cleveland franchise attempted "to mine a set of cultural images that resonated with the paying public" by adopting the name "Indians" in 1915, the exposition of the team's manipulation of its alleged Indian heritage must not be allowed to obfuscate the vibrancy of Sockalexis's collegiate accomplishments, his short but pioneering professional career, and the lessons imbued by his struggles to assimilate into mainstream culture. These are the legacies of Louis Francis Sockalexis.[26]

Notes

1. Staurowsky, "An Act of Honor or Exploitation"; and Ellen Staurowsky, "Sockalexis and the Making of the Myth at the Core of Cleveland's 'Indian' Image," in *Team Spirits*, ed. King and Springwood, 82–106.

2. Biographical treatments of Louis Sockalexis are few and often romantic in nature. See T. Wellman, *Louis Francis Sockalexis: The Life Story of a Penobscot*

Indian (Augusta ME: Maine Department of Indian Affairs, 1975); J. Cohen, "The First Indian: Baseball Legend Louis Sockalexis," *Sports Illustrated* 83 (30 October 1995): 84; and John Phillips, *Chief Sockalexis and the 1897 Cleveland Indians* (Cabin John MD: Capital Publishing, 1991).

3. For Penobscot adaptation and survival, see Frank G. Speck, *Penobscot Man: The Life History of a Forest Tribe in Maine* (New York: Octagon Books, 1940); Peter Anastas, *Glooskap's Children: Encounters with the Penobscot Indians of Maine* (Boston: Beacon Press, 1973); and Paul Brodeur, *Restitution: The Land Claims of the Mashpee, Passamaquoddy, and Penobscot Indians of New England* (Boston: Northeastern University Press, 1985). For the historical experience of Native Americans in the greater New England region over the past three hundred years, see Colin G. Calloway, ed., *After King Philip's War: Presence and Persistence in Indian New England* (Hanover NH: University Press of New England, 1997).

4. For the boarding schools and their role in the cultural genocide of American Indian children, see Adams, *Education for Extinction*.

5. For the early history of baseball, see Harold Seymour, *Baseball: The Early Years* (New York: Oxford University Press, 1960); Benjamin G. Rader, *Baseball: The History of America's Game* (Urbana: University of Illinois Press, 1992); and Geoffrey C. Ward and Ken Burns, *Baseball: An Illustrated History* (New York: Alfred A. Knopf, 1994).

6. Patten authored over six hundred Frank Merriwell dime novels under the pseudonym Burt L. Standish, the first of which appeared in 1896. It is the best-selling American book series ever published, with over five hundred million copies of the various books printed. See John Levi Cutler, *Gilbert Patten and His Frank Merriwell Saga: A Study in Sub-Literary Fiction* (Orono ME: University Press, 1934); and Thomas M. Balchak, "A Study of the Use of Sport and the Image of Athletes as Depicted in the Writings of Gilbert Patten, 1900–1925" (Masters thesis, Bowling Green University, 1975).

7. In addition to his Hall of Fame status, Sockalexis was ranked number four in the spring 2000 edition of *Holy Cross Magazine* on a list of the college's ten greatest athletes. Available online at *http://www.holycross.edu/departments/publicaffairs/hcm.*

8. Blake and McAlee both saw severely diminished playing time in 1897 after the arrival of Sockalexis. For statistics, see Marshall D. Wright, *Nineteenth-Century Baseball: Year by Year Statistics for the Major League Teams, 1871–1900* (Jefferson NC: McFarland, 1996).

9. *Cleveland Plain Dealer*, 14 March 1897, p. 11 and 4 April 1897, p. 3; "The Indians Report to Their Big Heap Chief," *The Sporting News*, 22 March 1897.

10. Sockalexis's progress and the media's adoption of the sobriquet "Indians" for the Spiders can be followed in the 22 April–13 July editions of the *Cleveland*

Plain Dealer, the city's preeminent newspaper. For Cleveland's first victory, see *Cleveland Plain Dealer*, 1 May 1887, p. 3. For Sockalexis's rapidly escalating fame, see "Good Drawing Card: Sockalexis Is the Best Advertised Player in the Business," *The Sporting News*, 19 April 1897; "The Indian Player Catches On," *The Sporting News*, 24 April 1897. For the claim that Sockalexis attracted women to baseball, see *Cleveland Plain Dealer*, 17 June 1897, p. 3.

11. *Cleveland Plain Dealer*, 2 May 1897, p. 8 and 6 May 1897, p. 3.

12. For the abusiveness of late nineteenth-century baseball in general, see Seymour, *Baseball: The Early Years*; Ward and Burns, *Baseball*, 46–57.

13. *Cleveland Plain Dealer*, 24 April 1897, p. 3; *New York Sun*, 10 June 1897, p. 3.

14. Seymour, *Baseball: The Early Years*; Ward and Burns, *Baseball*, 25–40; "League Park," in Michael Benson, *Ballparks of North America: A Comprehensive Historical Reference to Baseball Grounds, Yards, and Stadiums, 1845 to Present* (Jefferson NC: McFarland, 1989), 105–9.

15. Wards and Burns, *Baseball*, 92; "As Sock Tells It," *The Sporting News*, 27 November 1897, p. 3.

16. Bates quoted in Willard Sterne Randall and Nancy Nahra, *Forgotten Americans: Footnote Figures Who Changed American History* (Reading MA: Addison-Wesley, 1998), 230. For Cleveland sports reporters' inconsistent treatment of Sockalexis, see the article written during the height of Sockalexis's success that accused him of drunkenness and characterized him as a "wooden [lazy] Indian": "A Wooden Indian: Sockalexis Played Very Much Like One," *Cleveland Plain Dealer*, 13 July 1897, p. 3.

17. *Cleveland Plain Dealer*, 13 July 1897, p. 3 and 22 July 1897, p. 8.

18. *Cleveland Plain Dealer*, 22 July 1897, p. 8 and 31 July 1897, p. 8.

19. *Cleveland Plain Dealer*, 18 May 1899, p. 6; Wright, *Nineteenth-Century Baseball*, 294, 300, 310; Franklin Lewis, *The Cleveland Indians* (New York: G. P. Putnam's Sons, 1949), 30–32.

20. Ward and Burns, *Baseball*, 92; Colin G. Calloway, *First Peoples: A Documentary Survey of American Indian History* (New York: Bedford/St. Martin's, 1999), 350–74.

21. Staurowsky, "An Act of Honor or Exploitation," 299–316. See also [Cleveland] *Plain Dealer*, 17 May 1999 and 18 January 2000.

22. [Cleveland] *Plain Dealer*, 17 May 1999; Staurowsky, "An Act of Honor or Exploitation," 309–11; and Staurowsky, "Sockalexis and the Making of a Myth," 98.

23. "Ki Yi Wangh Woop! Their Indians!" *Cleveland Plain Dealer*, 17 January 1915, sec. C, p. 1; "Looking Backward," *Cleveland Plain Dealer*, 18 January 1915, p. 8.

24. Morris Eckhouse, *Legends of the Tribe: An Illustrated History of the Cleveland Indians* (Dallas: Taylor, 2000), 21–23; "Looking Backward."

25. See Ward and Burns, *Baseball*; and Donald Honig, *The American League: An Illustrated History* (New York: Crown, 1987).

26. Staurowsky, "An Act of Honor or Exploitation," 309.

3. World Champions
The 1904 Girls' Basketball Team from Fort Shaw Indian Boarding School

Bum-a-ling! Bum-a-ling!
Bow-wow-wow!
Ching-a-ling! Ching-a-ling!
Chow-chow-chow!

The cheer that rose from the ranks of the uniformed students assembled on the parade ground on a Montana morning in early June 1904 was familiar enough, similar as it was to the kinds of nonsensical verses that floated over football fields across the country every fall. Familiar, yet singularly out of context, chanted as it was in the accents and cadences of the various Native peoples represented in this particular student body.

Bum-a-ling! Ching-a-ling!
Who are we?

the voices demanded. Then came the resounding response:

Fort Shaw! Fort Shaw!
Rah! Rah! Rah!

The volume and intensity of the those closing lines left no doubt as to the crowd's collective pride in the basketball team they were sending off that morning.[1]

Since the team's organization in 1902, the girls whose accomplishments engendered such pride had been virtually unbeatable in the fledgling sport of "basket ball," routinely defeating most of the state's college and high school girls' teams—and a few boys' teams as well. Now

Fort Shaw Indian Boarding School girl's basketball team. U.S. Government Indian exhibit, Louisiana Purchase Exposition, World's Fair Presentation Album II, plate 801. Courtesy Missouri Historical Society, St. Louis.

Superintendent Fred Campbell had decided it was time for a greater challenge. In less than twenty-four hours the girls from Fort Shaw Government Industrial Indian Boarding School would be on their way to St. Louis where, as students of the Model Indian School on the grounds of the Louisiana Purchase Exposition, they would be holding twice weekly intrasquad exhibition games and challenging all comers.[2]

En route to the world's fair, the girls would be sharpening their skills and increasing their visibility by playing exhibition and challenge games at whistle-stops along the way. And they would be financing their meals and lodging in the towns in which they played by changing from their basketball uniforms—wool serge middy blouses and bloomers—to ceremonial buckskin dresses and beaded breastplates and charging fifty cents admission to a postgame program of music, dance, and recitation.[3]

Superintendent Campbell's faith in his team was well placed, for the young women from Fort Shaw would prove to be worthy ambassadors of their school, their state, and their tribes, defeating every team they played over the next five months and returning from St. Louis with a trophy declaring them champions of the world's fair of 1904—in effect, champions of the world.[4]

Unfortunately, the Fort Shaw team had more staying power on the court than their story had on the page. Indeed, at the dawn of the twenty-first century, as girls' and women's basketball is drawing the attention of sports fans around the globe, relatively few of those fans realize that more than a hundred years ago full-court girls' basketball was already challenging long-held assumptions about women and sports. And that the best of the best, a team one Missouri reporter described as "eleven aboriginal maidens . . . from the Fort Shaw Reservation," overcame barriers of gender, race, and class to emerge as champions, thereby shattering stereotypes concerning the athletic, academic, and artistic capabilities of Native American girls and women.[5]

According to that same St. Louis reporter, the girls from Fort Shaw were "Lizzie and Mattie Wirth and Sarah Mitchell, Assiniboine Sioux; Belle Johnson, Blackfoot; Genevieve Butch, Yankton Sioux; Minnie Burton, Shoshone; Genevieve Healy and Katie Snell, Gros Ventre; and Emma Sansaver and Flora Luciro, Chippewa." That the reporter omitted Rose LaRose's name from the roster, called Nettie Wirth "Mattie Wirth," misrepresented (and misspelled) the tribal affiliations of several of the girls, and called Fort Shaw a "reservation" is not too surprising, since the story of this legendary team has long been riddled with contradictions and misinformation. That he referred to the girls from Fort Shaw as "aboriginal maidens" should also come as no surprise, unaccustomed as journalists of the day were to writing about Native Americans as anything but "the enemy" or "the exotic."[6]

As inaccurate and inherently—if unconsciously—racist as vintage journalistic accounts tend to be, they offer evidence that these skilled, energetic, and adventuresome young women not only went to the world's fair of 1904 but went, as Fort Shaw school officials were quick to point out, "not as an exhibit or anything of that sort" but as pupils of the Model Indian School the government maintained on the fairgrounds that summer and fall. Of course, the government's Model Indian School was, in and of itself, an exhibit designed to show the world how "civilized" American Indians were becoming under the tutelage of non-Indian teachers, how readily the younger generation had taken up their new language, how well they had mastered "white" homemaking and farming techniques that would assure their success as members of the larger society, and how accomplished they had become at "non-Indian" pursuits.[7]

Even so, interviews with descendants of the Fort Shaw team suggest that the girls were highly motivated participants in the government's game of "show and tell" and that they traveled east with hard-won confidence in their individual and collective abilities, looking forward to the coming adventure as a rare and wonderful opportunity to see the country and enjoy the sights and sounds of a world's fair while representing their school before an international audience. And since the government's interest in demonstrating the effectiveness of its programs and the team's interest in making the most of an unprecedented opportunity were not mutually exclusive, events at the 1904 world's fair provide a particularly vivid example of the ways in which Indian students were able to turn boarding school experiences to their own advantage.[8]

The trip to the world's fair had its beginnings a dozen years earlier—in 1892—with the establishment of an off-reservation government school for Indian children in the Sun River Valley, some thirty miles west of Great Falls, Montana. And, at almost the very same time—but on the other side of the country—with the invention of the game of "basket ball."

By 1892 most of Montana's Native American population was being served by mission and government day schools and boarding schools, all of which were part of a movement afoot at the time to "assimilate and acculturate" America's Indians. The dual goal was to strip Indian children of their language and culture and to teach them English, academic subjects, and vocational trades that would bring them into the "white world." Into this white world *with* the children, it was hoped, would come their elders and, eventually, their offspring.[9]

When the government school on the Fort Peck Reservation in northeastern Montana burned in 1892, federal authorities looked with interest at the recently vacated Fort Shaw military compound, some three hundred fifty miles to the west, realizing it could be easily—and economically—retrofitted as an off-reservation boarding school. Because of the beauty of its setting and the design and landscaping of its buildings—all of which faced inward on a four-hundred-square-foot green— Fort Shaw had long been known as the "queen of Montana's military posts." Now it would become the "queen of Montana's Indian schools." The administrators and faculty could be housed in the old officers' quarters; the children in the soldiers' barracks. The school would have its own chapel, mess hall, post office, store, laundry, and hospital.[10]

As an off-reservation school modeled after Carlisle in Pennsylvania, Haskell in Kansas, and Chilocco in Oklahoma, Fort Shaw would have the added advantage of being too far from the homes of most of its students to allow for regular visits from family members or for frequent trips home to the reservations, both of which educators feared would kindle nostalgia for Native languages and familiar customs. The school would also be sufficiently distant and isolated to discourage would-be runaways. Fort Shaw would serve the region's most promising Indian children, drawing its students—ages five to eighteen—from various tribes across the state as well as from Idaho and Wyoming.[11]

Such were the beginnings of Fort Shaw Government Industrial Indian Boarding School. Meanwhile, on the other side of the continent, in 1891, James Naismith, an educator at the International YMCA Training School in Springfield, Massachusetts, was developing a new sport— "basket ball." In the beginning there was only a soccer ball and a peach basket, and the rules of the game varied widely. There could be five, nine, or as many as twenty members of each team on the court at any one time. Designed for indoor play during the winter months, Naismith's sport became popular almost overnight. With popularity came some semblance of standardized rules: five to a team, two points per goal (or "field throw"), and fouls for intentional contact. By the end of the nineteenth century—less than a decade after its invention— basketball was being played on high school and college campuses across the country.[12]

Though originally intended as an indoor sport for men and boys enrolled in YMCA programs, the game immediately gained popularity with girls and women, and by 1892 gymnastics instructor Senda Berenson had introduced her own modified version of Naismith's new game to her students at Smith College in Northampton, Massachusetts. Soon thereafter women at Wellesley, Vassar, Radcliff, and other women's colleges and "normal schools" in the Northeast took up the sport. It was only a matter of time before basketball was being played by girls and women at high schools and colleges across America—including Montana.[13]

The game's instant popularity with girls and women is understandable, since it was one of the few active sports deemed acceptable for the "fairer sex" at a time when conventional wisdom held that "strenuous activity" could be harmful to female health. Welcome as the sport was to the girls and women who played it, opposition quickly arose from critics for whom the term "strenuous activity" included anything considered "unladylike." Running, for instance. Certainly running across a gymnasium floor in pursuit of a ball. In response to growing public outcry and fearful that the game would be banned altogether for women if it were not altered to curtail such unacceptable behavior as "snatching" the ball or attempting to block an opponent's shot, a committee headed by Senda Berenson established a uniform set of rules that would allow women to play basketball "safely." The court was divided into three sections—front court, center court, and back court. There could be six to ten players on each team. On most indoor courts there were two guards, two centers, and two forwards. Players could not step outside their designated zones and could dribble no more than three times before shooting or passing. These "girls' rules" so drastically altered the dynamics of Naismith's new sport that most high school and college teams—especially those west of the Mississippi—ignored them and continued to play by "boys' rules."[14]

Both basketball and Fort Shaw Indian Boarding School had come of age by the time Fred Campbell assumed the school superintendency in the summer of 1898. The three hundred students then enrolled represented all the tribes of Montana as well as the Bannock, Colville, Pend O'Reille, Shoshone, and Snake of neighboring states. They came, often as not, from families of mixed parentage, most often a non-Indian father and an Indian mother. And they came with different attitudes toward the school and their presence there. A goodly number—like Genevieve Healy from the Fort Belknap Reservation (who would become a guard on the 1904 girls' team)—came willingly, supported by parents who saw some advantage to educating their children in the ways of the white world. [15]

Other youngsters were taken to Fort Shaw over the objections of parents who feared that such an education would cause their children to forsake tribal and family customs. Such fears were not unfounded, for with assimilation and acculturation as its primary goals, Fort Shaw did its share of discouraging adherence to the traditional, Native ways of life. One of the school's first pupils, Lone Wolf, a Piegan who was eight years old when he was taken from his home on the Blackfeet Reservation in 1892, recalled the trauma of that experience: "It was very cold the day they loaded us into the wagons. . . . [W]e cried for it was the first time we were to be separated from our parents. . . . [When we arrived at] the school at Fort Shaw . . . our belongings were taken from us, even the little medicine bags our mothers had given us to protect us from harm. Everything was placed in a heap and set afire." [16]

Lone Wolf and others in similar situations suffered from what one Indian scholar has described as "the homesickness that would not go away." Yet still others, like Gertrude LaRance of the Little Shell band of the Chippewa, had nothing but fond memories of their years at Fort Shaw. Taken by her mother to the school when she was five years old, little Gertie, who was destined to become the "mascot" of the 1904–5 girls' basketball team, had long anticipated the day when she'd join her older sisters at Fort Shaw. By her own report, she suffered not a single moment of homesickness and recalled some ninety years later that she had been the "pet" of the school's staff, all of whom were "just wonderful" to her. [17]

Perhaps the experiences of Louis Youpee, a Chippewa youth brought to Fort Shaw as an eight-year-old in the fall of 1900, are more typical, beginning as they did with apprehension and ending in Youpee's expressed appreciation for the "patience and kindly advice" of Superintendent Fred Campbell, the man who "practically raised that then Indian boy against his own wishes and educated him." [18]

A visionary under whose leadership Fort Shaw Indian Boarding School continued to grow, Superintendent Campbell quickly realized that "assimilation and acculturation" was a two-way process. If Fort Shaw students were ever to make the cultural transition for which they were being educated, then the white world needed educating, too. The non-Indian settlers and ranchers of Sun River Valley and the residents of nearby Great Falls needed to see for themselves the caliber of the students at Fort Shaw, and, toward that end, Campbell began to invite area residents to visit the school.

In the spring of 1901 he convinced U.S. senator Paris Gibson of Great Falls to come and inspect the government boarding school that was practically in his own backyard. In honor of that visit by Gibson and several other Montana politicians, the *Great Falls Daily Tribune* devoted front-page coverage to what its feature editor hailed as "one of the largest and best of the Indian boarding schools." Of particular interest to the editor was the exemplary behavior of the students, especially since there were "but 30 employees and teachers all told to control [316 children] . . . most all of [whom had] . . . come from the tepees of savage parents . . . and ha[d] ever been free to go and come when they chose," making their "resignation to the necessary restraints at the school" all the more amazing.[19]

In addition to the discipline displayed by the children—both in their general behavior and in the elaborate precision drills performed on the parade ground by the boys' and girls' battalions—the visitors were equally impressed by the academic achievement of Fort Shaw students. Though admitting that "it [was] hardly a pleasant thought," the reporter duly noted that "for the number of hours of study and not [even] taking into consideration the difficulties consequent upon a poor understanding of the English language," the Indian children at Fort Shaw were "much further advanced than [the state's] . . . white children of the same age."[20]

Such academic success seemed doubly impressive since pupils spent only half of each day in the schoolroom and the other half engaged in "other necessary and useful employment." That "employment" not only constituted the vocational arm of the curriculum at Fort Shaw but also provided the school with vegetables and meats for its tables; uniforms and shoes for its students; chairs and other wooden furniture for use and for sale; and crochet, lace-making, and other needlework that consistently took top prizes at the annual state fair in Helena. The school's vocational education was gender specific. The girls were taught "to cook, to sew, to cut out and manufacture their own clothing, and to do everything necessary to the maintenance of a happy home"; the boys were trained in carpentry, blacksmithing, and the mechanical arts deemed appropriate for the man of the house. And while the future farmers were taught "to milk and take care of the [cows] and the calves," the future farmers' wives were "instructed in the care of the milk and the manufacture of butter."[21]

"To say that the statesmen and those who accompanied them were astonished" by all they observed during their tour of Fort Shaw was, according to the *Tribune* reporter, "putting it mildly." Yet as impressed as the distinguished visitors were that day, neither they—nor Superintendent Campbell—could possibly have imagined that in a few years representatives from this very school would become Montana's most impressive—if unofficial—ambassadors to the world's fair of 1904, where their academic, artistic, *and* athletic accomplishments would astound some three million of the nearly twenty million people who attended that exposition.[22]

The athletic accomplishments of the students at Fort Shaw were of special concern to the school's superintendent. Hailed as the best catcher ever to play for the University of Kansas, Fred Campbell knew from experience the self-esteem sports could impart to young athletes. That knowledge motivated him to expand Fort Shaw's athletic program by strengthening the baseball, football, and track teams. And since he, like James Naismith, needed an indoor sport to keep his students physically fit through long, cold winters, he introduced them to the new sport of "basket ball."[23]

The game seemed perfect for his purposes. The dance hall of the original Fort Shaw military establishment was of sufficient length—125 feet—to allow for indoor play, and its dirt floor, hard-packed by legions of heavy-booted soldiers, was ideal for bouncing a ball. Not only did Campbell have the right facility, he also had some receptive players—girls as well as boys, for almost universally in Indian cultures there was a long history of female participation in games. Girls' games—lacrosse, shinny, double ball—like boys' games, were central to the spiritual as well as the sporting life of Indian communities. And girls and women played their games with as much intensity as did men and boys.[24]

By 1902 Superintendent Campbell was acting as Coach Campbell, and the Fort Shaw girls were working seriously on their game, running up and down the dirt court in the old dance hall, practicing the dribble, the pass, the "field throw," and the free throw. The ball they used was the standard equipment of the day. Made of leather, it had lacings and was about 12 inches in diameter—or approximately 38 inches in circumference, considerably larger than the balls used by today's women's teams (29 inches in circumference) or even today's men's teams (30 inches). The basket, an iron ring with a net, was suspended some 10 feet above the floor. The net held the ball in place until the goal had been duly noted by the referee who then pulled a chain that released the ball and allowed play to resume with a jump ball at center court.[25]

Over the weeks of practice, as the players' individual aptitudes became more apparent, the starting lineup evolved. Though not the tallest girl on the team, Nettie Wirth played center, earning that position by virtue of her prodigious leaping ability. At a time when the ball came back to the middle of the court for a "center jump" after every score, a player with a vertical leap like Nettie's was an obvious asset. The daughter of an Assiniboine mother and a German immigrant father, Nettie had barely begun her schooling on the Fort Peck Reservation in 1892 when fire destroyed the Poplar school she and her siblings were attending. Shortly thereafter she became one of Fort Shaw's earliest students—and, at age six, one of its youngest. Now, ten years later, she was an outstanding student and a natural at the game of basketball.[26]

At right guard was Josephine Langley, daughter of a Piegan mother and a Metis father who had once served as a scout at Fort Shaw. Born on Birch Creek near Valier around 1877, Josie, like Nettie, had come to Fort Shaw Indian Boarding School the year it opened. Four years later, at age nineteen, she had been recommended for the position of assistant matron. Now, in 1902, because of her leadership skills and her maturity—at twenty-five she was by far the oldest of the girls—she became the team's captain.[27]

The tallest girl on the team was Minnie Burton, an eighteen-year-old transfer from the agency school on the Lemhi Reservation near Salmon, Idaho. Her mother, a Western Shoshone from Nevada, had died when Minnie was nine, and she and her younger brother were thereafter raised by their Lemhi Shoshone father and their Bannock stepmother. Though she had barely arrived on campus when Coach Campbell began to choose his players—many of whom had by then been classmates at

Fort Shaw for several years—the newcomer was readily accepted by the other members of the team and promptly dubbed "Big Minnie." While her skills as a defensive player seemed almost instinctive, Campbell saw that it would take her a while to develop the offensive skills for which she would eventually be known. Biding his time, he put her at left guard.[28]

At right forward he placed eighteen-year-old Emma Rose Sansaver. Daughter of a Metis father and a Chippewa-Cree mother, Emma was born near Havre. She and her younger sister Flora had attended St. Paul's Mission School at Fort Belknap Agency before transferring to Fort Shaw in 1897, shortly after the death of their father. The shortest girl on the team—and one of the quickest—Emma compensated for her lack of height by her energy and agility. She could always be counted on to sink her "field throws" or to get the ball to someone who could.[29]

Often that person was left forward Belle Johnson, who was sixteen during her first season with the team. Belle was born near Belt, the child of a Piegan mother who had met and married a white miner from Fort Benton. She was still a young child when her parents took up ranching near Browning, and she and her two sisters began their education at the Blackfeet Agency School before transferring to Fort Shaw around the turn of the century.[30]

Rounding out the roster that first year were substitutes Delia Gebeau and Genie Butch. Like Minnie Burton, with whom she often shared the position of left guard, sixteen-year-old Delia was a first-year student at Fort Shaw. Her mother—a Spokane Indian from the Colville Reservation—had died when Delia was two. Since that time she had lived with her French Canadian father and seven older siblings on the Flathead Reservation, where she had attended school prior to her enrollment at Fort Shaw.[31]

The daughter of an Anglo rancher and an Assiniboine mother, Genie Butch grew up on the Fort Peck Reservation and attended school there during her early years. Able to play offense as well as defense, fifteen-year-old Genie gave depth to the Fort Shaw team during its first year of competitive play, and her persistence made it evident she intended to earn her way to a starting position. Indeed, all the girls on the team demonstrated similar dedication and determination, and they were soon showing more promise than the boys.[32]

Perhaps because the boys at Fort Shaw were already involved in football, track, and baseball while the girls had no such outlet for physically challenging team play; perhaps because this particular group of girls was composed of unusually talented athletes; perhaps because they enjoyed the freedom of running up and down the old dance hall and the exhilaration of sending a ball flying through the air and into an iron hoop; or perhaps for individual and collective reasons we'll never know a magical meld developed between these young women and the fame of "basket ball."

Their talents did not go unnoticed by their coach. As an educator dedicated to increasing public awareness of the abilities of his Indian students, Fred Campbell knew the public relations benefits that could come from fielding a winning team. But to showcase his girls, he had to come up with some worthy opponents against whom to test their skills. With basketball not yet broadly established in Montana, Campbell set about organizing a girls' team in nearby Sun River to introduce the Fort Shaw girls to interscholastic play and ready them for competition at a higher level. When he thought the Sun River team was capable of giving his Indian girls a game, he brought them by wagon to Fort Shaw for the first of several one-sided matches.[33]

By late November 1902, sensing his team was ready for tougher competition, Campbell arranged a game with Butte Parochial. On their first long-distance road trip, he and the Fort Shaw girls traveled by wagon to the rail junction several miles distant and then by train to Butte, where they defeated the home team 15–9. While such a score seems low by today's standards, it was typical in the early days of basketball, due in large measure to the fact that the clock continued to run while the ball was being retrieved from out of bounds after an errant pass or shot *and* while the ball was being returned to center court for a jump ball after every score. Eager to avenge the loss, W. J. Adams, Butte Parochial's young coach, pushed for a rematch, and Coach Campbell set about making arrangements for what was to be "the first basketball game ever played in Great Falls."[34]

On Thursday evening, 15 January 1903, Luther Hall was "crowded to its limit with spectators," few of whom were familiar enough with the rules of the game to realize that the opposing teams would ordinarily have played two twenty-minute halves rather than the three twelve-minute periods agreed upon because Coach Adams had felt his girls were "[not] equal to longer periods of play after their journey from the smoky city." In their navy blue uniforms trimmed in white, the Fort Shaw girls took the floor against the girls from Butte Parochial, and the game was underway.[35]

Though "the nimble maidens play[ed] like lambent flames back and forth across the polished floor," there were no successful field throws, and the first period ended in a score of 1–0 in favor of Butte, the lead having been gained on a free throw assessed for "holding" on the part of one of the Fort Shaw girls. The following period saw the "little maids from Butte" explode, scoring five goals from the field to bring the score to 11–0 before "the ball suddenly sped down the room, thrown by an Indian girl. Another dusky maid caught it and before anyone could block her she had deftly tossed it in the goal basket." At that point "thunderous applause broke forth, 500 voices cheered . . . [for] local sympathy was with the Indian school girls." In the final period "the Indians went on the warpath" and the "the leather globe was hurled about as fast as a ping pong ball," but time ran out and the game ended at 15–6 in favor of Butte Parochial. Reflecting the partisanship already evident among the fans in Great Falls, the *Tribune* reporter noted that "the short periods of play probably afforded the Butte players some advantage" since the Fort Shaw girls were "credited by their supporters with more staying power than their white opponents."[36]

Despite the fact that "their" team lost, basketball was obviously a hit with the fledgling fans of Great Falls, and "a good patronage [wa]s assured for future contests." Indeed, some two weeks later on the evening of Friday, 30 January, when the college girls from what was then known as Montana State University in Missoula played Fort Shaw in Luther Hall, "numbers of persons who desired admission to the hall . . . [had to be] sent away, it being impossible to accommodate them." This time the home team came through for the local fans, crushing the college girls 19–9.[37]

Impressed by the "fearlessness with which the Indian girls entered into the game," the *Tribune* reporter noted that "despite a few hard falls they never flinched or ceased for a moment in . . . [their] effort to score a point." And score they did. This sudden surge in scoring might well have been tied to a subtle but significant change in the team's original lineup. Belle Johnson had been moved to left guard, making way for Minnie Burton to begin playing forward opposite Emma Sansaver. The front line of Minnie, Emma, and Nettie combined for six points in the first half and then exploded for thirteen more in the second.[38]

That the Great Falls fans were hooked on the game and on "their" team was evident from the changing tone of the press coverage the girls were beginning to draw. Up until this point, reporters had made little effort to name individual players, though Nettie Wirth's many center jumps, her role as the team's designated foul shooter, and her constant involvement in the offense made her readily identifiable by fans and reporters alike. But in newspaper reports of games played from this point on, individual girls began to be credited for outstanding plays. The *Tribune* even ran the team's picture, along with thumbnail sketches of the players: Emma Sansaver, "the little one," was "quick about her schoolroom . . . work"; Minnie Burton was "a general favorite with employees and pupils"; and Josie Langley was "reliable and trustworthy." This was a journalistic turning point of sorts—though reporters continued to use such phrases as "dusky maiden" and "on the warpath." Whatever they were called by contemporary reporters, in a few short months the young women from Fort Shaw had, in effect, transformed an activity once seen as merely "good exercise" for high school and college women into a standing-room-only spectator sport.[39]

During the rest of that 1902–3 season, the girls played—and won— at least six more games. They twice humbled the "Farmerettes" from Montana Agricultural College in Bozeman, first by a score of 36–9 in Great Falls, then by a score of 20–0 in Bozeman. At the second game over eight hundred people—"probably the largest crowd that ever attended a college game"—squeezed into Story Hall for their first glimpse of "the Indian girls." The girls from Fort Shaw also traveled to Missoula for a game at the Union Opera House, where the audience "filled every foot of standing room allowed them between the walls and the players." The balcony, too, was "filled to its capacity . . . [and] every good play, whether by a university girl or a Fort Shaw player, was loudly applauded." There was much to applaud, but ultimately the "more accurate throwing, . . . splendid catching," and balanced attack of Fort Shaw carried the day: "Belle Johnson threw three baskets from the field, Minnie Burton threw two from the fifteen-foot line, and

Nettie Wirth one from the same place." In the end it was a 17–6 victory for the girls from Fort Shaw.[40]

Perhaps their sweetest victory was a 28–10 win over the girls of Helena High School, a win that avenged an early season defeat played on the home court of "the capital city girls." The rematch in Great Falls was reported to be "the prettiest, fastest and most enthusiastic [game] ever played in the state." In late March Fort Shaw returned to Butte to take on the girls from Butte Parochial in the rubber match of that series—and came away with a resounding 18–8 win. On that same road trip they crushed the girls' team from Boulder High, 37–6.[41]

Having run up a record of nine wins and two losses (both of which had come at the outset of the season), the Fort Shaw team concluded its first year of interscholastic basketball as the sport's undisputed—if unofficial—state champion. In the process the team had become the acknowledged favorite of fans across Montana. And by season's end the cheers and applause of the Fort Shaw stalwarts were joined not only by the curious folk who had come out just to see what all the publicity was about but also by the originally partisan fans of their opponents, so that the team's rallying cry, "Shoot, Minnie, shoot! Shoot, Minnie, shoot!" rose to the volume and intensity that made it the stuff of legend.[42]

The Fort Shaw girls had become "Montana's team." Furthermore, their exemplary conduct in the course of their athletic achievements had earned them an entrée into social as well as athletic arenas in the non-Indian world. When the Fort Shaw girls traveled to Bozeman to meet the Farmerettes in late March 1903, they were special guests at a school-wide assembly followed by a luncheon where "each Indian was seated beside the white girl who was to be her opponent [that] . . . evening," giving the girls "a good opportunity to get acquainted." And during a postgame dance held that evening, the victorious "dusky bell[e]s had no cause to complain of a lack of partners among the college boys."[43]

From the standpoint of Superintendent Campbell and his colleagues, the fact that the girls on the Fort Shaw team could move easily and gracefully in the white world provided ample evidence that Fort Shaw was meeting—even exceeding—the goals of the government's Indian education system. Other educators in the system took notice. In late May 1903 Campbell received an invitation from S. M. McCowan, superintendent of the Chilocco school and the newly appointed director of the Model Indian School that was to be constructed in St. Louis in conjunction with the upcoming world's fair. The school would house 150 students selected from among the various Indian boarding schools located within the boundaries of the Louisiana Purchase Territory, and McCowan wanted Campbell to send a cadre of Fort Shaw's best students to reside at the Model Indian School from the fair's opening on 30 April 1904 to its closing on 1 December.[44]

Choosing those students was a relatively simple matter for Superintendent Campbell, who immediately turned to the girls on the basketball team. If they met all their classroom and workroom requirements, he told them, if their conduct was in every way beyond reproach, and if they played as well in the upcoming season as they had in the season just concluded, he would take them to St. Louis the following year to represent the school at the Louisiana Purchase Exposition. The girls responded with "the greatest enthusiasm, unanimously determined to make themselves worthy of the honor." And they welcomed Coach Campbell's proposal to expand the roster to ten so that when there was no competition to take the floor against them—a situation that was to become increasingly common—Fort Shaw could field two teams to engage in scrimmages against each other.[45]

The front line of the first team—center Nettie Wirth and forwards Emma Sansaver and Minnie Burton—remained in place. The back court, however, underwent a major change. Josephine Langley, who was now planning her marriage to Harvey Liephart, the school's baker, left the team to become a full-time employee of Fort Shaw. Genie Butch, the substitute who had seen the most playing time in the recently concluded season, took Josie's place at right guard. And into Josie's place as captain stepped Belle Johnson, who remained the starting left guard.[46]

The anchor of the team formed with the new recruits was Delia Gebeau, the other substitute of the 1902–3 season. Genevieve Healy was assigned to one of the guard positions on the scrimmage squad. The daughter of "Colonel" W. H. H. Healy, an adventurer and army scout, and White Eagle, a full-blood Gros Ventre, Gen had first attended the mission and agency schools on the Fort Belknap Reservation with her siblings. But in 1896 after the death of their mother, Colonel Healy had sent Gen and her two sisters to Fort Shaw. At fifteen Gen was among the youngest of the team members—and apparently the liveliest, known for her pranks in classroom and dorm as well as her fierce play on the court. [47]

The other guard position was assumed by seventeen-year-old Catherine Snell, who had also begun her education at Fort Belknap Agency School before transferring to Fort Shaw with her three sisters. Like Nettie Wirth, Katie was the daughter of a German immigrant father. Her mother, Fannie Black Digger, was Assiniboine. One of eleven children, Katie was by nature a quiet girl, and she brought a quiet strength to the team. [48]

Playing forward on the expanded roster was fifteen-year-old Sarah Mitchell. Like many of her teammates, Sarah had followed siblings to the school at Fort Shaw. The youngest of six, she had been born in Wolf Point to an Assiniboine-Chippewa mother and an Anglo-Assiniboine father. Another fifteen-year-old, Flora Lucero, was paired with Sarah at forward. Born near Choteau, Flora was the daughter of a Chippewa-Cree mother and a father of Spanish descent. With Healy and Snell, Mitchell and Lucero now lining up with Gebeau, Fort Shaw could field two teams worthy not only of giving each other some spirited practices but also of giving any audience a fine introduction to the game of basketball. [49]

With additional girls came the need for more uniforms, and several of the members of the team were among the domestic science students who crafted the middies and bloomers for the members of the "red" team. The new uniforms were much like those worn by the veterans— navy blue wool serge bloomers, matching long-sleeved blouses with striped dickies, sailor collars, and tight cuffs—though, to distinguish between the players, the uniforms of the red squad were trimmed in red rather than white, including the monogrammed "F" and "S" on the collar. Black cotton stockings and black gym shoes completed the outfits. [50]

In late June with schoolwork done for the year, the girls headed for Havre for "a clever, fast, and snappy" exhibition game in Swanton Hall, playing before "a large audience, many of whom had never seen a basket ball game" and most of whom "[had never] seen the Indian girls [who] exemplify the sport." This intrasquad exhibition game—like all the team's earlier games—gave Superintendent Campbell a platform for his favorite cause, and he spoke briefly to the crowd on the "benefits of Indian education." With that game concluded, the team members returned to Fort Shaw only long enough to pack their belongings before heading off to their respective homes for the summer, full of excitement over what the coming year would bring.[51]

Back in place on campus by 1 September, they began to work seriously, both in the classroom and on the gym floor, intent upon meeting Campbell's expectations. To help Coach Campbell conduct practices, Sadie Malley, a young woman who had been teaching at the school since 1899, took on the duties of assistant coach. By the time the season opened, the players were more than ready to defend their title as state champions, but they were to be denied that opportunity. Whether Coach Campbell's inability to secure "consecutive dates [for games] in different cities," as he had done the previous year, was simply one of the scheduling difficulties "managers of athletic aggregations in the Northwest [had] to contend with" or whether the difficulties were due to an understandable reluctance on the part of other coaches to put their programs on the line again against the team from Fort Shaw may never be fully known. Making the best of a frustrating situation, Campbell scheduled instead intrasquad contests around the state that still allowed fans to see the girls play—and gave his "second team" a chance to gain experience before large crowds.[52]

If the fans wondered why their local teams had not included Fort Shaw on that season's schedule, so be it. He could not let himself be concerned about something over which he had no control. But he had to feel some justification when the *Anaconda Standard* noted that Fort Shaw's "famous girls' basket ball team" was coming to town to give "an exhibition of how that exciting game should be played. This team has not been playing much throughout the state this season," the reporter continued, "for the reason that there is no girls' team in the state that can give them anything like a tussel [*sic*]. They stand alone and unrivaled. This may not be [welcome] . . . reading for the white girls, but it is true."[53]

In Anaconda, as elsewhere through February and March, the girls not only impressed the sellout crowds with their athletic skills but also entertained them after each game with a program that included music, recitations, dance, and calisthenics. The program was a preview of things to come, for though they had been selected to go to the world's fair because of their athletic abilities, as students at the Model Indian School they would also be giving weekly literary programs, pantomimes, musical concerts, and gymnastics demonstrations.[54]

To assist the girls in mastering exercises involving Indian clubs and dumbbells, Superintendent Campbell brought in Lizzie Wirth, Nettie's older sister and a recent graduate of Carlisle Industrial School in Pennsylvania. At twenty-three Lizzie had the experience and maturity Campbell to be a steadying influence on the team during their summer at the fair.[55]

Preparing the girls' musical program for St. Louis fell to Fern Evans, the school's music teacher and an accomplished violinist. The task was not a difficult one, as most of the players on the team had studied instrumental and choral music ever since their arrival at Fort Shaw, and several of them had become skilled musicians. Miss Evans organized a mandolin club that fostered the girls' talents, and they were soon playing in concert as smoothly as they played on court.[56]

If Miss Evans's task was a relatively easy one, the assignment that fell to Lillie B. Crawford—training the girls in "pantomime and recitation"—was, by Miss Crawford's own report, "most disconcerting." Before the fall of 1903, the girls had never been required to speak in public, and their beginning efforts at recitation were "very crude." But by spring they had surpassed their teacher's "most sanguine expectations," perfecting an intricately choreographed recitation of "The Famine" from Longfellow's *Hiawatha*, an act they performed in ceremonial buckskin dresses and beaded breastplates representative of their respective tribes.[57]

For these performances Miss Crawford added another member to her troupe, Rose LaRose, a Shoshone-Bannock from Idaho's Fort Hall Reservation. A talented dancer who excelled in the Delsartian techniques favored by Miss Crawford, Rose was not particularly interested in basketball. However, she agreed to join the "traveling squad" when Delia Gebeau decided to leave Fort Shaw and return to her home in the Flathead Valley.[58]

Training in music and public performance was not just the privilege of the girls' basketball team. It was a part of the curriculum for all students at Fort Shaw, and the school's orchestra and marching band were frequently invited to perform at special events around Montana. The band also appeared at the girls' basketball games, especially through the spring of 1904 as the team played in cities across the state. Eleven-year-old Louis Youpee was often a part of the entourage. A "natural-born actor," the youngster's recitations of pieces like "Grandpa's Meddler" kept the audience "in a continual [uproar]." Little Gertie LaRance, the team's seven-year-old "mascot," appeared with Louis during these halftime shows. While he did comedy, she did tragedy, performing heart-rending versions of "The Culprit's Plea." Team, band, and junior troubadours played to full houses in Anaconda, Butte, and Missoula, with each appearance billed as the residents' last chance to see the Fort Shaw girls in action before they left for the world's fair.[59]

The Louisiana Purchase Exposition officially opened on 30 April 1904 when the fair's president ceremoniously touched a golden telegraph key that flashed a message to President Theodore Roosevelt in Washington, D.C. However, the Model Indian School did not open until 1 June. And it opened without the delegation from Fort Shaw, since school commitments kept the team in Montana until the end of May. On the first day of June the long-awaited trip finally began with a festive send-off on the school campus as wagons laden with the team, faculty chaperons, and all their trunks rolled off toward the rail junction several miles distant. A last-minute addition to the group was Louis Youpee, for Superintendent Campbell had been asked to bring the youngster along to "make medicine for . . . audiences" in St. Louis. He had also been asked to bring samples of the handiwork that consistently won blue ribbons for the school at the Montana State Fair, and packed away among the gear loaded onto the train that morning were not only the girls' basketballs, musical instruments, and Indian clubs, but also a proud collection of the beadwork, needlework, and leather work crafted by the students of Fort Shaw.[60]

That evening the team performed in Great Falls, and on evenings thereafter, as the train made its way across Montana, they played exhibition games in Bozeman, Livingston, Billings, Miles City, and Glendive. Across the state line they played challenge games in Dickinson, Bismarck, and Valley City, North Dakota, defeating an All-Star team in the latter city by a score of 34–0. Pressing on, they played another game in the Twin Cities before turning south toward St. Louis.[61]

Arriving in that city to much fanfare on Tuesday, 14 June—coincidentally, "Montana Day" at the fair—they were immediately escorted to the Model Indian School for their first performance, a musical program that led a St. Louis reporter to exclaim, "One of the unique features of the U.S. Government Indian exhibit at the fairgrounds was seen for the first time yesterday afternoon when the Fort Shaw Indian girls' mandolin club . . . furnished the music for the daily literary programme in the chapel [of the Model Indian School]."[62]

The "literary programme" was not the only thing the girls participated in on the very day of their arrival. Having been on the train for almost two weeks by the time they pulled into St. Louis, they were obviously ready to stretch their legs and take in the sights. With their first performance behind them, they asked to be taken to the fabled Pike, a mile-long stretch of amusements on the northern boundary of the fairgrounds. There they found such exhibits as "The Temple of Mirth"; Jim Key, the educated horse; "Hagenbeck's Zoological Paradise and Animal Circus"; daily reenactments of a battle in the recently concluded Boer War; and "Cummins' Indian Congress"—a Buffalo Bill–style display of cowboys and Indians, in this case some eighty Dakota Sioux "warriors" who traveled the country with the Cummins group.[63]

The girls' first visit to the Pike would not be their last, though their free time was limited during their five-month stay at the fair. Their daily schedule, if not as rigorous as the one back at Fort Shaw, was heavy enough to keep them close to Indian Hill, the name given to the area of the fairgrounds designed to show off the "types of the aborigines of the present United States, and especially of the Louisiana Purchase Territory." The focal point of Indian Hill was the Model Indian School, a beautiful three-story building whose elevation and surroundings made it one of the most conspicuous structures on the fairgrounds. The building faced an open plaza, surrounded by an area designated as "The Indian Reservation," where representatives of fourteen different tribes set up camps resembling those in their homelands. There were Acoma and Santa Clara peoples from New Mexico in their respective "pueblos"; Navajo in hogans; Minnesota Chippewa in birch bark houses; Pawnee in ceremonial earth lodges; Rosebud Reservation Sioux in their tipis; and Wichita from Oklahoma in grass lodges, each group wearing the clothing and preparing the foods preferred by their respective tribes. In all, some 550 North American Indians—including the 150 students at the Model Indian School—were, in one way or another, "on exhibit" at the fair.[64]

Fairgoers were left to draw the conclusion that students at the Model Indian School were much further "advanced" than the Native peoples living on the neighboring "reservation." The students were, after all, an example of the progress being made by the government's educational programs. From 9 a.m. to 5 p.m. visitors were free to walk through the school and observe academic classes attended by seventh-grade pupils from the Chilocco school in Indian Territory (present-day Oklahoma) and kindergarten students from Pima Indian School in Sacaton, Arizona Territory, plus domestic science activities, blacksmithing, woodworking, and farming and ranching demonstrations. Visitors strolling the wide central hallway of the school building could look into the open-door classrooms and workrooms on one side of the hall, then turn to look into the open stalls on the other side, where the "blanket Indians" plied their ancient—and seemingly "primitive"—crafts.[65]

Afternoons were given to literary and musical programs in the chapel of the Model Indian School, though within a few weeks audiences had outgrown that space, and, weather permitting, the programs were moved to the east porch of the building. Performances given by the girls from Fort Shaw included pantomime, dance, recitations, and mandolin concerts. The reporter who covered one such program in early September for the *St. Louis Globe-Democrat* was dazzled by the "pantomime performance" of "Song of the Mystic," a rhythmical dance performed by nine of the Fort Shaw girls garbed in ethereal white outfits. A woman from Boston declared the exercises in the Model Indian School chapel that day "the finest of the kind" she'd ever seen.[66]

But the Fort Shaw girls were not in St. Louis merely to provide cultural entertainment. They had been brought to the fair to demonstrate their skill in the sport of basketball—and that they did, engaging in exhibition games twice a week, most often on the plaza in front of the school, playing in mid-afternoon, in the heat and humidity of the St. Louis summer, in wool bloomers and middies. Their first exhibition game, on the day after their arrival at the fair, was reported in the *St. Louis Republic*. The writer who covered the event was impressed. The girls, he said, were veritable "streaks of lightning," and the excellence of their play that afternoon had more than "justified their title of basket ball champions of the northwest." His opinion as to the probable origins of such excellence gave equal weight to both sides of the old question of nature versus nurture: "The natural agility of the Indian maiden . . . [had] been developed by the training of . . . Fort Shaw . . . to surpassing excellence."[67]

Over the course of the summer, as the first Olympic Games staged in the United States were carried on just a few blocks away and AAU, YMCA, college, and scholastic men's and boys' teams competed for trophies offered through the fair's Physical Culture Department, the girls from Fort Shaw afforded exposition attendees their only opportunity to observe women's team sports. And this despite the relatively positive response of the fair's athletic director, James Sullivan, to those who had proposed adding a women's component to the competitions in St. Louis. "It would be a great thing for girls' sport," Sullivan had said, "and I believe [it] would prove a drawing card at the Fair"—provided, of course, participating institutions and organizations were prepared to violate the gender taboo against allowing female athletes to compete in a public arena. Predictably, deep-seated prejudice had prevailed, sparing Sullivan the need to make good on his offer.[68]

Thus at the world's fair of 1904, team sports for "the fairer sex" were exemplified only by the hard-driving intrasquad games played twice a week by the young women from Fort Shaw—and these games, contested in a very public arena, did indeed prove to be "a drawing card." Somewhat less public were the games in which the girls competed against Missouri and Illinois high school teams that summer, most of which were apparently held indoors and on the home courts of the opposing teams. One notable exception to the indoor rule was a game played in late July against O'Fallon (Illinois) High School before "a crowd . . . so great that ropes had to be used to keep the field clear." From the opening whistle, play was "extremely fast" and the Indian girls displayed an adeptness at feinting and dodging that amazed the eastern fans. The Model Indian School band that had accompanied the team and provided their only support in that partisan crowd sent up cheers of "Shoot, Minnie, shoot" as the girls ran up a halftime lead of 10–0 before Emma Sansaver sprained her ankle and had to leave the game. With Katie Snell taking her place at forward, Fort Shaw held its lead through the second half, winning by a score of 13–3. After the game the band "gleefully . . . escorted both teams from the field and played concerts all evening."[69]

Shortly thereafter the Anthropology Department of the fair staged an "anthropological athletic meet" in which "natives from the four quarters of the globe" engaged in track and field events. "Won" by the American Indian contingent, this "meet"—rightly described decades later as "the lowpoint of the entire summer"—was, at the time, hailed by Dr. W. J. McGee, head of the fair's Anthropology Department, as having demonstrated "what [scientists] have long known, that the white man leads the races of the world, both physically and mentally."[70]

The "anthropological games" and the comments they evoked were widely publicized and could not have escaped the notice of the Fort Shaw girls, who must have considered themselves lucky, for once, to have been excluded from the field of play. Their moment was coming, however, for an "authority on basketball" in Missouri, one Philip Stremmel, had decided there had to be some way of defeating the Indian girls from Fort Shaw. Early in August he began putting together a St. Louis "alumnae team" made up of young women who had played for that city's Central High School over the course of Central's reign as the champions of Missouri and Illinois. By month's end Stremmel's challenge to Fort Shaw had been issued and answered, and the teams prepared for a three-game series that would determine the championship of the world's fair of 1904.[71]

The pending face-off drew the immediate attention of the St. Louis media. Apparently James Sullivan had stood by his earlier requirement that all official fair competitions had to be played in a public arena, since the *St. Louis Republic* announced that "for the first time in the [city's] history" a girls' basketball game would be played in the open—at Kulage Park on Saturday afternoon, 3 September, phrasing that effectively dismissed the demonstration games played all summer by the "Indian girls team . . . that [would be] representing the Louisiana Purchase Exposition."[72]

The Fort Shaw lineup that afternoon was a familiar one: Nettie Wirth at center, Minnie Burton and Emma Sansaver at forward (though Emma was still suffering the effects of the ankle sprain), Belle Johnson and Genie Butch at guard. The weather was described as perfect, "delightfully cool, [with] a cloudless sky and a gentle breeze," by Fort Shaw teacher Lillie B. Crawford, who filed a report of the game with the hometown *Tribune*. "The referee ordered everybody back from the lines," Crawford wired, "the umpire tossed a coin to decide goals and the game was on." Nettie controlled the tip. And the Fort Shaw girls controlled the game. Minnie finished the first half with two free throws and three field throws. Emma, as if to discount the effects of the sprained ankle, "nonplussed her opponents . . . by dodging here and there with the rapidity of a streak of lightning." Nettie made "four brilliant field throws," Belle Johnson made "one of the finest plays . . . ever seen," and Genie Butch "covered herself in glory" by holding the St. Louis girls to a single basket. The final score was 24–2.[73]

Miss Crawford's superlatives aside, the final score spoke for itself. The local press was equally fulsome in its praise: "To the great surprise of several hundred spectators . . . the girls from Fort Shaw [were] . . . more active, more accurate, and cooler than their opponents," the reporter for the *St. Louis Post-Dispatch* wrote, concluding that they simply "outclassed the girls of St. Louis in every way."[74]

Perhaps Coach Stremmel had come to that same conclusion, for he and the St. Louis alumnae team failed to show the next Saturday for the second game—technically forfeiting the series. However, on Saturday, 8 October, in response to a last-minute plea from the St. Louis players, the teams faced off again, this time on the plaza in front of the Model Indian School, the "home court" for the Fort Shaw girls. Despite the short notice, so many people thronged the site that game officials had to call on the Jefferson Guard, the fair's security police, to push back the spectators so the game could begin. Again, Miss Crawford wired home a colorful dispatch, full of descriptions of Nettie's phenomenal leaps, Belle's skillful passes, Minnie's field throws, and Genie's steals. The crowd seems to have been a factor in this match, for early in the game when Emma "made quite a brilliant field throw" the St. Louis team seemed "disconcerted at the applause." Indeed, each time the Indians made a basket the audience "went wild with enthusiasm." There was plenty to cheer about as the score at the final whistle stood at 17–6, leaving no doubt as to the superiority of the Fort Shaw team.[75]

The girls from Montana were the undisputed champions of the Louisiana Purchase Exposition. And Coach Stremmel was gracious in defeat. The Fort Shaw girls "play[ed] a wonderful game," he conceded. "They are so skillful, so fleet, and . . . their powers of endurance are simply marvelous. . . . My girls . . . [were] unprepared to cope with such formidable opponents."[76]

With the championship secured, the girls from Fort Shaw soon joined their classmates at the Model Indian School in the task of closing down the classrooms and workrooms, for despite its magnificence, the school building, like most of the other structures on the fairgrounds, had been built to last but a season. Now, with no way to heat the facility against the late autumn chill, Superintendent McCowan reluctantly announced its imminent closure. The students would be on their way home before Thanksgiving. The news was bittersweet. Eager as they were to take home the trophy declaring them basketball champions of the world's fair of 1904, the girls from Fort Shaw were reluctant to say good-bye to the friends they had made in St. Louis. Addresses were exchanged and autograph books were passed around to be filled with reminders of the friendships formed and experiences shared at the fair.[77]

The citizens of St. Louis were equally reluctant to see the fair close. Although the closing meant an end to noise and congestion, it also meant an end to the Pike and the Palaces, the Ferris wheel, and the fairy tale world that had for one short season seemed more real than life beyond the exposition's borders. So much of what had been grand and glorious would be gone forever, and yet, as William Reedy editorialized in *The Mirror* on 1 December 1904, "[I]t is over—the Fair—Yet much of it remains with us, . . . [including] a broader tolerance [and] a keener appreciation of the good in all the world. . . . We have learned to be humble before the achievements of other peoples whom we have fancied we long ago left behind in the march of progress."[78]

Perhaps no other group at the fair had contributed to the appreciation of the achievements of other peoples as much as had the students at the Model Indian School, including the group of young women from Fort Shaw, Montana, who had gone to St. Louis to prove their abilities in the concert hall and on the playing field. Though they were but one small part of the "Indian Exhibit" as a whole, they had developed a loyal following among visitors from around the world, many of whom would have agreed with one Montanan's assertion that the fair "just wouldn't have been the same without them."[79]

The girls were no longer in St. Louis when Reedy's editorial appeared in print, having already left for home, taking with them the gleaming trophy that signified their status as champions of women's basketball. Welcomed home by jubilant classmates, they quickly settled back into the campus routine. But they had their stories. And their memories. And the promise of still more challenges. The next summer they set out for Portland, where they planned to take on all comers at the Lewis and Clark Exposition of 1905. But their reputation had preceded them, and the competition was thin in Oregon. The girls were able to pick up only one contest—a game against Chemawa Indian School just outside Salem. Said to be the only game they ever played against another Indian school, that match-up ended as had so many others, in a clear victory for the girls from Fort Shaw.[80]

The world champions played as a unit only one more year, going undefeated through the 1906 season, which once again included games against the women from the university in Missoula and the college in Bozeman as well as against high schools across the state. Of the girls who had gone to St. Louis, by 1907 only Emma Sansaver, Katie Snell, and Genevieve Healy were still playing basketball for Fort Shaw, the others having left school to begin their adult lives. At season's end Emma and Genevieve followed suit. And the following year, having served the school for nearly a decade, Superintendent Campbell himself left Fort Shaw to accept a position in another area of the Indian Service.[81]

Facing declining enrollment in 1910, Fort Shaw Government Industrial Indian Boarding School was closed. And over the course of the century, the institution itself, along with the basketball team that had given the school a moment of international fame, was largely forgotten. Yet the legacy of the team lives on, for, in the prophetic words of a young *Anaconda Standard* reporter, the "particularly entertaining" style of the Fort Shaw girls had "much to do with making the game so popular in Montana."[82]

Evidence of the broader implications of the team's legacy was expressed in spring 2000 by Turtle Woman, a descendant of Genevieve Healy, who spoke for many when she noted that the Fort Shaw girls were "more than a skilled basketball team. . . . They were a rare gathering of young female warriors who, facing the same . . . [barriers] that caused many Indian people to become discouraged and defeated, chose a path that made them victors."[83]

Notes

A modified version of this article appeared in *Montana The Magazine of Western History* in 2001.

1. "Big Victory for Fort Shaw Girls," *Great Falls Daily Tribune*, 9 September 1904.

2. "Indian Girls Will Play Many Basketball Games En Route," *Great Falls Daily Leader*, 2 June 1904; Gertrude LaRance Parker, interview by Barbara Winters, November 1990. According to Don Evans, who coached the boys' team at Great Falls High, his teams and "other boys teams in Montana" were "severely trounced" by the Fort Shaw girls (" 'Shoot, Minnie, Shoot': Famous Battle Cry Carried by Fort Shaw Indian Belles to 1904 World Title," *Montana Sports Magazine*, spring 1968, 222).

3. "Indian Girls Will Play."

4. This trophy is held by Valerie Goss, granddaughter of Belle Johnson Arnoux Swingley Conway, captain of the team during their 1904 season. Thought for years to be lost, the trophy was located by three Simms (MT) High School juniors—Tana Fleming, Sarah Green, and Ashle Wheeler—in the course of their research on members of the Fort Shaw championship team of 1904. The research was carried out as part of their school's Montana Heritage Project under the guidance of their teacher, Dorothea Susag, and of the authors. See *Stories in Place III: Our Sun River Valley Heritage*, Simms High School student literary magazine, spring 2000.

5. "Eleven Aboriginal Maidens, Champions of the West, Arrive," *St. Louis Republic*, 15 June 1904. On the evolution of women's basketball, see, in particular, Joan Hult and Marianna Trekell, *A Century of Women's Basketball: From Frailty to Final Four* (Reston VA: National Association for Girls and Women in Sport, 1991).

6. "Eleven Aboriginal Maidens."

7. "Indian Girls Draw Very Large Crowd," *Great Falls Daily Leader*, 2 June 1904.

8. Newspaper stories based on interviews conducted with Nettie Wirth Mail and Genevieve Healy Adams in their later years convey positive attitudes toward the team's experiences at Fort Shaw and at the world's fair. John Bye, " 'Shoot, Minnie, Shoot': Lusty Cry of Unbeaten Indian Girls," *Montana Post*, August 1965, 1–2; "She Was Born to Be a Basketball Star," *Great Falls Tribune*, 3 April

1977. In the course of their research, the authors conducted a series of interviews with descendants of team members. In every case, these descendants conveyed the impression that, from the stories they had heard from their mothers and grandmothers, the team members saw that summer in St. Louis as their own individual and collective moment of glory. Among descendants interviewed between 1997 and 2000 were Betty Bisnett, daughter of Emma Rose Sansaver; Barbara Winters, granddaughter of Emma Rose Sansaver; Valerie Goss, granddaughter of Belle Johnson; Rose Stuart, daughter of Catherine Snell; Thelma James, granddaughter of Catherine Snell; Donita Nordlund, granddaughter of Genevieve Healy; Rita Nordlund, great-granddaughter of Genevieve Healy; Jessie James Hawley, great-niece of Genevieve Healy; Terry Bender, grandniece of Nettie Wirth; Elsie Bennett, daughter of Lizzie Wirth; Grace Dawson Lavendis, niece of Flora Lucero; Dorothy Courchene Smith, daughter of Sarah Mitchell; Greg Courchene, grandson of Sarah Mitchell; and Drusilla Gould, great-granddaughter of Minnie Burton. As of spring 2005 more than fifty descendants have shared their memories and memorabilia with the authors in a cross-cultural collaboration that has added depth and breadth to portraits of the girls from Fort Shaw.

9. The idea that students "were not passive consumers" of boarding school education but took advantage of the opportunities offered "while retaining their tribal values" is perhaps best delineated by K. Tsianina Lomawaima in *They Called It Prairie Light: The Story of Chilocco Indian School* (Lincoln: University of Nebraska Press, 1994). In the past decade a number of other excellent books on various aspects of Indian education in government boarding schools have been published, most notably Adams, *Education for Extinction*; Brenda Child, *Boarding School Seasons: American Families, 1900–1940* (Lincoln: University of Nebraska Press, 1995); and Margaret Archuleta, Brenda Child, and K. Tsianina Lomawaima, eds., *Away from Home: American Indian Boarding School Experiences* (Phoenix AZ: Heard Museum, 2000). For an insightful article-length study, see Michael Coleman, "Motivations of Indian Children at Missionary and U.S. Government Schools," *Montana The Magazine of Western History* 40 (winter 1990): 30–45.

10. Built on the Sun River in 1867, Fort Shaw took its name from Col. Robert Shaw, who had met his death four years earlier while leading the 54th Massachusetts Volunteers, a regiment of black soldiers, in an engagement at Fort Wagner, South Carolina. Originally established to protect the region's Euro-American settlers from "marauding Indians," Fort Shaw housed units that participated in the infamous Baker Massacre, engaged in the great Sioux wars that culminated at the Little Big Horn, and marched against Chief Joseph and the Nez Perce in the Big Hole Basin. Don C. Miller and Stan B. Cohen, *Military and*

The Girls' Basketball Team from Fort Shaw

Trading Posts of Montana (Missoula MT: Pictorial Histories Publishing, 1978), 76–79; "U.S. Army's Killing of about 200 Peaceful Indians Memorialized," *Great Falls Tribune*, 21 June 2000; photo caption, *Great Falls Tribune*, 11 July 1999; Bill Thomas, "Early Life and Times of the Montana Smith Family: A Biography of Tom Smith," unpublished manuscript in possession of the authors, 66.

11. The school officially opened on 27 December 1892 under Dr. William Winslow, who was superintendent, physician, and principal teacher. It opened with an enrollment of 52 students, but by the end of its first year of operation there were 176 children in residence (Jeffrey Cunniff, "Fort Shaw Indian School," 5, FS Vertical File, Montana Historical Society, Helena [hereafter MHS]; Dorothy Baldwin, "History of Fort Shaw," 9, FS Vertical File, MHS). The "buildings and reservation of the abandoned military post" were transferred for use by Fort Shaw Indian Boarding School on 23 June 1892 (Field Office Records of the Bureau of Indian Affairs for Fort Shaw Indian School [hereafter Field Office Records], Cashbooks, 1892–1900, entry 1362, PI-163, RG 75, National Archives, Denver, Colorado [hereafter NAD]).

12. James Naismith, "Basket Ball," *The [YMCA] Triangle*, January 1892, 145–46; David Anderson, *The Story of Basketball* (New York: William Morrow, 1988), 4–17; Zander Hollander, ed., *The Modern Encyclopedia of Basketball* (New York: Fourwinds Press, 1969), 3–5.

13. Joanne Lannin, *A History of Basketball for Girls and Women: From Bloomers to Big Leagues* (New York: Lerner Sports, 2000), 10; Betty Spears, "Senda Berenson Abbott: New Woman, New Sport," in Hult and Trekell, *Century of Women's Basketball*, 24. College basketball came to Montana in 1898, when the women of Montana Agricultural College in Bozeman began practicing their game twice a week in the drill hall on campus and "urg[ed] the men to form a team too" (*The Exponent*, November 1898).

14. Formulated in 1899, the first standardized rules for women and girls appeared in "Spalding's Athletic Library" series in 1981. Spears, "Senda Berenson Abbott," 28–31; Lannin, *History of Basketball*, 10. For an excellent overview of "girls' rules," see Joanna Davenport, "The Tides of Change in Women's Basketball Rules," in Hult and Trekell, *Century of Women's Basketball*, 83–108.

15. Baldwin, "History of Fort Shaw," 9; Fort Shaw School, from Indian Census Rolls, 1885–1940, MHS. In his 1901 annual report to officials in Washington DC, Campbell noted that only 17 percent of the children enrolled at Fort Shaw came from full-blood Indian parents, adding that it was "a very difficult matter to secure as many full bloods as desired." Report of School at Fort Shaw, Montana, 1901, Records of Office of Indian Affairs, RG 75, National Archives, Washington, DC (hereafter NAW); W. H. H. Healey to Indian Commissioner, 19 September 1894, Incoming Correspondence, 1894–95, #36194,

Records of Office of Indian Affairs, RG 75, NAW; "She Was Born to Be a . . . Star." Born in Shawnee, Kansas, in 1864, Fred Choteau Campbell graduated from the University of Kansas, taught at a nonreservation boarding school in Genoa, Nebraska, and served as superintendent of the agency school on the Fort Peck (Montana) Reservation before moving to Fort Shaw. LaRue Smith, "Campbell Mountain in Glacier National Park," *The Sigma Nu Delta*, March 1943, 164; "F. C. Campbell, Veteran Indian Worker, Retires from Service," clipping in family scrapbook held by Campbell's grandson Fred DesRosier; "Personal Statement of F. C. Campbell," January 1918, from DesRosier's files.

16. Cunniff, "Fort Shaw Indian School," 7; John Greer, "A Brief History of Indian Education at Fort Shaw Industrial School" (master's thesis, Montana State University, 1958), 39; Paul Dyck, "Lone Wolf Returns to That Long Ago Time," *Montana The Magazine of Western History* 22 (winter 1972): 24. Lone Wolf, or Hart Merriam Schultz—later a leading artist of the West—was the son of Fine Shield Woman, a Piegan Blackfeet, and James Willard Schultz, who lived among the Blackfeet and was known for the books he wrote about the tribe and its history.

17. Peter Iverson, "Introductory Essay," *From Trout Creek to Gravy High: The Boarding School Experience at Wind River*, exhibit catalog, Shoshone Episcopal Mission's Warm Valley Historical Project, 1992–93. Born near Choteau, Gertrude LaRance arrived at Fort Shaw in 1901 and was there nine years later when the school closed (Parker interview).

18. Louis Youpee, "A Friend of the Indian," *The American Indian Journal* 1 (May 1938): 6. Appearing in the first issue of the journal Youpee himself established, this tribute concedes that Youpee's appreciation for Superintendent Campbell's efforts on his behalf came only "in the light of mature reasoning and understanding." Of equal interest is the fact that Youpee refers to himself as "that *then* Indian boy" (authors' emphasis). While this would seem an admission of Youpee's loss of "Indianness," his lifelong activism on behalf of Indians across the country suggests that the word "then" was used to refer to his no longer being a boy rather than to his no longer identifying himself as Indian.

19. While Superintendent Winslow had cultivated the support of Sun River Valley's non-Indian residents early on, Campbell's 1901 invitation expanded outreach efforts to include Great Falls and beyond. "Town and Country," *The Rising Sun*, 28 June 1893; "Indian School at Fort Shaw, Montana," *Great Falls Daily Tribune*, 26 May 1901. In marveling at the children's "resignation to the necessary restraints," the *Tribune* reporter did not mention that Fort Shaw had its share of runaways, most of whom were boys. Field Office Records, Records of Non-Reservation Schools, Records of Runaways, 1907–8, RG 75, NAD.

20. "Indian School at Fort Shaw." According to John Greer's study, Fort

Shaw students spent the first two years of their school life "mainly in acquiring the English language and . . . the white man's way of living" ("Brief History," 46). The discrepancy the reporter noted between the work of Indian and white students of the same "grade" could be attributed in part to the fact that students at Fort Shaw were expected to master the work of each grade before being promoted. There was no notion of being "too old" for one's grade, nor was any stigma attached to remaining in a grade until one's performance merited promotion. Though many students stayed at Fort Shaw through their late teens, the school's curriculum ended at the eighth-grade level. F. C. Campbell, Report of School at Fort Shaw, Montana, 27 March, Records of 1901, Office of Indian Affairs, RG 75, NAW.

21. "Indian School at Fort Shaw"; Greer, "Brief History," 46; "Shaw at State Fair," *Anaconda Standard*, 12 October 1903. In 1899 Fort Shaw Indian Boarding School, which comprised five thousand acres, had 425 head of cattle and 50 milk cows (*Reports of Inspection of Field Jurisdiction of Office of Indian Affairs, 1893–1900* [Washington DC: National Archives and Records Service, 1980], 12).

22. "Indian School at Fort Shaw"; *Report of the Anthropological Department*, a publication of the Louisiana Purchase Exposition, Missouri Historical Society, St. Louis, 22; report of W. C. Buskett, Special Agent in Charge at St. Louis, 30 January 1905, MC35, Governor's Papers, box 315, folder 10, MHS. From 1 June through mid-November, some three million people—or twenty thousand on any given day—toured the Model Indian School and saw the programs given there. By contrast the Montana Building on the opposite end of the fairgrounds drew some five hundred people a day. The Fort Shaw girls were, indeed, Montana's most visible ambassadors.

23. "Montana Senator Remembers Heydays [*sic*] of Baseball," *Montana Daily Record*, 18 February 1939.

24. Baldwin, "History of Fort Shaw," 5. See Stewart Culin, "Games of the North American Indians," *Twenty-Fourth Annual Report of the Bureau of American Ethnology* (Washington DC: GPO, 1907), 647–64.

25. "Butte Girls Beat Indian Maidens," *Great Falls Weekly Tribune*, 22 January 1903; Davenport, "Tides of Change," 98, 97.

26. "Indian Maidens and University Girls to Play This Evening," *Great Falls Daily Tribune*, 30 January 1903. Born in 1886, Nettie was the next-to-youngest of six children born to Jacob Wirth, a native of Wuertenberg, and Woman That Kills Wood, sister of a local Assiniboine chief. Nettie followed two older sisters to Fort Shaw. It is said that before the Poplar school burned down, Woman That Kills Wood attended classes with her daughters not only to learn English but to make sure the girls were attentive to their lessons (Thomas, "Early Life and Times," 23, 26, 28, 37–38, 67, 72, 74).

27. Josephine Langley's birth date remains a mystery, with various records indicating she was born in 1872, 1875, 1879, and 1880. "Death Claims Mrs. Josephine [Langley] Leiphart," *Browning Chief*, 7 September 1951; Blackfeet Agency Records, 1907–8, Browning, Montana; Blackfeet Agency Census, 1891, Browning, Montana; Montana Territory Census, 1880; U.S. Manuscript Census, 1900, Fort Shaw; W. H. Hailman, superintendent of Indian Schools, to Dr. W. H. Winslow, superintendent of Fort Shaw Indian School, 21 August 1896, #32131, Outgoing Correspondence, 1895–96, Records of Office of Indian Affairs, RG 75, NAW; "Indian Maidens and University Girls to Play." Josephine Langley was the daughter of a Piegan mother, Many Kills, and a Metis father, Louis Langley. Blackfeet Records, courtesy of Joyce Spoonhunter, cultural officer.

28. Register of Indian Families, Lemhi Agency, 1901, Shoshone-Bannock Library, Fort Hall, Idaho; "Indian Maidens and University Girls to Play." William Burton, Minnie's father, served as an interpreter for the Lemhi Agency. Minnie's mother was Jemima Osborn Burton; her stepmother was Maggie Tingo Burton. Records of Shoshone-Bannock Library, Fort Hall; interviews with and family records supplied by Drusilla Gould, 24–25 July 2000. The *relative* sizes of the team members have been established through news accounts and descendants' memories of the height of their mothers and grandmothers. The vital statistics available for almost every other student enrolled at Fort Shaw in 1904 are missing for the basketball players, who were en route to the world's fair in St. Louis that week in June when the measurements were taken.

29. "Indian Maidens and University Girls to Play." Emma's father, Edward Sansaver (St. Sauveur), had died when she was seven years old, and by the time she turned fifteen she had lost her mother, Mary Rose, as well. Emma and Flora's older brother Isadore, who had earlier been with them at the mission school, followed them to Fort Shaw in 1898. According to Emma's granddaughter Barbara Winters, from that time on Emma looked upon the school's students and staff as her "family." F. C. Campbell, superintendent of Fort Shaw School, to Commissioner of Indian Affairs, 24 October 1901, Incoming Correspondence, 1900–1901, #61154, Records of Office of Indian Affairs, RG 75, NAW; Family Group Record compiled by Barbara Winters; Barbara Winters to authors, 3 January 2000.

30. Belle Johnson's mother was Nearly Died (Jennie) Johnson, a Piegan; her father, Charles Johnson, was a miner turned rancher. She was the fourth-born in a family of six. Valerie Goss, interview by the authors, 13 March 2000; Indian Census Rolls, Blackfeet, 1890–96; Blackfeet Agency Rolls, 1900, Browning, Montana; "Indian Maidens and University Girls to Play"; "Death Claims Belle Conway at Helena Hospital," undated news clipping from family scrapbook;

Nora Connolly Lukin, "My Early Years," unpublished manuscript in possession of authors.

31. The daughter of Henry Gebeau (Geboe) and Cecille Shaw, Delia was the youngest of ten children, two of whom died in early childhood. Register of Flathead Families, 1905, Pablo, Montana; Delia Gebeau Ladderoute obituary, *Char-Koosta*, November 1957, courtesy of Gene Feldsman, archivist at Salish-Kootenai College, Pablo, Montana.

32. Genie was the youngest of three daughters of Joe Butch, a British immigrant, and Steps On, an Assiniboine woman. Census of the Assiniboine, 1897, Poplar, Montana; Joe Butch obituary, *Wolf Point Herald*, 27 March 1931; "Indian Maidens and University Girls to Play"; Donald Clark, great-nephew of Genie Butch Hall, phone conversation with the authors, 25 April 2001; "Two Games to Be Played Tonight," 6 February 1903, clipping in Nettie Wirth scrapbook in possession of Terry Bender.

33. For an overview of the public relations role of athletics at Indian boarding schools, see Bloom, *To Show What an Indian Can Do*. Fort Shaw played games against the Sun River school for several seasons. Edna Blossom Jenkins, "Reminiscence," in *Montana Centennial* (1864–1964) (Sun River Valley MT: Centennial Committee, 1963), 8.

34. Parker interview; "Fort Shaw Indian Girls Too Fast for High School Lassies," *Butte Inter Mountain*, 28 November 1902. Scores in the early days of basketball—in both men's and women's games—were characteristically low because of the running clock. When two of the earliest "powerhouses" met in the finals of the Championship of America tournament in April 1896, the men of the East District (New York) YMCA defeated Brooklyn Central YMCA by a score of 4–0. Until the center jump rule was repealed in 1937, scoring twenty points was generally enough to assure a win. The exception to the rule was the famed Buffalo Germans, a semi-pro YMCA team that regularly defeated its opponents by a spread of fifty to eighty points. Hollander, *Modern Encyclopedia*, 6; Anderson, *Story of Basketball*, 9; Bill Mallon, *The 1904 Olympic Games* (Jefferson NC: McFarland, 1999), 214.

35. "Butte Girls Beat Indian Maidens." Luther Hall was located at the corner of Fourth Street and First Avenue South. "Parking Garage Dig Unearths Tales from Great Falls' Past," *Great Falls Tribune*, 8 June 2000.

36. "Butte Girls Beat Indian Maidens."

37. "Butte Girls Beat Indian Maidens"; "The Indian Girls Win," *Great Falls Daily Tribune*, 31 January 1903; "Indian Girls Win Out," undated news clipping in Nettie Wirth scrapbook.

38. "Indian Girls Win Out"; "Indian Maidens and University Girls to Play."

39. See, for instance, "Indian Maidens and University Girls to Play"; "Uni-

versity Girls Lose," *The Missoulian*, 31 January 1903. Until a rule change in 1923, all free throws could be taken by one player, the team's best shooter; in 1903 that was Nettie Wirth (Anderson, *Story of Basketball*, 9).

40. "Fort Shaw Wins Again," undated (likely late March 1903), unattributed news clipping in Nettie Wirth scrapbook; "The Indians Win," *Avant Courier*, 3 April 1903; "Fort Shaw 36, M.A.C. 9," and "Indian Girls 20, College Girls 0," *The Exponent*, April 1903; "Dusky Damsels Win the Game," *The Kaimin*, April 1903. Story Hall was located in downtown Bozeman on the southeast corner of South Third Avenue and Main Street (Derek Strahn, Historic Preservation Officer, Bozeman, Montana).

41. Fort Shaw had lost the 28 November 1902 game in Helena by a score of 13–6. "Won the Game from Indians," *Helena Independent*, 29 November 1902; "Indian Girls Win Out"; "U. of M. Girls Basketball Team Leave for Great Falls," *Great Falls Daily Tribune*, 28 January 1903; "Dusky Damsels"; undated, untitled news clipping in FS Vertical File, MHS; "Shoot, Minnie, Shoot," 222.

42. "Play Basketball," *Havre Plaindealer*, 27 June 1903; "Indians Win." The team's popularity had financial benefits for the schools that scheduled home games with them, for when Fort Shaw came to town, there were capacity crowds and record ticket sales. Edna Tracy White, "Women's Activities as I Knew Them at M.S.C. from 1904–8," reminiscence in Special Collections, Montana State University, MHS.

43. "Fort Shaw 36, M.A.C. 9."

44. "Indians To-Night."

45. "Indians To-Night"; "St. Louis Is Their Goal," *Montana Daily Record*, 29 February 1904.

46. Field Office Records, Records of Non-Reservation Schools, Roster of Employees, 1891–1910, Fiscal Year 1901, vol. 1, entry 1361, RG 75, NAD.

47. "Reminiscence of William H. Healy, 1869–1916," Special Collections 814, MHS; W. W. Healy to Indian Commissioner, 9 September 1894, Incoming Correspondence, 1894–95, Records of Office of Indian Affairs, #36194, NAW; Field Office Records, Records of Non-Reservation Schools, , Register of Pupils, 1892–1908, vol. 1, entry 1358, RG 75, NAD; Donita Nordlund, interview by the authors, 20 March 2000.

48. *Thunderstorms and Tumbleweeds: Blaine County (MT), 1887–1987* (Visalia CA: Centennial Book Committee, 1989), 314; Manuscript Census, 1900, Fort Shaw School; Rose Stuart to authors, 22 March 2000.

49. Dorothy Courchene Smith, telephone interview with the authors, 14 March 2000; Greg Courchene, interview by the authors, 17 March 2000; Smith to authors, 8 June 2000; Grace Dawson Lavendis, telephone interview with

the authors, 21 May 2001; Emma Toman, Sun River Valley Historical Society secretary, to authors, 10 February 2000.

50. "Three Survivors in This Area of Famous Indian Girls' Team," undated *Phillips County* (MT) *News* clipping in family scrapbook kept by Donita Nordlund. The girls made their own uniforms in sewing class, and the boys made their gym shoes in shoemaking class. Confidential communication to authors by descendant of Fort Shaw student cobbler.

51. "Play Basket Ball," *Havre Plaindealer*, 27 June 1903.

52. Sadie Malley was new to the Indian Service when she came to Fort Shaw in 1899 at age twenty-seven. Field Office Records, Records of Non-Reservation Schools, Roster of Employees, 1891–1901, Fiscal Year 1901, vol. 1, entry 1361, RG 75, NAD; "Can't Secure Date Wanted," *Montana Daily Record*, 26 February 1904; "Basket Ball Game," unidentified Choteau news clipping, 6 November 1903.

53. "To See Fort Shaw Indians," *Anaconda Standard*, 1 March 1904.

54. "The Indians Are Coming," *Anaconda Standard*, 20 March 1904; "Entertained by Indians," *Anaconda Standard*, 25 March 1904.

55. Thomas, "Early Life and Times," 74, 82, 91–103; Terry Bender, interview by the authors, 23 March 2000.

56. Field Office Records, Records of Non-Reservation Schools, Roster of Employees, 1891–1910, Fiscal Year 1901, vol. 1, entry 1361, RG 75, NAD; "Indian Girls Will Play."

57. Field Office Records, Records of Non-Reservation Schools, Roster of Employees, 1892–1910, Fiscal Year 1899, vol. 1, entry 1361, NAD.

58. Parker interview; Ardith Peyope, librarian, Fort Hall Resource Center for Shoshone-Bannock Tribe, Fort Hall, Idaho, interview by the authors, 25 July 2000. Though Rose LaRose was never listed in team lineups, she is shown in a basketball uniform in a picture taken of the girls in St. Louis. The photo is in the possession of Terry Bender.

59. "To See Fort Shaw Indians"; "The Indians To-Night," *Anaconda Standard*, 25 March 1904; "At Fort Shaw," *Great Falls Daily Tribune*, 31 May 1904; "Fort Shaw Girls Entertained Convicts at State Penitentiary," *Montana Daily Record*, 6 May 1905; "Indians Are Coming." Three years earlier the *Great Falls Daily Tribune* had touted the Fort Shaw band as "better than most of the amateur bands heard throughout the land" ("Indian School at Fort Shaw").

60. The Model Indian School opened a month late due to construction delays. *Daily Reports of the Department of Anthropology* (St. Louis: Louisiana Purchase Exposition Company, 1904), 26; S. M. McCowan to the Commissioner of Indian Affairs, 2 June 1904, Incoming Correspondence, #36905, NAW. Traveling with the team were Superintendent Campbell and instructors Lizzie Wirth, Fern Evans, Lillie Crawford, Sadie Malley, and John Minsinger, a twenty-one-

year-old graduate of Fort Shaw who had stayed on as maintenance staff and now served as a companion and chaperon for young Louis Youpee. "Indian Girls Will Play"; "Shaw at State Fair"; "Indian Girls at the Big Fair," *Great Falls Daily Tribune*, 21 June 1904; W. J. McGee, "Universal Exposition of 1904, Division of Exhibits: Report of the Department of Anthropology," 26, typed transcript, Missouri Historical Society. The Fort Shaw handiwork was displayed with other anthropological items in a large exhibit hall on the fairgrounds. Telegram from S. M. McCowan to Commissioner of Indian Affairs, 25 June 1903, Incoming Correspondence, #3933, RG 75, NAW.

61. "Indian Girls Will Play"; "Fort Shaw Girls Win," *Great Falls Daily Tribune*, 11 June 1904. W. J. Adams, coach of Butte Parochial and a firm believer in the invincibility of the Fort Shaw team, was determined to give the girls the publicity they deserved as they made their way toward St. Louis, and he scheduled in advance most of the games and exhibitions they played across Montana, North Dakota, and Minnesota. These appearances also assisted in defraying the girls' incidental expenses in St. Louis.

62. "Eleven Aboriginal Maidens"; "Indian Girls at the Big Fair"; *Report of the Anthropological Department*, 22.

63. "Noteworthy Event at the Fair," *St. Louis Globe-Democrat*, 16 June 1904; "Indian Girls at the Big Fair"; Timothy Fox and Duane Sneddeker, *From the Palaces to the Pike: Visions of the 1904 World's Fair* (St. Louis: Missouri Historical Society, 1997), 221, 223, 229.

64. *Daily Reports of the Department of Anthropology*, 33; "Indian Exhibits at the St. Louis Exhibition," *Department of Interior Report to Congress, Part I* (Washington DC: GPO, 1905), 51–56.

65. "Indian Exhibits at the St. Louis Exhibition," 55; *Official Catalogue of Exhibitors: Universal Exposition, St. Louis, U.S.A., 1904*, rev. ed. (St. Louis: Official Catalogue Company, 1904), 19; *Daily Reports of the Department of Anthropology*, 35; Martha Clevenger, ed., *"Indescribably Grand": Diaries and Letters from the 1904 World's Fair* (St. Louis: Missouri Historical Society, 1996), 11.

66. *Daily Reports of the Department of Anthropology*, 39; *Official Catalogue*, 20; "Ability of Indian Students Amazes World's Fair Audience," *St. Louis Globe-Democrat*, 11 September 1904, Louisiana Purchase Exposition, newspaper scrapbook, p. 289; *Report of the Anthropological Department*, 28.

67. "Indian Girls at the Big Fair"; untitled article, *St. Louis Republic*, 16 June 1904.

68. "A Chance for Girl Athletes to Achieve Fame," *Colorado Springs Telegraph*, 6 September 1903. The Olympic YMCA Championship in basketball in 1904 was won by the famous Buffalo Germans, who defeated the Missouri Athletic Club by a score of 97–8; Hiram College won the Olympic College Basketball Champi-

onship, defeating Wheaton College, 25–20. Mallon, *1904 Olympic Games*, 213–14, 217.

69. "Fort Shaw Indians Really Take the Show," *Great Falls Daily Tribune*, 16 August 1904; "High School and Indian Girls to Play Basketball," *St. Louis Republic*, 24 August 1904; "Unbeaten Basketball Teams," *St. Louis Post-Dispatch*, 27 August 1904. The O'Fallon game was played not in O'Fallon but in nearby Belleville, Illinois, on 27 July. On 10 August the *Great Falls Daily Tribune* carried a reprint of a *St. Louis Republic* report of 29 July. By this time Superintendent Campbell had returned to Montana and Sadie Malley was coaching the team in his absence.

70. "A Novel Athletic Contest," *World's Fair Bulletin*, September 1904, 50; Allen Guttmann, *The Games Must Go On* (New York: Columbia University Press, 1984), 19–20.

71. "Unbeaten Basketball Teams."

72. "High School and Indian Girls"; "Big Victory for Fort Shaw Girls." Kulage Park was at the corner of Newstead Avenue and Penrose Street.

73. "Big Victory for Fort Shaw Girls." The St. Louis alumnae team was composed of Flem Messing at right forward, Pauline Fisher at left forward, Lillian Randall at center, Laura Strong at right guard, and Birdie Hoffman at left guard ("Unbeaten Basketball Teams").

74. "Indian Girls Win Basketball Game," *St. Louis Post-Dispatch*, 4 September 1904.

75. The St. Louis team failed to show for a second time. The captain of their team finally contacted the Fort Shaw girls more than a month after the first game had been played, to arrange the 8 October meeting. "Great Victory of Fort Shaw Girls," *Great Falls Daily Tribune*, 14 October 1904.

76. "Great Victory of Fort Shaw Girls."

77. S. M. McCowan to Commissioner of Indian Affairs, 15 October 1940, Incoming Correspondence, #72479, NAW; autograph book in possession of Barbara Winters.

78. William Reedy, "The End of the Fair," *The Mirror*, 1 December 1904.

79. Dr. C. I. Jones, a dentist of Great Falls, as quoted in "Fort Shaw Indians Really Take the Show."

80. The return to the campus routine was so swift and immediate that years later Genevieve Healy Adams would recall that, with no fanfare whatsoever, the world champions, like every other Fort Shaw student, "went back to work tending the school's pigs . . . and digging weeds" ("She Was Born to Be a . . . Star"). For the team's experiences in Portland, see "Fort Shaw Girls at Portland Fair," *Great Falls Daily Tribune*, 5 September 1905; "Basketball Team Arrives," *Oregon Journal*, 21 August 1905; Bye, "Shoot, Minnie, Shoot," 2.

81. Bye, "Shoot, Minnie, Shoot," 2; 1907 team photo, with identifications, in possession of Thelma James.

82. "Passing of the Fort Shaw Indian School," *Great Falls Daily Tribune*, 18 April 1910; Greer, "Brief History," 58. The school was closed under the superintendency of John B. Brown, who succeeded Fred Campbell. Campbell left Fort Shaw in 1908 to take up duties as special allotting agent for the Fort Peck Reservation. He was later superintendent of the Blackfeet Reservation and subsequently held several posts in the Indian Service, including district superintendent of Montana, Wyoming, and North Dakota. "Fort Shaw Indian School Has a New Head," *Great Falls Daily Tribune*, 25 October 1908; "F. C. Campbell, Veteran Indian Worker, Retires from Service," undated news clipping in DesRosier family scrapbook. See "Indians To-Night" for the context of the reporter's prophetic comment.

83. Turtle Woman (Jessie James Hawley), letter to authors, 26 March 2001.

4. "Winnebago Is a Great Nation!"
George Howard Johnson's Life in Baseball

George Howard "Chief" Johnson, a member of the Ho Chunk (or Winnebago) of Nebraska, is occasionally recalled as the second half of a baseball trivia question: "Who hit the first home run in Wrigley Field?" It was Art Wilson, catcher for the Chicago Whales Federal League team, on 23 April 1914. "Who did he hit it off?" Yes, it was George Johnson. [1] But George Howard Johnson was far from a trivial figure in his fourteen-year career in professional baseball, three of which were spent playing in the Major Leagues. Indeed, from his trade to the Cincinnati Reds in April 1913 to his jump to the Federal League in April 1914, and to his violent and tragic death in Des Moines in 1922, Johnson often captured headlines. A hefty 5'11½" spitballer (who usually weighed in between 200 and 220 pounds), Johnson won 40 games and lost 43 in three Major League seasons, notching a 2.95 ERA. [2] He pitched nine Major League shutouts, two minor league no-hitters, and had a career winning percentage in the Major Leagues (.482) well above that (.466) of the teams for which he played. [3] Broad shouldered and muscular, he was consistently described as a "great physical specimen" and "strong as an Ox." But perhaps the most interesting story about Johnson does not concern his size and pitching prowess, or even his notorious contract jumping to the Federal League, but his paradoxical assertion of his American Indian identity, the dignity of his people and heritage, through the Anglo game of baseball.

Johnson was born on the Winnebago Reservation, along the Iowa-Nebraska border, on 30 March 1886. He would live there, on a farm in Walthill, Nebraska, for most of his adult life, and he would be buried in the agency cemetery nearby. He was one of five children, the two

George Howard Johnson, with the Kansas City Packers, circa 1914. Courtesy of Michael Mumby.

sons and three daughters of Louisa Johnson, and his Carlisle records describe him as one-quarter Native. [4] Various records list "Murphy" as Johnson's nickname, middle name, or last name, but his daughter Elaine explained, "My father was part French and Winnebago Indian with his strain of Irish that made him 'Murphy' to the newspaper wags." [5] Johnson apparently did tell a newspaper reporter from the *Kansas City Star* that "Murphy" was his true surname; the story reads: "A bunch of bugs [i.e., fans] approached Johnson at the hotel last night and implored him to give them his right name. They expected a 'Rain-in-the Face' answer, or at least 'Boy-Afraid-of-His-Dog.' His answer was a surprise even to his teammates when he said: 'George Murphy.' That's his real name, too. His father was a real Irisher." [6]

The *Boston Evening Globe* stated that his paternal grandfather was an Irishman named George Washington Murphy who left his son in the care of a family named Johnson during the Civil War. [7] Whatever the precise details of Johnson's parentage, he faced a struggle in defining his name and identity. Winnebago (Ho Chunk) names were ridiculed by the press of the day and the idea of an Irish Indian was even more warmly hooted. Thus, like so many others, he was given the facetious epithet of "Chief," but his teammates also called him "Murphy" or "The Big Murph."

Starting with Louis Francis Sockalexis in 1897, many Native players in professional baseball were nicknamed "Chief." In addition to "Chief" Charles Albert Bender and "Chief" John Meyers, there were "Chief" Mose YellowHorse, "Chief" Louis LeRoy, "Chief" Ike Kahdot, "Chief" Euel Moore, "Chief" Ben Tincup, "Chief" Emmett Bowles, "Chief" Jim Bluejacket, and "Superchief" Allie Reynolds, among others. The historian John P. Rossi calls the epithet "a perfect reflection of the naivete and racism of the age."[8] Joseph Oxendine, the author of *American Indian Sports Heritage* and a Lumbee from North Carolina, was himself called "Chief" as a minor league baseball player in the 1950s.[9] He explains:

It is really used by non-Indians to say, "Hey, you're an Indian. Therefore, that's how I can define you and keep you in your place."... They used to call me "Chief" because I was the only Indian in school.... Nobody believed that you were chief of a tribe.... Billy Mills, the long-distance runner, reacted very testily to people calling him "Chief." Most Indians do not want to be called "Chief" because it demeans the significance of the [tribal] chief, and it's a constant reminder, like saying, "Hey, Indian."[10]

So, too, might George "Chief" Johnson have reflected on his baseball name with distaste, frustration, or perhaps with a victorious irony.

George Johnson attended the Winnebago Reservation school where he learned to read and write, but his father's death (apparently when he was seven years old) interrupted his education. According to the *Boston Evening Globe*, Louisa Johnson moved with George to Philadelphia and enrolled him in Lincoln Institute, but he later attended Flandreau Institute in South Dakota.[11] Other newspaper accounts place him at the Carlisle Industrial School, and school records confirm his brief tenure there from 8 February to 6 October 1903, where he performed outing tasks for a printer named James S. Rich and may have played outfield briefly for the school baseball team, just before Jim Thorpe's arrival at the school. On 6 October he was discharged for "running away." Before entering Carlisle, Johnson had also briefly attended Haskell Indian Institute in Lawrence, Kansas: he enrolled on 14 October 1902 but deserted on 9 December 1902 and was dropped from the school rolls on 30 June 1903.[12] Apparently the military discipline, academic studies, and culture at the federal boarding schools did not sit well with Johnson, and he rebelled in the most common way, by running away.

Newspaper accounts, however, mention Johnson's Carlisle experience prominently as a great tribute to his character, and he may have exaggerated his time there (instead of his time at less famous schools) to burnish his reputation with the writers. Like his fellow Carlisle student and Major Leaguer, Frank Jude (an Ojibwe from Minnesota), Johnson was a natty dresser, appearing for team photos in a tweed coat, bow tie, and driving hat. Harold D. Johnson described Johnson as a "gentlemanly, well-read Indian," and Harry A. Williams called him "that splendid child of nature, Chief Johnson, who prefers public life to the reservation with free food and government chewing tobacco" and who pitches "a highly civilized grade of ball."[13] The racism in these accounts, which consider reservation Indians as degenerate and in need of a program for civilization, is blatant and one that George Johnson struggled against throughout his life.

In 1905 Johnson played outfield for a semi-pro team in Oakland, Nebraska, and he married another Winnebago student from Carlisle, Margaret LaMere. They had three children, Elaine, Catherine, and Joseph. George played professional baseball during the summers and tended his homestead and barbered in Walthill during the winters. He played his first professional ball with Guy W. Green's Nebraska Indians, a nationally recognized barnstorming team, in 1906 and early 1907. In fact in 1907 Johnson pitched thirty-eight games for the Nebraska Indians and won thirty-two, earning him a mention in *Sporting Life* magazine.[14] The travel and playing conditions of the Nebraska Indians were tough, even for the time. The twelve Indian players would travel by Pullman car together, sometimes assemble, when necessary, for a parade in Indian headdress to drum up a crowd, and play night games under their crude portable lighting equipment against college, semi-pro, and town all-star competition. The team often slept on the baseball fields they played on—to economize and because some hotel keepers refused to lodge Indians. On various occasions the players were pursued by town constables who accused them of theft. In 1906 the team traveled to well over one hundred towns in fifteen states, from New Jersey to Nebraska. By Guy Green's account, the team won 151 games, lost 31, and tied 2, and shut out their opponents 44 times. In addition to his turns in the pitcher's box, Johnson also played outfield. [15]

It is from Guy W. Green's interview with the *Sioux City Journal* in 1909 that we can learn the most about Johnson's experience with the Nebraska Indians and with teams in the Western League. [16] A meticulous and unusually sympathetic observer, Green commented on the racist epithets and abuse that Johnson endured wherever he pitched:

Johnson, my Indian twirler . . . pitched for my Nebraska Indian team three seasons. During that time we played an average of 150 towns annually in the United States and Canada. That makes 450 towns. Johnson is now pitching his second season in this league. He has never yet stepped to the mound to pitch a game anywhere on earth that three things have not happened. Numerous local humorists have started what they imagine to be Indian war cries; others have yelled "Back to the reservation," and the third variety of town pump jester has shrieked "Dog soup! Dog soup!" If you were at the game Tuesday you heard this. If you see him pitch in Pueblo or Sitka or Kamchatka you will hear the same thing. You would think people would get all that kind of patent inside stuff out of their systems after awhile, wouldn't you? But they never do. [17]

Of course mock war chants, "Back to the reservation," and "Dog soup!" were not the only racist barbs hurled at George Johnson. The newspapers themselves contributed their share: "Injun," "Heap-Big Injun," "Big Chief," "Plenty-Saliva," "Indian buck," "Poor Lo," "Redskin," and on they would go for his entire career, providing Johnson's "fight spirit" with plenty of fuel.

In 1907 Johnson advanced to the minor league ranks, signing briefly with the Joplin Miners of the Class C Western Association. He did not stay in Joplin long, though, once Guy Green purchased the Lincoln Tree-Planters (and renamed them the Greenbackers) of the Class A Western League in 1908. [18] Green signed his former star in 1908, and Johnson impressed Western Leaguers immediately with his hard fastball and intimidating presence on the mound, recording a 19–16 record in his first year. [19] Johnson's early success proved sporadic, however. Most Western League teams played with pitching staffs of five or six, and three or four starters. The brutal schedule made it difficult to rely heavily on a fastball, as pitchers were often called to pitch on successive days or to relieve in the second game of a doubleheader after starting the first. In his sophomore year he slumped, and Lincoln (now owned by Don Despain) traded him to the Sioux City Packers. But the trade did allow Johnson one moment of glory among his people. Sioux City was scheduled to play the Walthill semi-pro team, a Winnebago team featuring other talented Carlisle and Haskell players, at Walthill on 30 September 1909. In that game Johnson pitched his team to victory, 5–2, in front of "nearly 500 fans coming from all parts of the reservation." He must have been proud not only of his own performance but of the Indian team's talented play against the Class A Packers. [20]

In 1910 Johnson made a pitching breakthrough when he began to use his curve more and to learn the spitball. Some of the best pitchers in the Western League, including Red Faber and Fidgety Phil Douglas, were spitballers, and Johnson learned the pitch quickly, experimenting with different brands of slippery elm. Even though his light-hitting team provided little run support in 1910, he managed eighteen victories, including a string of impressive shutouts. [21] On 5 April of that year in an exhibition game he faced the American Association's Minneapolis Millers, a team that featured slugger Gavvy Cravath in the center of its lineup, and he pitched five scoreless innings, allowing only one hit. [22] His shutout victories included a twelve-inning 1–0 thriller against Lincoln on 28 June, a three-hitter against Lincoln on 6 August, a 2–0 whitewash of Wichita on 10 September, and a two-hitter against the Topeka Jayhawks on 19 September.

Although Johnson's 18–17 record sounds mediocre, he was the most effective pitcher on his team, which went 76–91 overall. The sports editor of the *St. Joseph Gazette* noted, "Chief Johnson sure is having hard luck this year. He is losing more games in which he holds his opponents to a fewer number of hits than the Drummers [to whom he got traded in 1909] get than any other twirler in the league." [23] Soon photos of the "Indian twirler" who was "pitching excellent ball" became a staple of the press coverage. He was recognized and cheered by crowds of fans, and he became clubhouse leader for the Drummers. One tidbit about Johnson, provided by the *St. Joseph News-Press*, is especially interesting:

Chief Johnson, it is said, is the motion picture critic of the squad. He takes them all in and it is on his report that the other members depend. If Chief says that the pictures are good, then there is a sale of the 10-cent size, but if he says, "Heap bum," then it is a quiet game of billiards or pitch for the Drummers. They say Chief has had more than one offer to show his face and form as a warrior before the machine of the moving picture man.[24]

Here the writer's mock-Indian dialogue, "Heap bum," is typical of stereotypes of the time. What makes the note fascinating is the information that Johnson was a curious observer of celluloid images during the silent-film era and that he was recruited to appear in some of the first Westerns. Rather than choosing to "show his face and form as a warrior" to the camera, however, Johnson choose to remain a warrior on the baseball diamond. It was a deliberate choice of creating an oppositional image of himself in an Anglo game, rather than creating one in an Anglo film.

By this time Johnson was making $200 per month pitching for the Drummers, and he had acquired a handsome house and farm in Walthill, where he raised wild ponies and thoroughbred horses. If Johnson had never made it to the Major Leagues he still would have been regarded as a success story by his boarding school teachers. The superintendent of Carlisle, Moses Friedman, wrote to Mrs. Margaret LaMere Johnson in December 1910 to ask her for a photo of the family's house.[25] The collection of photographs that Friedman was assembling was one of many that Carlisle administrators assembled and submitted to the Department of the Interior and Congress to demonstrate the institution's educational value. Richard Pratt had begun the practice by taking photographs of his students, first in their Native clothes and hairstyles, and then again after they had been forcibly barbered and dressed in European apparel. These pictures showed convincingly to the legislators of the time that the civilizing process was at work at Carlisle or, as Pratt put it, "This will show whence we started." The purchase of a home was more proof of Carlisle's success as a civilizing institution.[26]

The 1911 season started brilliantly for Johnson. On 21 April he faced his former team, the Sioux City Packers, before a crowd of 8,000, and he pitched the first no-hitter of his professional career. He struck out six Packers, allowed no hits, and collected one hit himself in the 7–0 victory.[27] The promise of the 1911 season faded, as Johnson apparently suffered an injury in July and missed more than a month of the season, but he was at full strength again for 1912.[28] Johnson appeared ready for Major League stardom. He had his finest season in professional ball, going 24–12.[29] Johnson was clearly one of the most dominating pitchers in the Western League in 1912: his fastball came plenty fast, his spitball danced and darted, he fought for every strike, he displayed fine control, and he used a tricky half-balk motion to first base. On the strength of Johnson's pitching, St. Joseph found itself in first place for the first two months of the 1912 season, and fans knew why. When the Drummers returned from a road trip in first place on 17 June, members of the team's boosters' club met them at the Union train station, serenading them with a brass band and calling out for speeches. George Johnson retreated from the crowd, but to no avail. According to the *Gazette* report, "After repeated calls, 'Chief' Johnson was dragged from an automobile but enjoyed the welcome so much that he only bowed and shed a few tears."[30] It is hard to know exactly what emotions George Johnson's silent tears expressed, but I imagine them as tears of confused joy and pain, joy for his newfound glory, and pain for the hard times behind. Johnson seldom articulated his emotions in public, but the broad smile he sometimes flashed and his silent tears refuted the old stereotype of the stone-faced Indian.

As Johnson proceeded to compile his 24–12 record in 1912, scouts from three Major League teams took notice: Bill Joyce of the Boston Beaneaters and Jim "Deacon" McGuire of the Detroit Tigers came to St. Joe to see Johnson pitch, and a representative of the Boston Red Sox also inquired about Johnson in June. The Boston Beaneaters then made an offer to Jack Holland, the owner of the Drummers, but it was Charley Comiskey, owner of the White Sox, who bought Johnson for the 1913 season on the recommendation of Western League president James "Tip" O'Neill.[31] Comiskey had bought James Gossett, the Drummer catcher, from St. Joseph the year before, so Johnson reported to spring training in California in 1913 with one familiar face and plenty of competition. The White Sox began 1913 with a full stable of pitchers, including several spitballers. Whether Comiskey ever intended to keep Johnson is uncertain, but he was saved another stint in Class A by a last-minute deal with the pitching-starved Cincinnati Reds. Reds scout Tom O'Hara recommended Johnson to manager Joe Tinker, who worked out a "probationary" deal, allowing him to send Johnson back to St. Joseph if he did not stick on the Reds' roster.[32] But stick Johnson definitely did.

The 1913 Reds, led by player-manager Tinker, Ohio speedster Bob Bescher, and Cuban sensation Armando Marsans, were an interesting team but a bad one, finishing with a .418 winning percentage, $37\frac{1}{2}$ games out of first place.[33] The team included a number of former Cubs stars—Tinker, Mordecai "Three-Finger" Brown, Johnny Kling, and Jimmy Sheckard—most of whom were well beyond their prime. The pitching staff was cobbled together at best and was soon to be uncobbled by the incursions of the Federal League. Johnson secured his place on the team almost immediately by pitching brilliantly in his first starts. After Cincinnati lost its first two games of the season, Johnson stepped to the mound at Redland Field on 16 April and produced the following headlines:

Winnebago Is a Great Nation
Chief Johnson Steps to Red Mound and Proves It
First Red Victory Due to Indian's Fine Hurling[34]

He had shut out Miller Huggins's St. Louis Cardinals on three hits. The headlines were further amplified by Jack Ryder's description of Johnson's pitching:

The game was over when the sturdy and conscientious red man took up the burden. He came through with a collection of shoots and benders, which had the Cards standing on their giddy little top-knots. . . . The Chief showed big league form in the box right from the jump. Never rattled, always there with the first ball over the plate, and following it with a spitter that broke a good foot or more, he outguessed the enemy at every stage. . . . The Indian's best showing was in the way of nerve and control. It was his first game in the big ring, but he acted as if he had pitched as often as Chief Bender.[35]

Here the noun "nerve" was especially apt, as it fit Johnson's fearless determination to win, whatever the occasion. It was what Warner called "fighting spirit," and what Ernest Hemingway called "grace under pressure," or courage. It was to become one of Ryder's favorite words for

Johnson, and he used it in various forms, such as, "The big Indian . . . has the nerve of a lion and likes his game hard rather than easy," and "the Chief . . . is well supplied with the good old nervine."[36]

In spite of suffering a brief letdown in June, George Johnson was unquestionably Cincinnati's best starting pitcher in 1913. He led the pitching staff in almost every category, including wins (14), games pitched (44), games started (31), complete games (13), innings pitched (269), strikeouts (107), shutouts (3), and ratio (hits + walks/innings pitched) (1.25).[37] Had he been pitching for the first-place New York Giants, he might have won more than twenty games. Giants pitcher Jeff Tesreau would certainly have preferred that, since "the Arkansas Bear" lost twice to Johnson in shutouts. Johnson himself lost a 1–0 heartbreaker to Christy Mathewson on 26 August and could take consolation only in the headline, "Indian Johnson Outpitched the Great Mathewson."[38] After Johnson's considerable successes against the Giants, New York manager John McGraw ordered his players to take more pitches and "wait the limit every time one of them went to bat and endeavor to tire out the twirler."[39] Yet, perhaps Johnson's most remarkable pitching accomplishment in 1913 is not recorded in any book of statistics and is mentioned only briefly in a news account.

Apparently Johnson brought a Winnebago medicine rite into Cardinal Park in St. Louis. The rite was described by Jack Ryder in his baseball notes on 27 May 1913:

Chief Johnson is anxiously awaiting his next turn in the box to try a new method of discomfiting the enemy, which was sent him by an old Indian doctor on the reservation in Nebraska, where the Winnebago tribe holds forth. The venerable medicine man forwarded to the Chief a package of potent herbs, with instructions for their use. The method of applying them is unusual, but the Indian doctor says that it cannot fail. George is to chew up a mouthful of three different kinds of roots and then blow his breath in the direction of the opposing players, who will immediately wilt, lose their eye at the bat, and not have a chance to beat him. The package was accompanied by a letter from the ancient doctor describing just what George must do. . . . The essence of the treatment, however, is blow the breath on the enemy, after chewing up the mixture. "This old doctor," said the Chief tonight, "is a great character. I have known him a long time and he is an expert on herbs and roots. He used to tell me that he had stuff which would make a hunter tireless and at the same time take the strength away from the game he was after, if the wind is blowing in the right direction. . . . I am willing to take a chance."[40]

This note, which Ryder appears to have written for his readers' amusement, is only one of several mentions of Johnson's interest in Native medicines, and it clearly shows his reverence for Winnebago tribal elders: "I am willing to take a chance," he says, noting his white audience's disapproving attitude toward Native medicine as superstition. The rite that appears to be described is a medicine bag ceremony, a kind of medicine bundle typically used by the Apache, Winnebago, and other Plains tribes. The herbs would be carried in a small buckskin pouch, suspended by a drawstring, and worn around the medicine man's neck or waist.[41] The use of herbs in the rite displays the magical power of herbs, known to the Winnebago (Ho Chunk) as *wasê*, rather than the medicinal power of herbs, known as *ma kan*.[42]

In its way, Johnson's medicine rite is also example of a syncretism (a blending of Winnebago and Euro-American cultures) that resists the extermination of American Indian culture and religion. While Johnson clearly accepted the game of baseball, he did so from the spiritual viewpoint of a Winnebago leader, determined to incorporate the game into his own culture. Baseball, as practiced in the rite, is seen as a "little brother of war," and the space of the diamond is sacralized by the mixture of the herbs, the human breath, and the winds. Without the power of the four winds, the rite has no efficacy, and so the practitioner prays for the power of the winds to assist him. Here, as Vine Deloria, Jr., notes, a sense of the sacredness of space, rather than time, separates Indian religious ceremonies from modern Christianity: "It must be spaces and places that distinguish us from one another, not time or history."[43] Ultimately the four winds mark out the sacred spaces of the tribe, and they express the power of the one great spirit that makes all nature sacred. Although Jack Ryder makes no further mention of Johnson's medicine bag rite, the game record shows that Johnson won his next game in relief in St. Louis on 29 May and his next start in St. Louis on 31 May. Perhaps he did so by making more than his usual application of medicine to the ball.

Although the *Enquirer*'s baseball beat writer Ryder was one of the more sympathetic journalists toward Indians, Johnson confronted harsh epithets and cartoonish depictions of Native Americans in Cincinnati as elsewhere. Anti-Indian caricature flourished in the daily baseball cartoons and headlines printed in the *Enquirer*. During the teens, when Indian team names and logos were becoming increasingly popular, the Reds seized on the trend, often forgetting the stockings in their own team name. *Enquirer* headline writers and cartoonists often referred to Joe Tinker as the Red Chief, and there the jokes began. For example, when Johnson's relief pitching combined with a Tinker hit on 18 April to gain a tie with Pittsburgh, the headlines read, "Two Chiefs Stopped the War Dance. . . . Joe Drove Two Runs in for Our Boys in Ninth. Then the Redskin Held Pirates to a Tie after Three More Rounds."[44] And if the headlines were in bad taste, the cartoons were offensive in the extreme. When the Reds faced the Cubs in April, *Enquirer* cartoonist Shafer presented the Reds as a band of savagely grinning Indians in war paint, brandishing tomahawks, knives, and bows and arrows, headed by "Chief Tinker." Shafer's cartoon spokesman, "Old Man Grump," also appears in the cartoon, saying, "Here's one time when I'm pulling for th' Reds," meaning the Cincinnati Redskins.[45] When the Cubs took three of four games from the Reds, Shafer responded with another Indian cartoon, showing a gloating bear carrying off an Indian's bow, arrows, headdress, blanket, and moccasins, leaving the bruised and naked Indian standing in a barrel, with the dialog bubble, "Ugh! Well, anyway, he didn't get th' barrel!"[46] This anti-Indian bigotry also included specific affronts to Johnson himself. When manager "Buck" Herzog vilified George Johnson in April 1914 for jumping from his contract with his Reds, and when Reds president August Hermann secured an injunction that prevented Johnson from pitching for Kansas City, writers and cartoonists also took up the theme. Russell, another *Enquirer* artist, pictured "Chief" Johnson, dressed in a blanket, moccasins, and headdress, in a cartoon panel with the caption, "All dressed up and no place to pitch."[47] For his part, George Johnson reacted to press accounts with considerable restraint. His one laconic comment on his contract problems was wry and defiantly ironic: "I should fret!"[48] Johnson didn't fret, as he turned any personal animus he harbored into victories on the baseball diamond.

Johnson's period with the Reds also brought to light something he struggled with on and off throughout his career: alcohol. Fairly or unfairly, he was branded as a "booze-fighter," the phrase commonly used for alcoholics. [49] Whether Johnson drank often is uncertain, but over his career he established a pattern of binge drinking, especially on the nights before his scheduled starts. One news story tells of Johnson being conned by an opposing manager in the Western League to go drinking the night before a start, but he arose late and "ashamed" the next day, took a quick bath, and then threw a shutout for the Drummers. [50] It is unlikely that Johnson was ever so credulous, but he, like many other Major League pitchers, used alcohol to relieve stress. On 14 August Johnson missed a start against Philadelphia, and he returned to the team the next day with "a terrifying account of a siege of ptomaine poisoning far from the reach of a telephone." Joe Tinker, who was known to tie one on himself, winked at the offense, levied a small fine, and started Johnson the next day with good results. [51] The same pattern occurred again on 18 April, and it was a crucial factor in Johnson's decision to jump to the Federal League.

Aside from the Wrigley Field trivia, George Howard Johnson's place in baseball history has largely been defined by his decision to jump from his Cincinnati Reds contract to a richer contract with the Kansas City Packers in April 1924. Johnson, along with Bill Killefer and Armando Marsans, became the subject of numerous lawsuits between the National League and the Federal League. After having taken $400 in advance money, Johnson abrogated his $3,300 contract with the Reds to sign a $5,000 contract with Kansas City. For this decision he has been described as the "1910's version of Andy Messersmith." [52] He was widely disparaged by the press of his time as greedy and disloyal. Ben Mulford, Jr., in *Sporting Life* described him as a "fellow with a price" and called him "Poor Lo" (a stock epithet for the un-Christianized savage): "Poor Lo will be scalped and kept out of the game." [53] Reds manager Buck Herzog described it as a case of "paying exorbitant salaries to men of that caliber," and Ernie Lanigan, in his "Casual Comment" column, bristled, "Let the Feds have their George Johnsons." [54] After a Chicago judge granted an injunction against Johnson and he was summoned from the mound by police on 23 April 1914, the first game in Wrigley Field, an anonymous poet in *The Sporting News* wagged his finger:

LINES TO WINNEBAGO JOHNSON
Mr. Johnson, it's no use!
That old Judge won't turn you loose.
Oh, Mr. Johnson please be good,
You can't hurdle from the Red
To the Kansas City Feds.
So, Mr. Johnson, you'd best be good. [55]

However, the assumption behind all these criticisms—that Johnson betrayed the Reds out of personal greed—is almost certainly mistaken. Johnson had a compelling reason to leave the Reds on 21 April 1914 and it had nothing to do with money.

In the early winter of 1914, Johnson had been courted by several Fed officials, including his former manager Joe Tinker, and probably offered considerably more than the $3,300 for which he signed a contract with Cincinnati in January 1914. If money alone were the object, he could have had it earlier rather than later from Baltimore, Chicago, or Kansas City. Johnson was concerned instead in early 1914 about his weight and possibly his drinking. He wrote to August Hermann, asking for an advance of $100 on his salary so he could travel to Hot Springs, Arkansas, and begin an early course of training. Johnson's letter reads:

Dear Mr. Hermann—

I have to have $100 to use on the trip to Hot Spring[s]. If you can forward it at once I will be very grateful of you. Understand this is advance money on my account.

I will send you all the details of each days work at the spring at the end of each week.

This is going to be a great help to me and I will do all I can to show you the great appreciation of an Indian during the season. I remain

Geo. H. Johnson [56]

This scrupulous request, with its promise to "show you the great appreciation of an Indian," hardly sounds like the words of a man planning to betray his employer for an extra buck. Johnson was taking an advance, after all, for his physical conditioning, on top of which he was sending reports to the Reds management. What happened, then, to make Johnson jump from the Reds on 21 April 1914?

The answer to the question is Charles L. Herzog, the new Cincinnati manager. "Buck" Herzog was a player-manager who modeled himself after his mentor with the Giants, John J. McGraw. Like McGraw, Herzog played ball tenaciously and managed autocratically. While his fellow players respected him as a gutsy and talented infielder, many bristled under his dictates. Armando Marsans, Dave Davenport, and Marty Berghammer all departed Cincinnati after Johnson, with similar complaints against Herzog. Marsans, smarting under a fine from Herzog, quit the team, returned, and then quit again, swearing he would never play for Herzog again. And Berghammer put it bluntly: "All this talk about Herzog being on good terms with his players is tommyrot."[57] Herzog had fined Johnson $50 earlier in the spring of 1914 for conditioning violations during a time when Johnson had the flu, and Herzog's comments in the press indicated he had a rather low opinion of Indians. While most writers and players considered catcher John "Chief" Meyers a vital part of the New York Giants' success, Herzog dissented: "Chief Myers is a great mechanical catcher . . . , but I tremble when I think of what might happen to him or his team if McGraw didn't exercise unfailing vigilance."[58] Here Herzog was more than hinting that Meyers (who had attended Dartmouth) was not smart enough to call pitches himself and was in need of McGraw's constant correction. And if anything, "Buck" Herzog's attitude toward "Chief" Johnson was considerably more hostile than his attitude toward "Chief" Meyers. The depth of this distrust became evident to Johnson on 18 April 1914.

On the evening of 17 April, Johnson was in Pittsburgh, facing a start the next day against Honus Wagner's Pirates. He thirsted for a drink and one led to another until he had broken curfew at some distance from the hotel. Early the next morning, Herzog sent a clubhouse attendant or a hotel detective to find Johnson. They found him, and Herzog issued Johnson a $100 fine:

Sir,

> *This is to notify you that you are fined One Hundred dollars (100.00) for being in a disreputable house with a disreputable woman, for drinking to excess, and for being away from your hotel the entire night on the night of April 17, 1914.*[59]

The wording of the fine suggests Herzog had caught Johnson in flagrante delicto and meant to shame him. For Johnson's part, he denied Herzog's published charges against him (that he was guilty of conditioning and rules violations), although it is clear that he was badly hungover and unable to pitch on 18 April. But despite the hangover, Herzog still started Johnson against the Pirates, and Jack Ryder reported the results: "When Johnson reported for duty Saturday, Herzog knew that he . . . was not in the best of shape, but sent him into the game [anyway]. Johnson pitched poorly and was knocked out of the box after four innings."[60] His manager had meant to show him up, and Johnson resented it, along with the fines leveled against him. Ryder also reported that Johnson "insisted that Manager Herzog had it in for him" and thereafter he defied Herzog's orders.[61] Although Johnson quickly repaid his $400 in advance money to the Reds when he signed his contract with Kansas City, he refused to pay the $150 in fines Herzog had issued to him. In the end Johnson's breach of his Cincinnati contract had almost nothing to do with money and everything to do with his pride. Yes, he had an alcohol problem, but he would not let his manager bully and humiliate him because of it.

The jump to Kansas City was also, as Johnson probably suspected, a jump into the courtroom. The sports pages were filled for the next two months with stories about the Reds' legal maneuvers to prevent Johnson from pitching again. He started on Thursday, 23 April 1914, against the Chicago Wales at their brand-new ballpark, called in the papers "the Northside plant," but stayed in the game just long enough to give up the first Wrigley homer, a two-run shot, to Art Wilson. At the end of the second inning, he was served with an injunction from Chicago Superior Court judge Foell.[62] Until it was dissolved, the injunction prevented Johnson from pitching, and for almost three months of the season it made him the best-paid batting practice pitcher in the Federal League. In need of pitching work, he even agreed to pitch one game for a local town team, Sweetwater, against the B'Goshes of Corder, Missouri. The episode, which reads like one of Satchel Paige's famous exploits, is one of the most colorful of Johnson's career:

Corder, Mo., July 16.—Indian Johnson, the Kawfeds' pitcher . . . disguised himself in a Sweet Springs uniform last Sunday and assisted the sporting citizens of that town in taking a ball game. . . .

Then the game started. The Sweet Springs pitcher didn't seem to be trained to a fine point, but appeared to have plenty of confidence. He lobbed one to the first batsman, and a hit was registered. When the dust and the cheers subsided, the Sweet Springs pitcher turned to the cocky Corderite on first and said:

"G'wan, steal. I won't spear you."

Then he turned his back on first and fiddled till the man did steal. Then the pitcher said: "That's right. Now steal third."

The Corderite refused to be kidded off the bag, so the big stranger calmly threw the ball away. While it was being recovered, the amazed runner took third. Then the pitcher said: "Now stay there." And he struck out three men with nine pitched balls.

Not till the game was over did the Corderites learn who the opposing pitcher was, and then they could hardly believe it. Now Corder is trying to figure out some way of securing Walter Johnson's services for a day without letting anyone know it. [63]

It is typical of Johnson that he performed this humorous feat not with Paige's circus-like exuberance but with his own broad smile and terse words. "Now stay there," he said, and Corder's B'Goshes did.

Johnson eventually did get to pitch for the Kawfeds in 1914. He logged 20 games, 19 starts, and 132 innings in the final two months of the season, making up for his lost time as much as possible. And while he was rusty at first, he pitched well in September. On 4 September he threw a four-hitter at the St. Louis Feds, beating Ed Willet, 1–0, and he came back two days later to defeat his old teammate, Dave Davenport, also of St. Louis, 2–0. Overall, he was 9–10 for the year, with a respectable 3.16 ERA, a strong conclusion to what had been a hard year. [64] It was tough personally, too, as the strains of alcohol and long periods away from home finally ended his first marriage. But Johnson began 1915 as hopeful as ever, on a new conditioning regime to lose weight, recommended by manager George Stovall. A feature in *Baseball Magazine* in June 1915 described Johnson as "one of the hurling mainstays of the Kansas City team" and said that he had adopted the exercise of "hoop rolling" in training camp "with such zest" that he was "in the best condition of his career."[65] The feature also noted, "The 'Chief' has found wolf-hunting in Iowa a pleasurable and profitable pastime. He has chased and caught wild horses, played lacrosse and taken part in all sorts of sporting carnivals promoted . . . by Redmen." This note is helpful, not so much because it establishes Johnson as a "picturesque character" but because it indicates his longtime interests in Native sports and values. The "sporting carnivals" were summertime tribal events, community homecoming celebrations that honored athletic prowess and outdoor skills. It is interesting that Johnson played "lacrosse" avidly, which was known in some tribes as "the Little Brother of War" for its fierce combativeness. Johnson brought that same mentality to baseball. Twice in his Major League career he was ejected from extra-inning games by the umpire for arguing balls and strikes. In both cases he was the batter.

The record book shows that 1915 was Johnson's best year in Major League ball. He pitched in 46 games, logging 34 starts, 19 complete games, 281 innings pitched, 17 wins, 4 shutouts, and a 2.75 ERA.[66] He led his team with 118 strikeouts, contributing significantly to a team that depended more on pitching than hitting for its winning record. Johnson's last shutout may have been especially memorable, as he faced a pitcher to whom he was sometimes compared, the Ojibwe Charles Albert Bender, and he won on a six-hitter. Attendance in the Federal League was poor in 1915, making its coming demise all but certain, but Johnson thrived. He met his future wife, a member of the Sac and Fox tribe, and bought a home in Kansas City while still maintaining his farm in Nebraska.[67] As the end of the season and of the Federal League arrived, he, like many of his teammates, began to make contacts with other baseball clubs.

In January 1916 Johnson began life in a new league, the AA Pacific Coast. He negotiated with both the Los Angeles and Vernon clubs before striking a deal with President Ed Maier of the Vernon Tigers. By March Johnson was running on Sunday mornings in a "rubber suit" in order, as always, to lose weight and prepare for the season.[68] As a proven Major League starter, Johnson graced ZeeNut baseball cards and occasionally the baseball pages of the *Los Angeles Times* and *San Francisco Chronicle*. Of course, in Los Angeles, as everywhere else in the America at that time, anti-Indian sentiment flourished. On 14 April 1916 Johnson had a tough outing against the San Francisco Seals, and beat writer Harry A. Williams wrote:

SEALS SCALP CHIEF JOHNSON

Washington Park was made uninhabitable for Indians yesterday. The Seals chased Chief Johnson to the underbrush in less than one round and later in the game a long foul went into the right field bleachers and almost hit a Washoe buck who came all the way from Inyo county on horseback to root for the Chief. The noble red man from Inyo then left the park, complaining that the white settlers had made this an unsafe place in which to live.[69]

Of course, George Johnson had long been inured to the clichés. Or as Green put it, "If you see him pitch in Pueblo or Sitka or Kamchatka you will hear the same thing." Fashioning an identity as an American Indian ballplayer was not easy, even in the sunny parks of California.

Of Johnson's three years in California, 1916–18, he was healthy only in the middle year, when he won 25 games. He split his 1917 season between Vernon and San Francisco, and he compiled impressive statistics, pitching 399 innings, striking out 147, and recording a meager 2.44 ERA.[70] That year he pitched the first PCL no-hitter of the season, against the Portland Beavers on 15 April. The Beavers' roster included a number of fine Major League players, especially the Browns' speedy slugger Ken Williams, the Cubs' hot-hitting shortstop Charlie Hollocher, and the veteran catcher Gus Fisher, once with Cleveland and New York. But to George Johnson that day, they were all alike—all goose eggs. Johnson walked only one and struck out nine. The *San Francisco Chronicle* gave Johnson his due, more or less: "The chief was in fine form and had everything there was, although he had good support as a big factor in his fine showing."[71] It was to be the last great game of his career, however, as overwork in 1917 took its toll on his aging arm. His shoulder was injured severely in 1918, and he fell to 2–6. He made a comeback attempt in early 1919 with the Dallas Marines in the Class B Texas League, but the shoulder injury was irreparable.[72] Yet Johnson had one more sad headline to make.

After baseball Johnson apparently went into the pharmaceutical business. The *Winnebago Chieftan* and other newspapers described Johnson in 1922 as an "Indian Medicine Man" who arranged exhibits at local drugstores, a description that seemed appropriate given his earlier interest in Native American herbs and shamanism. On the weekend of 10 June he "had been conducting a medicine show at the Blair & Haun

97

drug store" in Des Moines, Iowa, apparently with his nine-year-old son Joseph, and he was "expecting to leave for Omaha, and then go to his home on the Winnebago agency."[73] But in the early morning of 12 June, soon after 3 a.m., Johnson was shot twice at close range and killed. He was unarmed at the time. He had been playing dice and backing another player in the game as well, a woman described variously as a "negro" and "half-breed." As always, he was dressed neatly, and he was driving a new Ford coupe. The game took an ugly turn, however, when the host for the evening, Edward Gillespie, refused to pay for the alcohol consumed at the game. Johnson and Gillespie apparently began to fight and most of the other players bolted. When police arrived at the Gillespie residence, they found Johnson's body in "a clump of weeds" behind the house, and soon after they discovered a .32 caliber revolver. George Howard Johnson had been killed in a quarrel over $2.50 of hootch.

As far as the Des Moines police were concerned, the case was simple. Several witnesses stated they saw the pistol in Gillespie's hands soon after the shooting, and Johnson's pockets had been rifled, his car had been torn apart, and evidence, including the body, had been moved from the Gillespie house. Gillespie had shot and robbed Johnson, and he was charged with first-degree murder. Police quickly forced a confession from him, which he later denied. Although they did not locate a key witness (the black woman), they ceased their search for her on 14 June, just two days later. In its deliberation in October, the jury heard evidence that the gun did not belong to Gillespie and that whoever fired the weapon might have done so in self-defense against the hulking form of angry George Johnson. The jury deadlocked and then acquitted Gillespie of murder on 24 October 1922. In the end, Edward Gillespie's freedom owed not only to the sloppiness of the Des Moines police but also to negative stereotypes of Native Americans. Members of the jury readily believed that Johnson was "on a wild rampage from the effect of liquor" and were thus reluctant to convict Gillespie.[74] Johnson's murder was eerily similar to that of Roy Choteau, an Indian spitball pitcher who was shot in 1914 in a heated argument with his manager in a bar. Like Gillespie, Choteau's killer walked free because, as Mary Lou and August LeCompte said, "Apparently no one demanded justice for a 'Drunk Indian.'"[75] Racist statements about Johnson appeared in the papers, including: "Johnson . . . was . . . of splendid appearance being practically white," and "Johnson, it is reputed, is of great wealth from an Indian standpoint."[76] Johnson's death was summed up in a scanty paragraph in *The Sporting News*—a sordid end for a former Major League player.

The reaction to Johnson's death in Walthill, Nebraska, was vastly different. The *Winnebago Chieftan* ran two front-page stories on Johnson's death, including a lengthy obituary. It noted that Johnson's funeral was held at the Winnebago Agency church, and "The edifice was filled with a large congregation that came to pay their respects to the deceased chief."[77] "Johnny" was respected and admired by the Winnebago people, whatever the white newspapers might say. The life story of George Howard Johnson was not, however, a simple story of a saint. Even with his broad smile and in his finest clothes, Johnson was a flawed man. A loving father and uncle, he was often at a distance from his family (he learned of the birth of his second daughter by telegram), he was divorced from his first wife and charged with abandoning her in December 1914, and he struggled with alcohol. But rather than stereotype Johnson, as the newspapers did, as a "bad Indian," it is crucial, in conclusion, to place him in the context of his people and culture.

In the early nineteenth century the Ho Chunk of Wisconsin (or Winnebago) had been invaded by miners and white settlers. They had fought to keep their ancestral homelands, but in 1837, "through government trickery, the tribe . . . lost all its homeland east of the Mississippi." As a result the tribe was divided "on its own 'trail of tears'" between Wisconsin and Nebraska, losing hundreds of its members and splintering into separate communities.[78] When the Winnebago traded with white fur trappers, they were often paid with alcohol in a system intended to produce addiction and dependence. Their Siouan language, traditional religion, and culture were all under assault by Christian missionaries, government agents, and off-reservation boarding schools. George Howard Johnson was born into this confusing and tragic world, and for all his flaws he struggled aggressively to make a better life for his family while forging his own distinctive American Indian identity. It was a paradoxical identity: one that could fight bravely in the Native game of lacrosse, as well as in the white man's game of baseball; one who watched the first Westerns with fascination, but who demurred to be in them; one with a weakness for drink, but with the strength to defy a manager who had a low opinion of Indians; one that could bring Winnebago herbs on the diamond and apply them to his spitball; and one who could answer the hoots of "Back to the reservation!" with a strikeout. Finally, he was a man who wept silently when cheered by fans of any race.

Notes

1. Chicago Cubs, "Historical Information" (Wrigley Field), *http://www.cubs.com/wrigley/history.htm*.

2. John Thorn, Pete Palmer, et al., eds., *Total Baseball*, 6th ed. (New York: Total Sports, 1999), 1615.

3. Thorn et al., *Total Baseball*, 1615.

4. "Geo. H. Johnson," Carlisle Industrial School, student file, National Archives and Records Administration (hereafter NARA), RG 75, file 1327, Washington DC.

5. Elaine F. Johnson to Clifford Kachline, 26 June 1973, George H. Johnson Player File, National Baseball Library, Cooperstown NY (hereafter NBL).

6. C. J., "Stovall Needs a Catcher," *Kansas City Star*, 19 May 1914.

7. *Boston Evening Globe*, 24 May 1913. My thanks to SABR's Dick Thompson for supplying this article.

8. John P. Rossi, *The National Game: Baseball and American Culture* (Chicago: Ivan Dee, 2000), 82.

9. Joseph B. Oxendine, telephone interview by the author, 1 June 2001.

10. Oxendine interview.

11. "Geo. H. Johnson."

12. Marilyn Finke, NARA Archivist, Central Plains Region, Kansas City, Missouri, e-mail correspondence with the author, 12 May 2002. Ms. Finke refers not to a Haskell student file but to a transcription of a lost logbook from Haskell Indian Institute.

13. Harold D. Johnson, "George Johnson Is Master of the Saliva Ball," *Chicago Herald Record*, 6 March 1912, and Harry A. Williams, "Johnson Gives Great Attention to His Spitball," *Los Angeles Times*, 5 May 1916, sec. 3, both in George H. Johnson Player File, NBL.

14. "The Western League," *Sporting Life*, 18 January 1908, p. 10.

15. Guy W. Green, *Fun and Frolick with an Indian Ball Team*, 4th ed. (Lincoln NE: Woodruff Collins Press, 1907), 23.

16. Green, *Fun and Frolick*, 92–93.

17. Green, quoted in "Raps Bleacher Jokesters," *Sioux City Journal*, 3 June 1909, p. 9.

18. "Johnson, Geo. H.," player contract card, the Sporting News Archive, St. Louis; Lloyd Johnson and Miles Wolff, eds., *The Encyclopedia of Minor League Baseball*, 2nd ed. (Durham NC: Baseball America, 1997), 153, 158.

19. John B. Foster, ed., *Spalding's Official Baseball Record* (New York: American Sports Publishing, 1909), 178–81.

20. "Johnson a Drawing Card," *Sioux City Journal*, 1 October 1909.

21. "Western League Averages," *Sioux City Journal*, 9 October 1910.

22. "Drummers Easily Win from Millers," *St. Joseph Gazette*, 5 April 1910.

23. "Sports Editor's Notes," *St. Joseph Gazette*, 20 July 1910.

24. "Notes of the Drummers," *St. Joseph News-Press*, 23 March 1912.

25. M. Friedman to Margaret LaMere Johnson, 1 December 1910, Margaret LaMere [Johnson], Carlisle student file, NARA.

26. Pratt, quoted in Adams, *Education for Extinction*, 47.

27. "No Hit Game by Johnson," *Nebraska State Journal* (Lincoln), 22 April 1911, p. 3. This first no-hit game of Johnson's career has been listed mistakenly, without a date and score, in "1912 No-Hitters" in *The Encyclopedia of Minor League Baseball*.

28. "Western League Averages," *Sioux City Journal*, 29 September 1912.

29. "Western League Averages."

30. "Heroes Are Welcomed by Local Fans," *St. Joseph Gazette*, 18 June 1912.

31. "Johnson Is Sold to Sox," *St. Joseph Gazette*, 16 July 1912; "Comiskey Signs Up an Indian Twirler," 16 July 1912, George H. Johnson Player File, NBL.

32. "Indian Pitcher," *Cincinnati Enquirer*, 9 April 1913, p. 6; *Cincinnati Enquirer*, 18 May 1913, sec. 3, p. 1.

33. David S. Neft et al., eds., *The Sports Encyclopedia: Baseball, 1999* (New York: St. Martin's, 1999), 63.

34. Jack Ryder, "Winnebago Is a Great Nation," *Cincinnati Enquirer*, 17 April 1913, 8.

35. Ryder, "Winnebago Is a Great Nation."

36. Jack Ryder, "Brownie Is Himself Once Again," *Cincinnati Enquirer*, 2 May 1913, p. 6; Ryder, "Bad Luck," *Cincinnati Enquirer*, 28 April 1913, p. 8.

37. Neft et al., *The Sports Encyclopedia*, 63.

38. *Cincinnati Enquirer*, 7 August 1913, p. 8.

39. Ed A. Goewey, "The Old Fan Says," *Leslie's Illustrated Weekly* 117 (4 September 1913): 230.

40. Jack Ryder, "Berghammer Remembered," *Cincinnati Enquirer*, 27 May 1913, p. 6.

41. Arlene Hirschfelder and Paulette Molin, eds., *The Encyclopedia of Native American Religions* (New York: Facts on File, 1992), 176.

42. William S. Lyon, ed., *The Encyclopedia of Native American Shamanism* (Santa Barbara: ABC-CLIO, 1998), 382.

43. Vine Deloria, Jr., *God Is Red: A Native View of Religion* (Golden, CO: Fulcrum, 1992), 65.

44. "Two Chiefs Stop the War Dance," *Cincinnati Enquirer*, 19 April 1913, p. 8.

45. Shafer, "Loaded for Bear Today" (Cartoon), *Cincinnati Enquirer*, 20 April 1913.

46. Shafer, "Another 'Near Victory'" (Cartoon), *Cincinnati Enquirer*, 24 April 1913.

47. Russell, "Trolley Off" (Cartoon), *Cincinnati Enquirer*, 25 April 1914.

48. *The Sporting News*, 6 August 1914.

49. Edward R. Maier to August Herrmann, Western Union Telegram, 5 April 1916, George H. Johnson Player File, NBL.

50. "George Johnson, Indian Pitcher, Fooled Manager," *Chicago Record Herald*, 7 December 1912, George H. Johnson Player File, NBL.

51. Jack Ryder, "First Ball Pitched by the Indian," *Cincinnati Enquirer*, 16 August 1913, p. 8.

52. Dickie Thon Fan Club, "The Federal League, Part 1," *http://www.dickiethon .com/thoughtful/federal1.html*.

53. Ben Mulford, Jr., "The Fellow with a Price," *Sporting Life*, 9 May 1914, p. 9.

54. Herzog, quoted in "To Enjoin Jumper Johnson," *Sporting Life*, 25 April 1914, p. 1; Ernie Lanigan, "Casual Comment," *The Sporting News*, 3 September 1914.

55. "Poet's Corner," *The Sporting News*, 11 June 1914.

56. Geo. H. Johnson to August Hermann, January 1914, George H. Johnson Player File, NBL.

57. *Sporting Life*, 14 November 1915.

58. "Myers' Weakness," *Sporting Life*, 25 April 1914.

59. C. L. Herzog to Geo. M. Johnson, 18 April 1914, George H. Johnson Player File, NBL.

60. Jack Ryder, "Johnson Jumps to the Feds," *Cincinnati Enquirer*, 21 April 1914, p. 6.

61. Ryder, "Johnson Jumps to the Feds."

62. Harold D. Johnson, "Chiefs Open with a Victory," *Chicago Herald Record*, 24 April 1914, p. 10.

63. "Indian Johnson Goes in against B'Goshes," 16 July 1914, George H. Johnson Player File, NBL.

64. Thorn et al., *Total Baseball*, 1615.

65. "Who's Who in the Federal League," *Baseball Magazine* 15, no. 2 (June 1915): 64.

66. Neft et al., *The Sports Encyclopedia*, 71. For more on Johnson's Kawfeds, see Marc Okkonen, *The Federal League of 1914–1915: Baseball's Third Major League* (Garrett Park MD: SABR, 1989); and Lloyd Johnson, ed., *Unions to Royals: The Story of Professional Baseball in Kansas City* (Jefferson NC: McFarland, 1996).

67. "Chief Johnson Laid Away," *Winnebago Chieftain*, 22 June 1922, p. 1.

68. "Tigers Take a Day Off," *Los Angeles Daily Times*, 27 March 1916.

69. Harry A. Williams, "Seals Scalp Chief Johnson," *Los Angeles Daily Times*, 15 April 1916.

70. Dennis Snelling, *The Pacific Coast League: A Statistical History, 1904–1957* (Jefferson NC: McFarland, 1995), 35.

71. "No Hit Game for Chief George Johnson," *San Francisco Chronicle*, 16 April 1917.

72. "Johnson, Geo. H.," player contract card. My thanks to archivist Steve Gietschier of *The Sporting News* for his generous assistance.

73. "Think Murderer of Ball Player Escaped," *Des Moines Evening Tribune*, 13 June 1922, p. 10. My thanks to SABR's Alex Kleiner for supplying this and other stories about Johnson's death. George H. Johnson's death certificate states that he died on 11 June 1922, but the accounts in the *Des Moines Evening Journal*, the *Des Moines Register*, and in the October trial itself confirm that he was killed at about 3 AM on the morning of 12 June 1922.

74. "Assert Johnson on Rampage on Eve of Murder," *Des Moines Register*, 17 October 1922.

75. Mary Lou and August LeCompte, quoted in Harold Seymour, *Baseball: The People's Game* (New York: Oxford University Press, 1990), 392.

76. "Think Murderer of Ball Player Escaped," 10.

77. "Chief Johnson Laid Away," 1.

78. David Lee Smith, "Winnebago," *Encyclopedia of North American Indians*, ed. Frederick E. Hoxie (Boston: Houghton Mifflin, 1996), 682–83.

5. The Forgotten Irish Indian
Ethnicity, Class, and Football in the Life of Tommy Yarr

When American sports journalists watched Indians play football in the early twentieth century, they saw reincarnations of Sitting Bull and Crazy Horse adorned in shoulder pads. The press described Indian-white football games as another frontier struggle, where savage Indians battled civilized whites for touchdowns. [1] What happened, though, when Indians played with, not against, whites on the gridiron? The story of Tommy Yarr's football career provides a different perspective on the relationship between the American press and Native American football players. While playing football at the University of Notre Dame, journalists emphasized Yarr's biethnic identity in order to make him one of the team. In the process they undermined the ubiquity of the frontier struggle on American sports pages and pointed out America's changing conception of mixed-blood peoples. Yarr was not a savage barbarian on the football field; he was an Irish Indian. [2]

People changed Yarr's ethnicity throughout his life. He was of Snohomish, Irish, and Finnish descent and observers emphasized one, two, and none of these ethnic identities as he grew up. Yarr was born in western Washington where, interestingly, many people did not consider him an Indian. When he moved to South Bend, Indiana, sportswriters treated his ethnicity with ambivalence. They and his peers described his Native American heritage with stereotypic nicknames and racial proclivities. In addition they disagreed about his ethnic identity. At times he was an Indian, Irish Indian, Irishman, and even a German Cherokee. After his football days ended, journalists and school officials described his Indian ethnicity without mentioning his other ethnic her

Tommy Yarr, Notre Dame football player. Courtesy Notre Dame Archives.

itages. Members of the dominant culture accepted Tommy Yarr because they constructed a bicultural and biracial identity for him.[3]

The ambivalence with which people treated Yarr in the Midwest provided him a great degree of social mobility. He grew up on a dairy farm in western Washington, moved to South Bend, Indiana, to play football for Notre Dame, wed a Chicago society girl, and enjoyed a prosperous, yet truncated, life after football. What is most remarkable about Yarr's story is that it occurred during the Great Depression, when most Americans faced extreme difficulties in maintaining a living. Football provided Yarr with stable occupations at Notre Dame and after graduation.

This ambivalence also conflicted with America's typical fear and loathing of mixed-blood people. In Yarr's time most members of the Anglo-American dominant culture feared "mongrelized" peoples because they threatened to undermine social stability. These anxieties often represented white middle-class concerns about their own unrestrained sexuality and the uncertain legal status of mixed-blood people.[4] However, multiethnic men and women were common throughout history. In studies of the fur trade, for instance, historians have shown that mixed-blood men and women served as mediators between Native American tribes and European traders and performed essential labor in the trade.[5] The people who watched Yarr play at Notre Dame accepted him as a person with mixed heritages. In fact, his mixed-blood was the reason why journalists accepted him as part of the football team.

In western Washington state Indians and whites constantly renegotiated the social, political, and legal definitions of "Indian."[6] Yarr was born in 1908 in Chimacum, Washington, into a family with strong ethnic Indian roots. Yarr's grandmother, Bodeah Strand, was a well-respected basket maker among the Snohomish. His mother, Josephine Strand-Yarr, provided information and songs in the Coast Salish language to anthropologists about Indian life in Washington.[7]

In the nineteenth century, federal Indian policy created two types of Indians in Puget Sound: on-reservation Indians who received benefits from the federal government and off-reservation Indians who did not.[8] Yarr's family did not live on the local reservation, Fort Tulalip. In 1918 the Strand family requested that federal officials recognize them as members of the Snohomish tribe. Government officials and on-reservation Indians often refused to recognize off-reservation Indians. The Office of Indian Affairs believed enrolling off-reservation Indians contradicted their assimilation efforts and held up on-reservation Indians as successful examples of the assimilation campaign. On-reservation Indians, on the other hand, worried about a loss of land or services that might accompany the enrollment of more Indians.[9] Even though Bodeah and Josephine spoke the Snohomish language and identified as Indians, their petitions were denied.

In 1924 Yarr's mother died from a heart attack.[10] Thereafter, Yarr's father, a dairy farmer who migrated from Ireland, raised Yarr. Yarr attended Chimacum High School, where he blossomed into an excellent athlete, participating in football, basketball, and baseball, and enjoyed a fine career.

West Coast schools actively recruited Yarr because of his athletic prowess, but he chose to attend the University of Notre Dame and play for Knute Rockne. During the 1920s Rockne developed a national recruiting system, bringing together scores of players from all over the United States. In order to maintain the team's success, Rockne solicited the help of eager alumni and Notre Dame football supporters across the country. The alumni recruited skilled football players in their area and paid for the players' tuition at Notre Dame. Once the recruits arrived on campus, Rockne secured summer jobs, tutoring programs, and financial packages for them. Former Notre Dame track athlete Morrie Starrett recruited Yarr, sponsored him while he attended Notre Dame, and took Yarr's father to Notre Dame games.[11] Notre Dame football players, as other players in big-time college football institutions, enjoyed a comfortable lifestyle on campus.

Although Murray Sperber faults Rockne's recruiting system because of its clandestine and corrupt aspects, it democratized college football. Rockne recruited middle-class Irish Catholics, Jews, and Italians to play against East Coast elites. The inclusion of Italians and Jews bothered some Notre Dame supporters and school officials, and they adamantly opposed including African Americans. Even though Big Ten schools recruited black players, Notre Dame officials did not allow blacks on the team and expressed some reluctance to playing schools that had black players.[12] Notre Dame's role in the Irish Catholic community in America accentuated feelings of ethnic solidarity and exclusion. Notre Dame's football team provided folk heroes, a rallying point and opportunities for middle-class Irish Catholics.[13] Rockne and Notre Dame officials did not express any concerns about Yarr and, as we shall see, he fit into the team's ethnic profile.

Before Yarr attended Notre Dame, the school endured a disastrous year on and off the field. The 1928 Notre Dame team posted a mediocre 4-4 record, much to the chagrin of the Fighting Irish faithful. In addition, Rockne sparred with school officials concerning the construction of Notre Dame Stadium and the administration's attempts to impose more control over the football program. Rumors of wrongdoing in college sports prompted the administration's increased interest in Rockne's team. In the late 1920s the Carnegie Foundation sponsored a report that excoriated college football and attacked its commercialization, corruption, and the coaches' cozy relationship with journalists. Notre Dame officials took the report seriously. They wanted to make the school known more for its academics than football, so they attempted to exert more control over Rockne's program.[14]

Yarr began his football career at Notre Dame amid administrative turmoil of which he knew little. During his first season Yarr played sparingly behind first-string center Thomas Moynihan. On 2 November 1929 Yarr saw his first action at center for the Fighting Irish, when he substituted for Moynihan in a 26–6 victory over Georgia Tech, the defending national champions. Yarr substituted at center against Drake University and Northwestern University and traveled to Los Angeles when Notre Dame all but sealed the 1929 national championship with a 13–12 victory over the University of Southern California.[15]

The Northwestern game provided Yarr's most embarrassing moment as a football player. Notre Dame had the game well in hand when Yarr entered the game at center. After the Irish lined up to punt, Yarr snapped the ball over punter Carl Cronin's head and the ball landed 35 yards downfield on the Notre Dame 12-yard line. The Notre Dame defense held Northwestern on four plays and the Irish regained possession. Again the Irish lined up to punt the ball and Yarr again snapped the ball over Cronin's head into the end zone, where a Northwestern player fell on the ball for a score.[16] Two years later Yarr remembered, "My heart sank to the general vicinity of my knees [when I realized I snapped the ball over Cronin's head]. It felt that the eyes of all the spectators were on me and that they were saying, 'What a dub he is.' I also feared that the players would think I was yellow and couldn't take it."[17] Yarr recalled this incident because it almost affected his standing with his teammates. In the early twentieth century, sports provided many ethnic Americans with opportunities for social advancement by gaining respect and showing intelligence on the field. [18] A gaffe such as the one he committed against Northwestern could have imperiled Yarr's future. After that game Yarr had to demonstrate to his teammates that he was not a cowardly "dub."

Before Yarr's first season on the Notre Dame football team concluded, the Depression mired the country in poverty, affecting sports as well. Attendance at professional baseball games declined precipitously, but college and professional football experienced mild success during the Great Depression. Between 1930 and 1937 fan attendance at college football games doubled, but Notre Dame felt the pinch of the Depression. [19] Games in metropolitan areas such as New York, Chicago, and Los Angeles still attracted hordes of fans, but gate receipts declined for Notre Dame home games and those played at rural colleges. Furthermore, alumni did not donate as much money to Notre Dame, which alarmed the school's administration. [20] Notre Dame's fortunes, as well as those of many Americans, were in a precarious state.

Aside from the Great Depression, Yarr's first season at Notre Dame ended quietly. Journalists paid little if any attention to his Indian ethnicity because he spent most of the season on the bench and possibly mixed in well with his Irish, Jewish, and Italian teammates. Even his mistake during the Northwestern game did not elicit a flurry of disparaging remarks. However, once he became a permanent fixture on the Notre Dame offensive line, journalists began to report on his ethnic makeup.

After his first school year ended in 1930, an alumnus provided Yarr and his teammates, including future Notre Dame football coach Frank Leahy, with jobs at the Waukegan power plant, earning $70 per week. The players brought football equipment and practiced during their off-hours. [21] Yarr and his teammates had comfortable jobs with a steady income, something many Americans did not have, and the boys had ample time to practice for the upcoming season.

In 1930 Notre Dame fans and journalists expressed some concern about the ethnic makeup of the team. Fans wrote school officials and complained about the number of Italians and Jews playing for Notre Dame, especially in the high-profile positions in the backfield. That year journalists and fans did not bestow nicknames on the talented, multiethnic backfield as they did for the all-Irish Four Horsemen in the 1920s. [22] Still, as training camp opened Rockne and the Notre Dame faithful were optimistic about the upcoming season. The defending national champions required contributions from all positions and Yarr stood in the middle of those plans. However, he faced competition for his position, as the campus magazine, *Scholastic*, reported, "Tommy Yarr appears to have the pivot job well stowed away but Frank Butler, huge sophomore, is giving him plenty of trouble."[23] Yarr successfully beat out Butler and assumed the position as the starting center for the Fighting Irish in 1930.

Before the season began, the *South Bend News-Times* profiled some of the Fighting Irish starters. The writer titled his article about Yarr "Rockne Has Heap Big Indian on Squad in Person of Yarr."[24] The article that followed combined Indian stereotypes about Indians with a discussion of Yarr's ethnic heritage: "Two years ago there came down to Notre Dame a big, broad-shouldered fellow from the town of Chinacum [*sic*] on the plains of northwest Washington state. The lad is Tommy Yarr, one-quarter Indian. His grandmother was a member of the Cherokee Indian tribe in the northwest territory years and years ago."[25]

The author had his own idea of what an authentic Indian was but like most people who employ stereotypes, he was wrong on many accounts. First, Yarr was not from a "plains" region but from western Washington. Second, Yarr was not Cherokee but Snohomish. Third, by placing his grandmother's tribal heritage some time in the ill-defined past, the report distanced Yarr from his Indian culture. Perhaps more important than the factual inaccuracies was the author's perception of real Indians. He thought that the only real Indians were Cherokees living on the Great Plains, comfortably in the past. The author wrote like many journalists who reported on Indian athletes in the early twentieth century, using stereotypic language and describing Yarr as an "other."[26] The writer also employed stereotypes to make sense of Yarr's Native American and Irish heritage:

"[Yarr] had plenty of fight, courage and the ability to make friends, but it seemed there was something else, a more impelling power behind him.

"Sure it was, he possessed the wit of an Irishman. An Irishman, yes, for it was soon discovered that Mr. Yarr, father of the now famous Tommy, was born and raised in Dublin, Ireland."[27]

The author placed Yarr's ethnicities in a racial hierarchy. Yarr's Irish heritage provided civilized intellect and cleverness, and his Native ancestry supplied untamed bravery. The writer successfully allayed any possible worries the Notre Dame faithful had about the heterogeneity of the Irish football team, including the addition of an Indian, by reaffirming Yarr's Irish ethnicity and the abilities of Irish Americans in the United States. Anglo-Americans treated Irish immigrants as they treated African Americans and Native Americans, believing that all three demonstrated childish and savage characteristics and lived licentious and idle lives.[28] As the author constructed the ethnicity of Indians, he also defined the ethnic characteristics of Irish Americans. Indians were bellicose and courageous, while the Irish were intelligent and civilized.

The article still had not reached its denouement; rather it took an interesting and unexpected turn. The author added, "Tommy Yarr's well-balanced proportions of brain and brawn, coupled with his natural and developed ability, have brought him up from the shock troops of 1929 to a permanent position on the first stringers this year."[29] Ironically, Yarr's mixed-race heritage did not debilitate him—as many proponents of scientific racism might believe—but he gained the best abilities from his Indian and Irish heritage.[30] The combination of "brain and brawn," "natural and developed ability," allowed him to become the starting center for Notre Dame. Even though the writer employed a racial hierarchy to discuss Irish and Indian ethnicity and used stereotypes in which to discuss Yarr, he did not disparage Yarr because of his mixed ancestry and accepted him as an equal member of the team by emphasizing his biethnic identity.

A few weeks later Notre Dame alumnus Arch Ward added more confusion to the discussion of Yarr's ethnicity. Ward compiled the ethnic composition of the Notre Dame football team for the *Chicago Tribune*. Ward described Yarr as a "German with Cherokee Indian blood." [31] Despite these inaccuracies, he did not degrade Yarr because of his dual heritages but accentuated them instead. Ward singled Yarr out as the only player with two ethnic heritages.

The Irish played their first game of the 1930 season against Southern Methodist University (SMU). This was the first game played in Notre Dame Stadium, though the university dedicated the stadium the following week against Navy, a higher-profile team. SMU boasted a prolific passing attack and many sportswriters wondered if the Irish could stop it. Rockne apparently did not have the same reservations as the scribes and started his second-team offense against the visitors. Much to Rockne's chagrin, SMU fought diligently. Notre Dame clung to a 20–14 lead in the fourth quarter when SMU unleashed its lethal passing attack. However, Yarr intercepted three passes in the fourth quarter and the Irish pulled away from SMU. The *Notre Dame Scholastic* reported, "Tommy Yarr's work was great on pass defense."[32]

Rockne often started his "shock troops" against inferior opponents during the 1930 campaign, usually inserting the first string to put a game away. Against Drake University the first string replaced the second string and, "An instant later, Metzger, Kurth and Yarr opened up a wide hole in the Drake defense and Hawley raced through it 34 yards for the first touchdown." Notre Dame went on to win comfortably 28–7 after Yarr and the first stringers widened the lead.

Winning and the expulsion of one of the Italian players smoothed ethnic tensions surrounding the Irish football team. In the middle of the 1930 season, Notre Dame officials expelled Italian halfback Joe Savoldi because he divorced the wife no one knew he had. Rockne attempted to cover up this event but decided not to challenge the Catholic priests on the issue.[33] The loss of Savoldi allowed an Irish American halfback to assume a starting role (journalists nicknamed the new fullback "Moon" Mullins) and Notre Dame did not skip a beat en route to its second consecutive national championship. In the biggest game of the year, Notre Dame traveled to Los Angeles and soundly trounced USC 27–0 to claim the crown. Savoldi's dismissal and another national championship ameliorated ethnic tensions but journalists continued to emphasize Yarr's dual heritage.[34]

The following season began favorably for Yarr and the team. In January 1931 Yarr's teammates elected him captain. Yarr stated that being selected captain was one of his goals as a football player and, predictably, the election elicited more scrutiny of and interest in the Indian player from Washington. The *Notre Dame Scholastic* wrote, "The secret is this: Tommy is one-quarter Indian, which explains why he had the nickname 'Chief' tacked on him by his teammates. And not to be outdone in that little matter his father was born in Dublin, Ireland."[35] This writer emphasized Yarr's biethnic identity but did not mention inherent racial characteristics of his Indian or Irish heritage. Yarr's teammates accentuated his Native American heritage with their apparently affectionate nickname. Yarr's peers, like journalists, described Yarr with a common nickname and stereotype of the era, but this did not mean that they ostracized him. Yarr's being elected team captain demonstrated the high regard in which he was held by his teammates.

Still, some Notre Dame writers seemed confused about Yarr's ethnicity. Two weeks later another campus writer authored a story about the team's new captain. He wrote that "a swarthy, black-haired Irishman" had traveled from Washington state to play football for Notre Dame. The author emphasized Yarr's connection to nature without mentioning his Indian heritage: "Quiet, smiling, rugged and clean, Tommy Yarr typifies the land from which he comes. He looks like a man who has lived in the outdoors and he looks like a man who can play football." The caption next to a picture of Yarr in his football stance read, "Quiet, smiling, rugged Irishman, typical Notre Dame gridder."[36] The ethnic concerns of Notre Dame supporters surfaced again, but writers continued to discuss Yarr as part of the team. This time it meant accentuating his Irish ancestry only. The effectiveness of this article is dubious considering the previous attention to Yarr's biethnic identity.

Two months later events quickly went awry for Yarr and Notre Dame. On 31 March Rockne's plane crashed in an ice storm in Kansas, killing him. Notre Dame and the United States mourned the passing of its coaching legend and an icon in American sports. Notre Dame officials replaced Rockne with co-coaches, "Hunk" Anderson and John Chevigny.[37] The team felt Rockne's loss immediately. In the final scrimmage of the spring, the reserve and freshman team trounced the starters 19–0.[38] Surely this was an ominous omen for the two-time defending national champions.

Before the 1931 campaign began, the *Notre Dame Scholastic* profiled the team captain. The writers described him as reticent and terse because he provided a one-sentence statement about the forthcoming season: "We will be ready when the time comes."[39] In order to obtain more information, the writers found an intermediary, Yarr's friend Boswell, to provide information about the captain. Yarr may have been too busy or reluctant to talk to the journalists, but it is also possible that the writers perceived Yarr as a product of another culture and sought out an intermediary to "interpret" Yarr. As anthropologist James Clifton has pointed out, some people found intermediaries to interpret and learn about people of different cultures and allay their fears.[40]

The article informed the Notre Dame community about its new captain. The writers provided a short sketch of Yarr's life before he came to Notre Dame and explained his biethnic identity: "The young chap in our picture is one of Irish-Indian ancestry. Yarr's mother was Squosomish [*sic*], a small tribe in Washington."[41] This was one of the few newspaper articles that accurately linked Yarr to an Indian group in Washington, suggesting that Yarr did not hide his Indian ancestry from his teammates.

The *Notre Dame Scholastic* article also provided some insight into Yarr's personal life. He lived in Sorin Hall and, like many Notre Dame football players in the 1930s, was earning a degree in physical education in order to coach football in the future. Off the field, Yarr was not active in extracurricular activities. In fact he apparently spent most of his day dormant: "sleeping is his hobby, his pastime, and his favorite sport—after football."[42] Yarr sounded very much like a modern student athlete, as he wanted to pursue a job in sports and focused all of his attention on athletics. However, emphasizing Yarr's sleeping habits made him sound like a "lazy Indian."

A few weeks later the *Chicago Tribune* published a piece on Yarr. The writer of this article also correctly identified Yarr's tribal roots: "In his veins is Indian blood, for Tommy is one-fourth Squoschomish [*sic*]." The writer also celebrated, rather than disparaged, Yarr's biethnic identity: "The Indian strain makes for endurance, but Yarr's Irish ancestors (his father was born in the old country) have willed him a fighting spirit."[43] Yarr's Irish roots supplied his fighting spirit, not his Indian ancestry, according to this writer. As with the previous writers, this one succeeded in placing Yarr within the Notre Dame community by emphasizing his biethnic identity.

The 1931 season disappointed Notre Dame fans. The team's twenty-game winning streak ended in a sloppy 0–0 tie with Northwestern. Notre Dame received a scare the day before the game when Yarr broke his left hand during tackling drills and played the game in a cast, but Yarr still played well, recovering a fumble and intercepting a pass.[44] Notre Dame did not lose a game until the end of the season, suffering embarrassing losses to USC and Army to end the unsatisfactory season.[45] *Literary Digest* named Yarr to its All-America team despite the team's lackluster record compared to previous seasons.[46]

One month later Yarr married his sweetheart, Rosemary Killeen, a "Chicago society girl."[47] Yarr's marriage was important on two accounts. First, the wedding demonstrated Yarr's acceptance into the wider society. Yarr did not seem to face the barriers to inclusion in society that many Native Americans experienced, as few Indians could claim they married into Chicago's social clique. Second, Yarr and Killeen wed during the Great Depression, a period when marriage rates declined.[48] Yarr and Killeen could marry during the Depression because the university was set to name Yarr an assistant head football coach.[49] His football experience, notoriety, and education secured a job and a livelihood for his young family.[50]

After the team's letdown at the end of the 1931 season, Notre Dame fans complained about the new coaching staff and directed most of their barbs at Anderson. Co-coaches Anderson and Chevigny performed poorly on the sidelines, battling for team control, which resulted in poor play and low morale. Anderson also lacked Rockne's gregarious personality. He could not cultivate the connections with alumni in order to secure jobs for recruits and he did not arrange for sympathetic officials to referee the team's games. These problems gravely affected the team's play. Against Carnegie Tech, for instance, the Irish amassed an unheard-of 104 yards in penalties. Fans and journalists demanded that Notre Dame fire Anderson after the 1931 season but the administration backed its man and let Chevigny go.[51]

Fans still worried about the team's coaching in 1932, but the administration expressed optimism about the forthcoming year, focusing especially on Yarr and other assistant coaches. Reverend Charles O'Donnell, the president of Notre Dame, wrote to an Irish booster, "Our coaching staff as established for next year is a fair topic for discussion. We admit it is experimental but are expecting it will be a successful experiment. The three young fellows are keen as can be on their assignment."[52] O'Donnell and others hoped that Yarr and the two new assistant coaches could return Notre Dame to its past glory.

Notre Dame began the year by trouncing Haskell Indian Institute, Drake, and Carnegie Tech by a combined score of 177–0. The Haskell game demonstrated that Notre Dame journalists had changed the way they wrote about Indian football, possibly because of Yarr. In 1921 Notre Dame had defeated Haskell 42–7 and the sports story followed the typical frontier formula. "Indian Massacre" was the headline and the writer began, "Cartier Field, Saturday was the scene of an Indian Massacre. When scalps had been counted, the toll was: Notre Dame 42; Haskell 7."[53] However, the temper of Notre Dame journalism differed in 1932. The headline read, "Irish Score at Will as Haskell Is Crushed, 73–0." The body of the story did not include the typical references to scalp taking, war, or other terms typically associated with Indian-white football. The writer noted the disparity in size between Notre Dame and Haskell as well as Haskell's trick plays, which were common topics in Indian-white football games.[54] It is possible that Yarr's abilities on and off the field led to the change. Writers minimized Indian and Irish racial qualities when they discussed Yarr, and he showed that an Indian played football as well as any other person.

After the Carnegie Tech game, Notre Dame's fortunes changed. The Irish dropped games to Pittsburgh and USC with uninspired and sloppy play. Furthermore, Anderson alienated the press, did not hire sympathetic referees, and failed to live up to the myth and reality of Knute Rockne. The 1932 team stumbled to a 7–3 record and the financial outlook for 1933 was not favorable. The Irish would host the big payday schools (like USC and Pittsburgh) and visit a number of smaller schools like Indiana during the 1933 season. During the team's declining fortunes, Yarr left his post as center coach at Notre Dame at the end of the 1932 campaign.[55]

A year later Yarr played professional football for the Chicago Cardinals, one of the worst teams in the National Football League. Yarr's playing time fluctuated throughout the season because he shared the center position with former Irish teammate Thomas Moynihan. Yarr started three consecutive games, including the Cardinals' only victory of the season against Cincinnati.[56] However, Yarr did not appear in the lineup for another month and when he returned to the lineup, he experienced déjà vu. In the Cardinals' second game against Cincinnati, the Cardinals prepared to punt, and "Yarr's pass went over Dick [Nesbitt's] head and while he jumped and touched the ball he couldn't stop it. It landed outside the end zone and automatically was a safety."[57] Yarr did not always enter the spotlight for his blunders. His play on defense against Brooklyn set up the Cardinals' offense so that they were in a position to win the game. Late in the game, "Tom Yarr threw Kelly for a 7 yard loss on third down" and forced the Dodgers to kick a field goal. Unfortunately the offense could not put the ball in the end zone and the Cardinals lost its last game of the season 3–0.[58]

Yarr played only one season with the Cardinals. In 1934 he found a job coaching John Carroll University, a Catholic college in Cleveland. Yarr's association with pro football did not hinder his ability to attain a job coaching in the college ranks as it did for others. College football purists considered professional football the "raggedly stepchild to the college game" because it corrupted the college game and the play was inferior.[59] Yarr's experience at Notre Dame probably alleviated any doubts about his affiliation with professional football in the minds of John Carroll officials. Much like his professional playing days, however, Yarr's record at John Carroll was lackluster. He finished with a 6–10-2 mark after two years of coaching, five wins coming in his first season.

After 1936 Yarr had had enough of football. He used his education, football fame, and various connections through his wife and Notre Dame to land a job with a loan company in Chicago owned by Fred Snite. On Christmas Eve 1941, Yarr died of a heart attack in his office, the same affliction that took his mother. A newspaper covering Yarr's death in 1942 stated, "Yarr, one of the great line of All-American centers at Notre Dame . . . rates with the great players of Notre Dame history." Even in death, however, Yarr could not evade the stereotypic nicknames that followed him throughout his playing days: "Part Indian, Tommy carried the nickname of 'Wahoo' throughout his career at Notre Dame."[60] This time journalists did not emphasize his biethnic identity but only his Indian roots. Perhaps accentuating Yarr's biethnic identity no longer served a purpose. At the end of his life he did not live in an environment where emphasizing both ethnicities was important, as it had been while he played at Notre Dame.

Yarr returned to some prominence in the 1980s. He was elected to the Native American Indian Athletic Hall of Fame in 1982 and the College Football Hall of Fame in 1987. At the halftime of the 1987 Notre Dame-usc game, Notre Dame president Reverend Monk Malloy presented

Yarr's widow with a plaque in commemoration of Yarr's accomplishments. After these events, however, Yarr again faded from view.[61]

People remembered and emphasized Yarr's biethnic identity while he played football at Notre Dame, but the school remembers him differently. While I worked on a senior thesis on Native Americans and sports at the University of Notre Dame, I entered the school's archives and mentioned my topic to the helpful staff. They provided me with a pamphlet from the Carlisle Industrial School and mentioned that a Native American played football for the Irish. They gave me a folder that read "Tommy Yarr [1929–31] One-Fourth Indian Football Player." It is ironic that the university archives accentuated Yarr's Indian heritage, even though contemporaries emphasized Yarr's biethnic identity and attempted to make him an indistinguishable part of the Notre Dame community. As with the reports that followed his death, people remembered Yarr for his Indian heritage and considered him a unique member of the Notre Dame football fraternity. Neither African American, Jewish, nor Italian football players have their ethnicities listed—only the Indian. That ancestry assured him a special ethnic place in Notre Dame history.

Notes

1. For recent works on Native American football that concentrate on players' ethnicity and journalistic impressions, see David Wallace Adams, "More Than a Game: The Carlisle Indians Take to the Gridiron, 1893–1917," *Western Historical Quarterly* 32 (spring 2001): 25–53; Bloom, *To Show What an Indian Can Do*; Oriard, *Reading Football*.

2. There are a few biographic sketches of Yarr's life, including Gene Machamer, *The Illustrated Native American Profiles* (Mechanicsburg PA, n.d.), 48; and Oxendine, *American Indian Sports Heritage*, 255.

3. This study accepts two current ideas concerning ethnicity: it is socially constructed and it is a product of internal identification and external ascription. Ethnicity, then, is subject to historical and environmental change. See Joane Nagel, *American Indian Ethnic Renewal: Red Power and the Resurgence of Identity and Culture* (New York, 1997); and Gerald Sider, *Lumbee Indian Histories: Race, Ethnicity and Indian Identity in the Southern United States* (New York, 1991).

4. The following works shaped my understanding of multiethnic people in America: Leonard Dinnerstein, *Anti-Semitism in America* (New York, 1994); James Clifton, *Being and Becoming Indian: Biographical Studies of North Ameri-*

can Frontiers (Chicago, 1983); Allen Kraut, *The Huddled Masses: The Immigrants in American Society, 1880–1921* (Arlington Heights VA, 1982); Ronald Takaki, *Iron Cages: Race and Culture in Nineteenth-Century America* (New York, 1979); and Winthrop Jordan, *The White Man's Burden: The Historical Origins of Racism in the United States* (New York, 1974).

5. The best example of literature on the fur trade that emphasizes the importance of mixed-bloods are Jennifer S. H. Brown and Jacqueline Peterson, eds., *The New People: Being and Becoming Metis in North America* (Lincoln, 1985); and Sylvia Van Kirk, *Many Tender Ties: Women in Fur-Trade Society, 1670–1830* (Norman, 1980).

6. For a history of the tribes in the Puget Sound, see Alexandra Harmon, *Indians in the Making: Ethnic Relations and Indian Identities around the Puget Sound* (Berkeley, 1998); and Brad Asher, *Beyond the Reservation: Indians, Settlers and the Law in Washington Territory, 1853–1889* (Norman, 1999).

7. Heather Bowers copied the petitions of the Strand family and posted them on the worldwide Web. Copies of the petitions are in the author's possession. The Center for Pacific Northwest Studies at Western Washington University holds Josephine's tapes of Native songs.

8. See Harmon, *Indians in the Making*.

9. Harmon, *Indians in the Making*, 139–69.

10. Merle Reinikka copied death certificates for people of Finnish descent in Washington. An excerpt of Josephine Strand-Yarr's death notice can be found at *http://www.genealogia.fi/emi/emi3d2ode.htm*.

11. For history of Notre Dame football and Knute Rockne, see Murray Sperber, *Shake Down the Thunder: The Creation of Notre Dame Football* (New York, 1993); Ray Robinson, *Rockne of Notre Dame: The Making of a Football Legend* (New York, 1994); Michael Steele, *Knute Rockne: A Bio-Bibliography* (Westport CT, 1983). For Notre Dame recruiting, see Sperber, *Shake Down the Thunder*, 296–301, 327; Morrie Starrett to J. Arthur Haley, 27 [June] 1930, University Athletic Business Manager, ca. 1900–1940, Correspondence Series, Haley Folder (UABM), University of Notre Dame.

12. Sperber, *Shake Down the Thunder*, 369. For general studies of sports in America during this period, see Donald Mrozek, *Sports and American Mentality, 1880–1910* (Knoxville, 1983); and Benjamin Rader, *American Sports: From the Age of Folk Games to the Age of Spectators* (Englewood Cliffs NJ, 1983).

13. Lawrence McCaffrey, *Textures of Irish America* (Syracuse, 1992), 26–27; Andrew Greeley, *That Most Distressful Nation: The Taming of the American Irish* (Chicago, 1972), 121; Rader, *American Sports*, 210.

14. Sperber, *Shake Down the Thunder*, 301–10.

15. See *Chicago Tribune*, 3, 10, and 15 November 1929. For more in-depth

discussions of the 1929 season, see Sperber, *Shake Down the Thunder*, 312–22; Robinson, *Rockne of Notre Dame*, 219–33; Steele, *Knute Rockne*, 44–47.

16. "Notre Dame on Rampage against Wildcats," *Notre Dame Scholastic*, 29 November 1929, p. 341.

17. Paul Host, "An Error Provided Yarr's Tensest Grid-Iron Moment," *Notre Dame Scholastic*, 25 January 1932, p. 25.

18. See Rader, *American Sports*, 88.

19. For a synthesis of America during the Great Depression, see David Kennedy, *Freedom from Fear: The American People in Depression and War, 1929–1945* (New York, 1999). For the condition of college and professional football during the Great Depression, see Rader, *American Sports*, 208; Robert Peterson, *Pigskin: The Early Years of Pro Football* (New York, 1997), 109–26.

20. Sperber, *Shake Down the Thunder*, 365–66, 396.

21. Arch Ward, *Frank Leahy and the Fighting Irish: The Story of Notre Dame Football* (New York, 1953), 108.

22. Sperber, *Shake Down the Thunder*, 339.

23. " 'We'll Have a Strong Team,' Says Rockne," *Notre Dame Scholastic*, 26 September 1930, p. 20.

24. "Rockne Has Heap Big Indian on Squad in Person of Yarr," *South Bend New-Times*, n.d., found in Notre Dame Athletics General Collection, Biographical Drop Files, folder "Thomas Yarr [1929–31] One-Quarter Indian Football Player," University of Notre Dame Archives.

25. "Rockne Has Heap Big Indian on Squad in Person of Yarr."

26. See Oriard, *Reading Football*, 229–47.

27. "Rockne Has Heap Big Indian on Squad in Person of Yarr."

28. For treatment of Irish Americans in America and their response, see Noel Ignatiev, *How the Irish Became White* (New York, 1995); Takaki, *Iron Cages*.

29. "Rockne Has Heap Big Indian on Squad in Person of Yarr."

30. For the half-breed character, see Clifton, *Being and Becoming Indian*, 27–29. For fear of miscegenation, see Takaki, *Iron Cages*, 59–60, 114.

31. *Chicago Tribune*, 7 November 1930.

32. Robinson, *Rockne of Notre Dame*, 241; "Southern Methodist Downed, 20 to 14," *Notre Dame Scholastic*, 10 October 1930, p. 82.

33. Sperber, *Shake Down the Thunder*, 335–36. Savoldi signed a professional football contract shortly after his expulsion and later became a professional wrestler.

34. For the 1930 season, see Sperber, *Shake Down the Thunder*, 323–46; Robinson, *Rockne of Notre Dame*, 235–55; Steele, *Knute Rockne*, 47–50.

35. James Keiner, "Yarr Football Captain," *Notre Dame Scholastic*, 16 January 1931, p. 399.

36. "Tommy Yarr Achieves His Goal as Star Gridder at Notre Dame," *Notre Dame Scholastic*, 31 January 1931, p. 449.

37. For the death of Rockne, see Sperber, *Shake Down the Thunder*, 347–62, 371–75; Robinson, *Rockne of Notre Dame*, 257–73; Steele, *Knute Rockne*, 47–50.

38. "Reserve and Frosh Win over Varsity in Final Scrimmage of the Season," *Notre Dame Scholastic*, 8 May 1931, p. 831.

39. "Introducing: Tommy Yarr," *Notre Dame Scholastic*, 25 September 1931, p. 25.

40. Clifton, *Being and Becoming Indian*, 19.

41. "Introducing: Tommy Yarr."

42. "Introducing: Tommy Yarr."

43. "Yarr Extends String of Star N.D. Centers," *Chicago Tribune*, 9 October 1931, p. 33.

44. Wilfried Smith, "Yarr Breaks Thumb in Last Drill—but He'll Play Today," *Chicago Tribune*, 10 October 1931, p. 21; *Chicago Tribune*, 11 October 1931.

45. For the 1931 season, see Sperber, *Shake Down the Thunder*, 371–85.

46. "N.D. Gridders Named to Concensus [sic] Eleven," *Notre Dame Scholastic*, 8 January 1932, p. 26.

47. "Yarr to Marry Chicago Girl," newspaper article, 5 February 1932, University of Notre Dame Archives.

48. Kennedy, *Freedom from Fear*, 165.

49. James Kearns, "1932 Coaching Staff Made Known by Athletic Board," *Notre Dame Scholastic*, 5 February 1932, pp. 7, 14.

50. Steven Riess argues that football players used their notoriety and college education (which the average American did not have) to obtain white-collar jobs after their playing days concluded. Riess quoted in Peterson, *Pigskin*, 211–12.

51. Sperber, *Shake Down the Thunder*, 375–85.

52. Rev. Charles L. O'Donnell to John H. Neeson, 11 February 1932, University Records, President Charles O'Donnell, 1928–34, folder 6/52, University of Notre Dame Archives.

53. Edwin Murphy, "Indian Massacre," *Notre Dame Scholastic*, 19 November 1921, pp. 141, 142.

54. "Irish Score at Will as Haskell Is Crushed, 73–0," *Notre Dame Scholastic*, 14 October 1932, p. 21. For earlier writers emphasizing Indian race, see Oriard, *Reading Football*.

55. For the 1931 season, see Sperber, *Shake Down the Thunder*, 388–96.

56. *Chicago Tribune*, 9, 16, and 23 October 1933.

57. Wilfried Smith, "Chicago Rally Falls Short in Fourth Period," *Chicago Tribune*, 13 November 1933, p. 21.

58. "Hickman Kicks Goal; Dodgers Beat Cards, 3–0," *Chicago Tribune*, 20 November 1933, p. 19.

59. Peterson, *Pigskin*, 6–7, 109.

60. "Funeral Is Set for Tommy Yarr," newspaper clipping, n.d., University of Notre Dame Archives.

61. Oxendine, *American Indian Sports Heritage*, 255; Machamer, *Illustrated Native American Profiles*, 48. For a picture of Yarr's widow receiving the award from Malloy, see University Photographer, Color Negatives (GPHR) 837, University of Notre Dame.

6. Playing Football, Playing Indian
A History of the Native Americans Who Were the NFL's *Oorang Indians*

While lying there listening to the Indians, I amused myself with trying to guess at their subject by their gestures, or some proper name introduced. . . . It was a purely wild and primitive American sound, as much as the barking of a chickaree, and I could not understand a syllable of it. . . . I felt that I stood, or rather lay, as near to the primitive man of America, that night, as any of its discoverers ever did. — Henry David Thoreau

As the sun fell on a mid-October evening in 1922, Jim Thorpe—along with a dozen or so other Native American athletes including Nick Lassa, Joe Guyon, Pete Calac, and Leon Boutwell—ran quickly through the dense woods along the east bank of the Scioto River. They were joined by several dozen dogs, specifically Airedales, a popular local pedigree. Because the animals needed daily exercise, these athletes would repeat this scene night after night, "running" the dogs several miles through the wooded countryside that surrounded the small Ohio town of LaRue, which had a population of 750 humans and many more dogs. The responsibility of caring for these animals was shared among a retinue of more than twenty-five American Indians, young men from as many as ten different tribes, hired that year to move to the previously all-white LaRue.

Training Airedales was but one of the duties this group of outsiders had been enlisted to carry out. They were also expected to advance the general popularity of this breed by fulfilling a public relations role. To be more specific, they were hired to play football, to form a professional team that would be known as the Oorang Indians, to compete in the new National Football League. [1] The world-famous Jim Thorpe, Sac

Advertisement for Oorang Indians game in the *Baltimore News*, 6 December 1923. Courtesy of the author.

and Fox, by this time thirty-four years old, accepted an invitation to coach this unique football team. To accomplish their charge to publicize the Airedale pedigree, the Oorang Indians of LaRue were saddled with unique and spectacular constraints. First, they were expected to play nearly all of their games on the road, in the larger cities of their opponents, since contests in tiny LaRue (lacking even a football field) would hardly serve the purpose of advertising Airedales. Second, during halftime and frequently even before the games began, the players were required to dress in Indian regalia and emerged on the field to stage particular versions of Native dances and war chants, as well as to demonstrate the abilities of the Airedales by leading the animals to perform stunts. On some days spectators might even see a tomahawk-throwing contest or Chippewa Nick Lassa wrestle a bear. Such antics likely compromised their performance as a football team. In two seasons they won only three games, and by 1924 the Oorang Indian franchise ceased to exist.

The few scholarly reports that have examined this football team[2] have offered merely thin accounts or undertheorized portraits,[3] and a number of media essays have provided overviews. In what follows I seek to develop a more detailed portrait of the Oorang Indians, lingering in particular on some of the individual Native Americans who came to LaRue and on the man who literally choreographed this spectacle of race, history, and identity: Airedale breeder Walter Lingo. Further, a series of interpretive readings emphasize the many competing voices that characterized the making of this short-lived football team. The

Oorang Indians franchise was constructed by the intersection of diverse American cultural practices, popular narratives, and social identities, just as it highlighted new forms of "playing Indian" and stagings of racial difference. [4] Further, its spectacles of Indianness were informed by expressive, creative, and repressive deployments of power and agency.

Theoretically, these readings turn on "spectacle," a nuanced concept developed by Guy Debord to explain how ideologies, images, and commodities animate contemporary media and society. [5] Douglas Kellner, elaborating on Debord, writes, "Spectacles are those phenomena of media, culture, and society that embody the society's basic values, serve to enculturate individuals into this way of life, and dramatize the society's conflicts and modes of conflict resolution." [6] In this instance, the staging of an all-Native American football team in the early 1920s brought into focus the process of spectacle in the construction of public culture, a process in which Indianness was produced as an allegory of play, but it was an allegory with multiple, contrasting meanings. In fact, it ultimately forged a dynamic space where Native American and Euro-American identities collided and colluded.

Crafting a Dog Race

LaRue's wealthiest citizen was Walter Lingo, whose life's passion was the Airedale breed, which was first developed in England and Scotland. Lingo established several large kennels in LaRue and by the 1920s had transformed the town into the virtual Airedale capital of the world. His extensive real estate was dedicated to these dogs, from kennels to mail-order puppy buildings, and he employed an array of trainers, crate makers, guards, and clerks. [7] Lingo's ultimate wish was for America to embrace Airedales the way he did.

For Lingo, breeding and raising these hunting dogs were activities connected to the processes of nature and the wilderness. He was raised to believe that Native American peoples embodied a unique relationship to nature, and ostensibly, for him, assembling a professional team of Native American football players as a way to help sell Airedales seemed logical. Indeed, he surmised a supernatural bond between Airedales and the American Indian: "I knew that my dogs could learn something from them that they could not acquire from the best white hunters." Born in LaRue on 12 October 1890, Lingo claimed to have grown up with the qualities of an adventurer, as a boy who loved the outdoors, animals, and Indians. Lingo was enamored by the lore that the town was built upon land once inhabited by Wyndotte Indians. He even recalled that as a teenager, he "skipped out west and spent the summer with the Indians."[8] In his mind American Indians were quintessentially masterful hunters and trackers, and he "considered [them] to be mythic people," believing there was "a supernatural bond between Indians and animals."[9]

As he matured into adulthood and began erecting an Airedale empire, Lingo never lost his robust enthusiasm for the outdoors, particularly hunting wild game, such as deer, raccoon, and opossum. Once he became wealthy he arranged numerous hunting engagements in Ohio and in other regions of the United States. During his hunting trips Lingo liked to tell stories; he especially liked to chronicle miraculous tales of Airedales rescuing children or performing acts of courage on the World War I battlefield. He brokered many friendships by inviting people to join him for hunting trips; those whose company he especially enjoyed would be invited again. One such hunting partner was Warren G. Harding, elected the president of the United States in 1921, who hailed from nearby Marion, Ohio. Lingo and, eventually, Thorpe considered Harding a good friend, and in 1922 the two of them "stopped in" to call on the president at the White House after the Oorang Indians had just lost the final contest of the season in Baltimore.[10]

It was in the context of Lingo's simultaneously entrepreneurial and magnanimous cultivation of new friendships that Jim Thorpe came to know the breeder. In 1919 Thorpe played for as well as coached the Canton (Ohio) Bulldogs when he was approached by Lingo, who rarely missed an opportunity to befriend a celebrity by either giving away a dog, sharing a meal, or arranging a hunting vacation. The two men quickly established a rapport, and Lingo shared with Thorpe his notion of assembling an all-Native American football team whose home would be LaRue. After Thorpe agreed to assist his new friend with his project, Lingo went to the owners' meeting of the new National Football League in June 1922 and for a sum of $100 purchased rights to a LaRue franchise (at the time, Lingo sold his highly trained Airedale police dogs for $500).

Thorpe immediately began to use his broad network of contacts among Native American athletes to locate potential recruits for the team. As the team's coach he earned $500 per week, a salary that also rewarded him for his role as the director of the Lingo kennels in LaRue. His search for players centered in the West on many Native American reservations, where he was able to find some of the men who had, in earlier years, played football with Thorpe at the Carlisle Industrial School in Pennsylvania. He also contracted players from the Haskell Indian Institute in Kansas and the Sherman Indian School in California. Two players of notable skill and reputation who agreed to join Thorpe and the others were Joe Guyon and Pete Calac. Guyon was inducted into the National Football Hall of Fame in 1966, based on a successful career that included early years with Carlisle and then Georgia Tech (where he was All-American), and a professional tenure that included the Canton Bulldogs as well as the Oorang Indians. A devout Catholic, Calac also played at Carlisle as well as for the professional teams in Buffalo, Canton, and LaRue.

Thorpe was not in town when players began arriving in LaRue in September 1922 to prepare for their first ever contest, scheduled for 1 October against the Dayton Triangles. On 26 September, just days before the first game, Lingo publicly introduced the players during a special dinner hosted by the Marion Athletic Association in Marion's Rider's Cafeteria. Describing the event, the *Marion Star* reported, "Chief St. Germaine, an Indian of giant size who graduated from Carlisle and Yale, gave an excellent talk to the members on the idea of raising the standard of his race. He related some interesting experiences of his career as a soldier in the World war [*sic*] and of his work in private life, telling of the Indian schools and what the race is doing." [11] On 28 September the *Marion Star* confirmed Thorpe's arrival in LaRue: "Mr. and Mrs. Thorpe, three children and maid, arrived last evening from Worchester, Massachusetts, having made their trip by automobile." [12] One day later the newspaper headline underscored the mythical prowess of Thorpe's coaching skills by proclaiming, "Thorpe Has Warriors in Excellent Condition" for the inaugural game that weekend. [13] Thorpe had, in fact, driven a Pierce Arrow touring sedan into LaRue and promptly checked into the Coon Paw Inn, where he would reside with his family. [14] Lingo advised Thorpe to use his Native American name, Brightpath, and specifically to add the moniker Chief before it. Chief Brightpath's team was housed in a converted clubhouse situated along the Scioto River, just south of town. Lingo was pleased to be able to merge the football-playing capacities of his players with the care and training of his animals. He began to claim in his advertisements that many of his dogs were trained by Indians, and those particular dogs were sold for a higher price.

It is noteworthy, too, that Lingo boasted that his veterinarian managed the dietary and medical needs of the players. The implications of this arrangement—suggestive of the discursive conflations of Native Americans and animals—are so obvious so as to render any extended analysis academic. Nonetheless, it *is* important to recognize that well before the twentieth century an historical, pervasive set of what I term "conditions of possibility" suggested the articulation of Indianness and animal. From the more general features associated with Indianness, such as wildness, savagery, physicality, and hypersexuality, to discourses literally equating Indian people with nature and animals and practices situating Indians as athletic "totems," white America had constructed a tissue-paper-thin line between the Native American and the animal. [15]

The most problematic aspect of the Oorang Indians' existence is probably the entertainment they were expected to stage during halftime and, on some occasions, before the game itself. Because variation and some degree of improvisation characterized the performances, each contest was unique. A typical halftime, however, might have seen the team members reentering the field in full "Indian" regalia, including feathered headdresses, to dance and sing an abbreviated rendition of a powwow. Throwing tomahawks, lariats, or even knives was added. Rifle shooting would have been a likely feature of the program, especially when the theme for the day centered on the prowess of the Airedales. Describing such moments, Robert Whitman wrote, "Lingo's dogs, handled by the Indians, trailed raccoons and coyotes, retrieved targets and brought to bay a black bear. Lingo's grand finale recreated the First World War, and his Airedales carried medicine to wounded United States Indian scouts, while a pitched battle between Indians and German soldiers raged over the football field."[16] Other times the performance highlighted the famed passing or punting skills of Jim Thorpe and some of his teammates. The following passage is from a 1922 *Chicago Tribune* article on the Sunday the Chicago Bears hosted the Oorang Indians: "The bleachers will be open to kids under 16 years of age at half price. Besides the grid battle proper, Jim Thorpe, famous coach of the invading outfit, will put on a punting exhibition, and a group of Indians will add a touch of the *wild and wooly* by staging a war dance before the game begins."[17] In pregame comments to his team, Lingo typically celebrated the Airedales and some of their miraculous life-saving rescues.

The presence of the celebrity LaRue residents enhanced the region's growing sense of self-importance, which had already been advanced, in particular, by Marion's prominence as a new industrial center and the autumn 1920 election of Warren G. Harding. The new Oorang Indians were not the first racial spectacle to parse the boundaries of Marion County; they entered a space already informed by the interpenetrations of racial signs and racialized social relations. LaRue was white, but Marion was marked by small neighborhoods of African American citizens who suffered from forced segregation and limited education opportunities. Black-face minstrel performances were commonly staged in downtown Marion and, in an effort to support Harding's presidential campaign, internationally famous black-face performer Al Jolson rolled into town to perform at the Chautauqua Auditorium. Further complicating this landscape of 1920s multiculturalism was the presence of many Amish homesteads in the areas surrounding LaRue and Marion. At this point it is nearly impossible to recover any reliable historical documentation about the everyday social relations that might have unfolded among the Native American players, their families, and the surrounding Amish community. Undoubtedly, however, when staying in LaRue, the Oorang Indian members saw Amish people and likely shared certain notions about them; to be certain, the Amish were aware of the presence of this embodied spectacle of Indianness that had "invaded" a nearby town. One can only imagine their reactions.

Healthy, Stealthy, and Brave

As other chapters in this volume argue, throughout the nineteenth and early twentieth centuries, Euro-Americans constructed Indianness in terms that mythologized the Native American's imagined physical prowess, stealth, and stamina. These cultural narratives animated the spectacle of the Oorang Indians, and an examination of the historical contexts that produced these myths will clarify important features of the Oorang team and its experiences. The project of American Empire continued apace through the nineteenth century—with more vigor and purpose than in earlier centuries—by increased surveillance, torture, imprisonment, relocation, and murder of the Native American body. In the late nineteenth century and into the twentieth century, the U.S. government, with the support of various Christian churches, endeavored variously to erase Native dance and religious expression from the daily lives of numerous American Indian peoples.[18]

An ambivalent array of sentiment, desire, and fear continued to characterize Euro-American colonial subjectivity in the early twentieth century. Once any potential for vigorous, sustained military resistance by the American Indian was erased, America began to enact an ethos of imperialist nostalgia for Indianness. This nostalgia—turning on an odd desire to "embrace" and appropriate that which has been effectively displaced—fixed the Indian at the center of a white America's fantasies through stagings of such spectacles as William Cody's Wild West Shows and Native American athletic mascots, as well as popular accounts of cowboys and Indians in the Wild West.[19]

During this time the Indian emerged as a key symbol in the development of a white, masculine, character-building movement. The "readings" of Indianness that enlivened this movement were produced in a popular series of youth novels, health manuals, and in the literature of the Boy Scouts of America. Specifically, this discourse encouraged boys to embrace various elements of Indian life to develop discipline, courage, healthy bodies, an intimate knowledge of nature, and a strong moral character. Ostensibly the aim was to teach white children Indian ways, but what constituted "Indian ways" were a set of highly idealized stereotypes of Indians as scouts, hunters, and craftspeople.[20] In 1930 Maud Smith Williams published a book that typified the discourses that proliferated during the preceding decades. Titled *Growing Straight: A New System of Physical Education with Mental Control*, it advanced a nineteenth-century temperance formula for building a sound mind and moral body with regimented discipline, but with the added element of reverence for the Indian. Williams anchored the proper inspiration for her program of breathing, posture, and relaxation exercises in "Indian prowess": "Of all races in the world today *the American Indian is the acknowledged superior in physical development*. He possesses vigorous strength and yet is lithe, graceful and straight as an arrow. He has the secret of keeping himself young, agile, strong and healthy, well into old age, and that without becoming senile."[21]

Ernest Thompson Seton offered perhaps the most paradigmatic encapsulation of imperialist nostalgia for Native American peoples and cultures in his popular series of Woodcraft books. Woodcraft was the name Seton gave to the general idea that the "character" of children could best be nurtured and developed by tapping into their natural instincts.[22] In 1903 he published *Two Little Savages: Being the Adventures of Two Boys Who Lived as Indians, and What They Learned*,[23] followed the next year by *Red Book: Or How to Play Indian*.[24] In these books he clarified his belief that it was *Native American* ways of living that were *authentically* ideal for advancing sound moral and spiritual character. Throughout his writing career, Seton repeatedly identified the Native American "body" as the authentic repository of all that is pure, beautiful, and healthy. Undoubtedly, young LaRue and Marion citizens had already engaged such materials growing up; whether or not Lingo actually read them, there is little doubt that he seemed to actualize Seton's writings as if they were his own credo.

These ideas about the American Indian existed in the context of a movement of a different sort led by the U.S. government to establish boarding schools designed, in a very real sense, to "take the Indianness out of Native American people" by teaching them elements of mainstream white American culture.[25] The administrators of these new institutions "saw their own optimism as symbolic of a benevolence they claimed to feel toward indigenous people," and they "believed themselves to be defenders of Native American humanity . . . proclaiming they were defending the 'right' of Indians to become 'civilized.'"[26]

Most of the Oorang Indian players had been students at Indian boarding schools, where they learned how to play football. Indeed, Thorpe began to achieve his fame while studying and playing football at Carlisle, where he helped transform the team into a dominant national force that routinely defeated the white universities with the strongest athletic programs. Although these federally operated boarding schools were designed to convert Natives to Christianity, teach them the importance of having a vocation, and show them how to be "civil," they unwittingly created new social relations between Indians and non-Indians. In terms of athletics, the American public and media drew on these well-worn discourses of pristine—even wild—Indianness in their efforts to engage these boarding school teams.

For the American public, and even for the Native Americans, contests pitting the Carlisle Indians or the Haskell teams against white college teams were viewed as racial battles, literally ideological performances framed by the lingering ethos of Manifest Destiny.[27] Michael Oriard has chronicled the way in which Carlisle's football team was constructed in the national coverage of the mainstream press.[28] Such coverage foregrounded the racial qualities of Indianness, and game headlines commonly incorporated such clichéd discourse as "The Redskins versus the Palefaces." The Oorang Indians were described in the same fashion, illustrated by following headline from the *Marion Star* on Saturday, 6 October 1922:

WHOOPIE! BIG INJUNS ON TOES FOR CONTEST . . . JIM THORPE HAS BEEN WHETTING SCALPING KNIFE . . . PALEFACES FROM COLUMBUS WILL BE BURNED ALIVE IN FOOTBALL PARLANCE—MAYBE!

Glenn "Pop" Warner, the Carlisle football coach from 1899 to 1914, who was very close to his star player Thorpe, is an important figure for understanding the complexity of white engagements with these increasingly visible boarding school Native Americans. In later years Warner would coach with great success at the University of Pittsburgh and Stanford University, although his prevailing image as a paternalistic leader who could get the best from his players—in terms of moral character and performance—assumed particular relevance at Carlisle with his Native American students.[29] In a series of essays published in *Collier's Weekly*, Warner remarked on his Carlisle teams:

Carlisle had no traditions, but what the Indians did have was a very real race and a fierce determination to show the palefaces what they could do when the odds were even. It was not that they felt any definite bitterness against the conquering white, or against the government for years of unfair treatment, but rather they believed the armed contests between red men and white had never been waged on equal terms. . . . "You outnumbered us, and you also had the press agents," a young Sioux once said to me. "When the white man won it was always a battle. When we won it was a massacre."[30]

Commenting on this passage, John Bloom argues that "Instead of helping to incorporate indigenous peoples into a fictive national unity, [football] seems to have symbolized the ways that Native Americans were defined by a national unity that through its very definition, systematically excluded and subjugated them."[31] Other reports indicate that during pregame speeches Warner implored Carlisle players to demonstrate their worthiness as "warriors."[32] Indeed, "Pop" Warner's paternal, sympathy-laced nostalgia turns on a desire for difference and a presumption to personally *know* Indian desire.

The Indian boarding schools served to stage what was, in the American imaginary, the very best in terms of determination and the natural, physical, athletic prowess of Indianness; what the schools had presumably done was to somehow tame the wilder, more dangerous elements of Indianness. However, such elements might be expected to rise to the surface during a football game, for even "white boys" were not expected to restrain their baser tendencies on the playing field. Athletics were a complicated cultural "technology," at once expected to offer Indians a space of rehabilitation, recuperation, and civil transformation. The imagined wildness of the Indian could be disciplined, reshaped, and even recontextualized on the court or playing field.

Native Americans were highly cognizant of the new identities—as educated, civilized Americans—they were being asked to actualize, and they appreciated how these new identities collided but also colluded with their identities as Native Americans. They understood the new forms of power these new identities might generate, and they also knew that elements of their Indianness could be staged to likewise generate opportunity. They enacted a sort of double consciousness in the early twentieth century; although this was often empowering, it was not always a comfortable process or one that easily transcended exploitation.

Oppression and Expression

Bill Winneshiek began attending the University of Illinois in 1996, majoring in recreational studies. A member of the Ho Chunk nation, Winneshiek's arrival on campus brought him in contact with other Native American students as well the university's (in)famous mascot, Chief Illiniwek. Troubled by this icon, he joined others in protest, demanding that the school retire the mascot. He and others commonly faced derision and even the threat of violence for their public stand. Like most Native American students who witness the stereotypical dances of Chief Illiniwek—ostensibly representing an Illinois Indian but dressed in Sioux regalia, including a war bonnet and a breastplate— Winneshiek was offended by this commercial appropriation of Indianness. Winneshiek is of interest here because his grandfather, known also as NahiSonwahika, attended Carlisle and played center and offensive guard for the Oorang Indians in 1923. Bill Winneshiek has designed a colorful Web site chronicling his family history and that of the Ho Chunk nation and offering numerous photographs of his living and deceased relatives. His grandfather, also named Bill, is featured in a snapshot alone and in another with Jim Thorpe and the rest of the Oorang team in 1923. Bill Winneshiek conveys great pride in his family and their accomplishments, including his grandfather's brief tenure as a professional football player. Near the bottom of his homepage he posts the following question in bold letters: "Is there a hostile environment at the University of Illinois?" [33] That link opens to a page in which Winneshiek provides details about the University of Illinois mascot controversy, outlining his own objections and offering readers a chance to view two letters of support for Chief Illiniwek that he received from the administration. He concludes, "We are not wanted at this university," and he then posts the contact information for several members of the University of Illinois board of trustees, who support the mascot.

Winneshiek conveys a healthy appreciation for the conditions of possibility and opportunity that brought his grandfather to LaRue. Like the other players, the senior Winneshiek undoubtedly relished the chance to parlay his skill and enthusiasm for the game of football into a high-profile job. At the same time Bill knows that his grandfather was aware of the larger contours of the performances of the Oorang Indians. His grandfather (in the 1920s) and Bill (in the present) likely share an ambivalence about the spectacle of Indianness that the LaRue team staged, a spectacle that was largely a projection of the fantasy of Walter Lingo and the nation.

This ambivalence, as well as confusion, surely informed numerous Native Americans hired to "play Indian" in the early twentieth century. But such stagings also gave Native Americans opportunities to exploit if not parody the fantasies of those who desired these stereotyped exhibitions of Indianness. In this volume Gerald Gems offers evidence that a fluid, polysemous cultural field framed these Native American athletic performances and that a prevailing trope of the "cultural trickster" defined the role of the American Indian football player. Indeed, Gems highlights an incident in which Carlisle students in 1905, while beating Dickinson 36–0, filled the chest of a mock Dickinson dummy with arrows after each score. Such antics add new layers of complexity to any analysis of Indians "playing" Indian and, for this essay, they suggest that the Oorang players had throughout their lives been at the center of such racialized play.

Everyday the Oorang Indian players confronted an array of racial and racist stereotypes and intersecting allegories of racial difference. It is impossible to draw conclusions about the personal interpretations of these athletes—in terms of their intersubjective response to this whirl of racial signs and symbols. They left behind virtually no personal diaries or other writings conveying their reactions and sentiments. A vast number of stories about the players are available, however, and many of them circulate as a body of oral folk knowledge among present-day LaRue locals.

The majority of these stories tend to highlight the zaniness, if not the unpredictable wildness, of the players. Hazel Haynes, LaRue's postmistress, served as the community's unofficial collector of oral memories of the players, which include numerous drunken escapades. The trope of the drunken Indian—even then, already a tired one—was conspicuous in the context of tales of players who would drink away, night after night. [34] Having emerged largely in the 1800s, this trope advanced conceptions of the Indian as wild, violent, and impetuous, and it spawned a rich colonial discourse of preoccupation and anxiety about Indian drunkenness. The "problem" drinking of Native American peoples became a complex symbol of Indians' inability to become appropriately acculturated by an ostensibly tempered white civilization. For example, after a game in Chicago several Oorang players allegedly stuffed a local bartender into a telephone booth because he attempted to close his bar early, and then they helped themselves to the liquor. On another occasion, in St. Louis, some Oorang team members left a bar and boarded a trolley, but the trolley happened to be facing in the opposite direction from their hotel. Improvising, the members lifted the car from its tracks and turned it around.

Emblematic of LaRue's perception that the Oorang Indians were mischievous, even potentially dangerous, police officers would meet the team at the train station to confiscate any guns or knives, and even to admonish the players about misbehavior.[35] Leon Boutwell, the team's quarterback, seemed to appreciate the importance of stereotypes and the possibility of exploiting and even parodying them. "White people had this misconception about Indians," he explained. "They thought we were all wild men, even though almost all of us had been to college and were generally more civilized than they were. Well, it was a dandy excuse to raise hell and get away with it when the mood struck us. Since we were Indians, we could get away with things the white men couldn't." To underscore his point, he added, "Don't think we didn't take advantage of it."[36]

Other narratives highlight more general impressions of Indian wildness. Faye Kurtz, who was interviewed in the 1980s, recalled, "We used to skate in the flooded field just north of the railroad tracks. One January several of the Indians came down. Toward the evening a big bonfire was started. After a while the Indians got up and started a war dance around the fire. Nick Lassa was obviously the loudest. Some say you probably could have heard him for five miles in the cold night air. All of us kids were fascinated, I can tell you that."[37]

The local memories of Nick Lassa, perhaps more than of any other player, embody the full range of the hyperbole of racial spectacle. A Kalispel tribal member, known by the moniker of Long Time Sleep, Lassa remained in LaRue for years after the Oorang Indians disbanded. Those who knew him talk about his drinking, his nonconformity, and his playfulness. Like Thorpe and his family, Lassa rented a room in the Coon Paw Inn, which was located next to the telephone office. Although many have remarked on his drinking, how much and how often he drank remain unanswered questions. Damon Leffler—who was about fourteen years old when he befriended Lassa—recalled, "He was quite a drinker, but he wouldn't hurt anyone. When he'd get drunk, he'd act like he was going to tear you all to pieces. . . . When he got drunk, he pulled his hair down over the front. It came just down to his eyes. It was blacker than coal. He looked real mean. Mostly he bothered the women at the telephone office. He'd go down there at night when he had a few drinks and peep through the window and scare them."[38] When residents grew concerned about Lassa's public behavior they would summon the mayor, who would have the player put in jail to "dry out." Marie English, who worked at the Campbell National Bank, painfully remembered one of these incidents, during which she claimed that the town marshal and several other men hoisted Lassa onto the back of a black pick-up truck. "I looked out the window from the bank and they had [the trunk] going down the town and up in the back of it was the marshal standing there hitting him over the head with a billy club. Blood was running down his head. It made me so mad."[39]

Other memories centered on Lassa's super strength, especially his ability to push cars out of snowdrifts or to perform the farmwork of several men. Resident Bob Greenwood remembers when Lassa stripped and jumped into the frozen river through a hole in the ice. Greenwood also claims that Lassa would carry him on the shoulders all the way to a town called Agosta, five miles up the river. People commented on Lassa's nakedness, claiming that when drunk he would often strip or citing other moments when he would remove his clothing. He apparently liked to wrestle, and town residents would drive him to regional carnivals to perform as a bare-chested strongman, fighting all willing opponents. Bill Guthrie, Jr., who lives just outside of LaRue, related a story his father told him:

One hot Sunday morning Jim Thorpe, Calac, and Nick all came out to the farm, still tipsy from the night before. Dad and his dad were going to castrate some boars, which weighed about 350 pounds. Normally, it would take four men using a rope to throw them so they could be cut. But those three jumped

*into that smelly pen and threw those boars by hand. . . . After they were done,
they climbed up on this 2,000 gallon concrete water holding tank we had . . .
and jumped in to wash off. Everyone except those three went away and a few
hours later when they got back, there was Nick, Thorpe and Calac, all stark
naked, lying on the water tank in the sun, still drying out.*[40]

This memory embodies several of the common narrative themes regarding Lassa, including excessive drinking, super strength, nakedness, and zany behavior. He fulfilled the cultural script—noted by Gems—of the indigenous trickster. Fittingly, a 1 November 1922 article in the *LaRue News* reported briefly on a Halloween masquerade party thrown by Lassa. As a trickster persona, Lassa straddled the chasm between civilization and wilderness, between human and animal, and between strength and weakness. While he lived in LaRue he worked occasionally for the kennels and on nearby farms, as well as touring regionally as a carnival strongman. He left for Montana about fifteen years later to work as an Indian agent on a reservation, where he died in 1965.

In a wonderfully personal, reflexive essay, Philip Deloria attempts to untangle the legacy of his grandfather, Vine Deloria, Sr., by examining his commitment to Episcopal Christianity as an ordained minister and his passion for American athletics. Specifically, Deloria wonders about his grandfather's wholesale investment in an American church and, with even more passion, in such mainstream sports as baseball, football, and basketball. He wonders whether attachments to white practices and institutions such as these had in effect erased the Indianness from his grandfather and many others like him. Deloria acknowledges that

Indians fit neatly into the nostalgic, antimodern image of professional and college sports. If athletes in general were emblems of post-frontier masculinity who embodied a reassuring sense of Gemeinschaft, *my grandfather and other Indian athletes proved to be even more complex, evocative symbols for White spectators. In the early twentieth century's tête-à-tête with cultural primitivism, "Indians" could be objects not simply of racial repulsion but also—as they reflected nostalgia for community, spirituality, and nature—of racial desire.*[41]

Deloria, however, avoids any simplistic readings of his grandfather's love of athletics. He suggests that a fifty-five-yard Hail Mary pass into the end zone, for example, is an event imbued with multiple meanings for both Native Americans and non-Indians, "some . . . shared, some . . . not."[42]

Noting the uneven relations of power that structured opportunity and shaped meaning, Deloria cautions against celebrating too uncritically the new forms of Indianness that characterized the early decades of the twentieth century, especially the ones that turned on Indians playing Indian. On the other hand, he insists on recuperating the sincerity and dignity of Native involvement in such practices as the Oorang Indian performances:

Again and again, [American Indians] created new Indian worlds, fusing diverse cultures or fitting themselves into the interstices between a core native "tradition" and new practices introduced from the American periphery . . . the same society that imposed . . . limits on Indians also offered [ironically] a certain power to native people who could find and push the right cultural buttons. The intercultural world that took shape in the early twentieth century formed in response to both Indian and non-Indian imperatives and constraints. [43]

Deloria refuses to view spectacles such as the Oorang Indians as simple, in any way, and insists on recognizing the vectors of power that created them. It is helpful here to appreciate "power" as a slippery force that resides within historically situated matrices of "signs and practices, relations and distinctions, images, and epistemologies."[44] Cultural analysts interested in "hegemony" often examine the various ways in which a more powerful, even oppressive bloc within a social structure is, in fact, able to generate popular consent among less powerful blocs. To suggest, however, that Native Americans were merely seduced into embracing stereotypical representations and narratives of Indian experience—such as those inscribed by the Oorang Indian spectacle—would be a flattened application of the idea of hegemony. It would fail to account for ethnic agency and overdetermined formulations of resistance, and would be an inaccurate perception that images and narratives are ultimately complete and effective.

Because no organic, essential Indianness exists and no monolithic form of whiteness prevails, we are forced to reckon the existence of the

Oorang Indians not as unproblematic (they were indeed problematic) but as hybrid and conflictual. In the early twenty-first century, as Native American people have secured new forms of postcolonial power, they would not likely stage Indianness as it was exhibited by Walter Lingo some eighty years ago. Nevertheless, even though they were exploited, the Native Americans who were *the* Oorang Indians were not mere puppets of white desire. The Oorang team requires our attention precisely because its existence provides significant insight into the structures of whiteness and the discourses of Indianness in the 1920s. The invention of this team reveals a political economy of Indianness that turned on popular understandings of race and history and that was defined by an uneven struggle over ethnic autonomy, economic opportunity, and (post)colonial (mis)representation.

Notes

I wish to acknowledge the research assistance of Cheryl Springwood, Jane Rupp, Robert Whitman, Grace Thorpe, Jim Anderson, Bill Winneshiek, and the National Football Hall of Fame. I also wish to thank C. Richard King for comments on an earlier draft.

1. In 1922 the league previously known as the National Football Association became the National Football League (NFL).

2. Deloria, "'I Am of the Body'"; Bloom, *To Show What an Indian Can Do*; King and Springwood, "Playing Indian"; Charles Springwood, "Playing Indian and Fighting (for) Mascots: Reading the Complications of Native-American and Euro-American Alliances," in *Team Spirits*, ed. King and Springwood, 304–27.

3. Robert L. Whitman, *Jim Thorpe and the Oorang Indians: The* NFL's *Most Colorful Franchise* (Marion OH: Robert Whitman and the Marion County Historical Society, 1984).

4. Philip Deloria, *Playing Indian* (New Haven: Yale University Press, 1998).

5. Guy Debord, *Society of the Spectacle* (Detroit: Black and Red, 1970), 10; see also C. Richard King and Charles Fruehling Springwood, *Beyond the Cheers: Race as Spectacle in College Sport* (New York SUNY Press, 2001).

6. Douglas Kellner, "Sports, Media, Culture, and Race—Some Theoretical Reflections on Michael Jordan," *Sociology of Sport Journal* 13 (1996): 458.

7. Bob Braunwart, Bob Carroll, and Joe Horrigan, "The Oorang Indians,"

The Coffin Corner, vol. 3 (Huntington PA: Professional Football Researchers Association, 1981).

8. Jim Borowski, "Tiny LaRue Was Once an NFL Town," *The Sunday Oregonian*, 8 January 1995, p. 1.

9. Quoted in Whitman, *Jim Thorpe and the Oorang Indians*, 33.

10. Quoted in Whitman, *Jim Thorpe and the Oorang Indians*, 66.

11. "Oorang Indians Guests at Athletic Dinner," *Marion Star*, 27 September 1922, p. 3.

12. "Thorpe Takes Charges of Oorang Indians," *Marion Star*, 28 September 1922, p. 6.

13. "Indians in Fine Shape for Game at Dayton," *Marion Star*, 29 September 1922, p. 6.

14. See Robert Whitman, "The Team That Went to the Dogs," *Ohio Magazine*, July 1986, p. 75.

15. See Vine Deloria, Jr., foreword to *Team Spirits*, ed. King and Springwood, ix–xi.

16. Whitman, "The Team That Went to the Dogs," 36.

17. "Redskins Invade Chicago Today to Battle Bears," *Chicago Tribune*, 12 November 1922.

18. See C. Richard King and Charles Fruehling Springwood, "Choreographing Colonialism: Athletic Mascots, (Dis)Embodied Indians, and EuroAmerican Subjectivities," *Culture Studies: A Research Annual* 5 (2000): 191–221; Carol Spindel, *Dancing at Halftime: Sports and the Controversy over Native American Mascots* (New York: New York University Press, 2000).

19. See Renato Rosaldo, *Culture and Truth: The Remaking of Social Analysis* (Boston: Beacon Press, 1989).

20. Jay Mechling, "'Playing Indian' and the Search for Authenticity in Modern White America," *Prospects* 5 (1980): 17–33; Shari Huhndorf, "From the Turn of the Century to the New Age: Playing Indian, Past and Present," in *As We Are Now: Mixed Blood Essays on Race and Identity*, ed. William S. Penn (Berkeley: University of California Press, 1997), 181–98.

21. Maud Smith Williams, *Growing Straight: A New System of Physical Education with Mental Control* (New York: A. S. Barnes, 1930), 7.

22. Mechling, "'Playing Indian,'" 19; see also Huhndorf, "From the Turn of the Century to the New Age."

23. Ernest Thompson Seton, *Two Little Savages: Being the Adventures of Two Boys Who Lived as Indians, and What They Learned* (New York: Doubleday, 1903).

24. Ernest Thompson Seton, *Red Book: Or How to Play Indian* (Privately published, 1904).

25. See Bloom, *To Show What an Indian Can Do*.

26. Bloom, *To Show What an Indian Can Do*, xv.

27. See King and Springwood, *Team Spirits, Beyond the Cheers*, and "Choreographing Colonialism."

28. Oriard, *Reading Football*.

29. See Bloom, *To Show What an Indian Can Do*, 18–19.

30. Glenn Warner, "The Indian Massacres," *Collier's Weekly*, 24 October 1931, p. 7.

31. Bloom, *To Show What an Indian Can Do*, 20.

32. See Gems's essay in this volume; also see Alexander M. Weyand, *The Saga of American Football* (New York: Macmillan, 1955).

33. Bill Winneshiek, *http://firstpeople.iwarp.com*.

34. Bonnie Duran, "Indigenous versus Colonial Discourse: Alcohol and American Indian Identity," in *Dressing in Feathers: The Construction of the Indian in American Popular Culture*, ed. Elizabeth Bird (Boulder CO: Westview, 1996), 111–28.

35. Shelby Strother, "Airedales, Indians, and Pro Football," *The Sporting News 1989 Pro Football Yearbook* (New York: The Sporting News, 1989), 147.

36. Braunwart, Carroll, and Horrigan, "The Oorang Indians."

37. Whitman, *Jim Thorpe and the Oorang Indians*, 46.

38. Ron Cass, "Long Time Sleep and LaRue's Oorang Indians," *Newslife*, 2 February 1981, p. 13.

39. Cass, "Long Time Sleep and LaRue's Oorang Indians," 15.

40. Cass, "Long Time Sleep and LaRue's Oorang Indians," 19.

41. Deloria, "'I Am of the Body,'" 329.

42. Deloria, "'I Am of the Body,'" 335.

43. Deloria, "'I Am of the Body,'" 325.

44. John Comaroff and Jean Comaroff, *Of Revelation and Revolution: Christianity, Colonialism, and Consciousness in South Africa* (Chicago: University of Chicago Press, 1991), 21.

ANN CUMMINS, CECILIA ANDERSON,
& GEORGIA BRIGGS

7. Women's Basketball on the Navajo Nation

The Shiprock Cardinals, 1960–1980

Thirty-three years ago a first-grade public school teacher in Shiprock, New Mexico, asked her class this question: "Who here has seen an Indian?" Shiprock is a large community just inside the northeast border of the Navajo Reservation. Ninety percent of the students in this classroom were Navajo. Initially, no one raised a hand. The teacher, an Anglo, asked again: "No one here has seen an Indian?" My sister, Patricia Cummins, also an Anglo, raised her hand. In 1962 my family moved to Shiprock where my father was a shift foreman at the Vanadium Corporation of America's uranium mill. We'd brought a television with us when we moved, and my sister had seen Indians on the TV. She told the teacher this, and then several others in the class raised their hands, too. They had seen Indians in John Wayne Westerns at the Chief Drive-in and at the Totah Theater in Farmington. The Indians wore feathers and carried tomahawks. The teacher said, "I have news for you. All you Navajos are Indians." The children were amazed.

Georgia Briggs (née Nelson) had a young nephew named Leonard in this classroom. Leonard went home that day and told Georgia's father—his grandfather, Woodrow D. Nelson—about the lesson. "Cheíí, did you know that Navajos are Indians?"

"They are?" Mr. Nelson said. "Who said so?"

"My teacher."

"Oh, well then," Mr. Nelson said. "If your teacher said so, it must be true."

The Shiprock Cardinals, 1960s. *Left to right*: Evelyn Garnanez, Ineth Diswood, Georgia Briggs, Cecilia Anderson, Joyce Ford, Katherine George, and Randi Hanova. Courtesy of the author.

Georgia's family and mine have been friends for many years. Georgia still tells this story when our families gather, and we always laugh and want to hear it again. We get a kick out of the fact that initially the only child in that reservation classroom who thought she'd seen an Indian was a white child. We get a kick out of Leonard's chat with his cheíí. Mr. Nelson passed away twenty years ago, and we all miss him. He was a smart, funny man on whom the irony of an Anglo teacher telling young Navajos what they were would not be lost. It would be added to his repertoire of teacher stories gathered over the years and translated into jokes for his daughters, sons, and their children. Still, he may well, in perfect earnestness, have been cautioning Leonard to listen to his teachers—and not necessarily because the teachers were wise. The English language and customs dominated the reservation economy then, especially the moral economy of the classroom. During the first half of the century, formal education had been brutal for many Navajos. By the 1960s most Navajo families had been touched by the boarding school experience, many of them ripped from their homes (one Navajo man told me how BIA agents came to his family's land and, when the family resisted orders to "turn him over" for schooling, lassoed him, as if he were a calf), transported to schools as far away as Kansas and California where educators systematically attacked everything that was familiar to the students. In 1969 when Leonard was in first grade, there were a few public schools on the reservation, but they were all staffed by Anglo administrators and teachers who taught from history books written by non-Native historians—books about Indians, not Navajos or Hopis or Apaches. Most public school educators did not teach, speak, or tolerate the Navajo language. I remember occasions in grade school where teachers spanked children for speaking Navajo; later, in high school, both teachers and students ridiculed Navajo-speaking students, calling them "johns." I understood this word to mean "primitive," "backward"—sheepherders. In the moral economy of a classroom that encouraged students to become English-speaking, moneymaking citizens, sheepherder did not trade very well.

Perhaps, then, Mr. Nelson cautioned Leonard to listen to and believe his teachers as a way of protecting him from physical or emotional pain. Or perhaps he was simply giving Leonard his own recipe for a good life. Mr. Nelson was a man who embraced life as an opportunity for learning. Everybody was a teacher, and though circumstances, environments, and lessons sometimes brought pain, the open mind brought consciousness, and consciousness empowered. Or perhaps he meant something altogether different by his off-the-cuff comment, something I cannot fathom. He is no longer here—I wish he were. I'd like to ask him.

When our families get together we tell stories that go back four decades; through the stories we re-create and celebrate our common history. It's a peculiar history. It features stories of my Irish Catholic family trying to make a home in the Navajo homeland. It features stories of Georgia's Navajo family negotiating the troubled terrain of a homeland overrun with Anglo systems. For the most part, my family interacted with Navajos from behind the skirts of Franciscan priests, and it is through the Catholic Church that many of our stories intersect with Georgia's—not because Georgia was Catholic, though my parents always hoped she would convert. My parents and she spent hours at our kitchen table, debating biblical points (Georgia likes to joke that everything she knows about the Bible she got from Cecil B. DeMille movies). The year I was a sophomore she went to mass with us several Sundays in a row; like her father, Georgia takes her education where she can, and that year a back pew at Christ the King mission was a classroom. My father, never a betting man, was close to wagering on Georgia's conversion but was severely disappointed when he found out she had signed the rosters at the Church of Latter Day Saints. She didn't tell us that she didn't intend to become a Mormon, any more than she intended to become a Catholic. She signed the Mormons' roster because that season the Mormons had a terrific basketball team.

Maria Allison, citing research by anthropologist K. Blanchard, suggests that the game of basketball was first introduced on the Navajo Reservation by Mormon missionaries in the mid-1940s as a tool for conversion,[1] though according to Georgia's mother, Lillian Nelson, who died in 2004, she and her friends were playing basketball twenty years before the Mormons "introduced" the game. Still, the churches did play a vital role in orchestrating competitive play on the reservation. By the 1970s public schools and interscholastic sports gave young people a format for organized play, but before then church youth leagues were extremely popular. From 1964 through 1968 my father and Georgia coached Shiprock's Catholic girls' team. As a coach Georgia had an opportunity to train young athletes whom she later recruited for her own teams.

Georgia and her sister, Cecilia Anderson, were playing basketball a decade before my family moved to the reservation. Their brothers, Gene and Buddy, played; Georgia and Cecilia learned from them first and began playing with the older girls in their early teens—with Mami Jim and her friends on dirt courts around Shiprock. In the 1950s adult community teams formed spontaneously across the reservation, some sponsored by local organizations, some simply groups of friends who liked to play. In October 1960 a coalition of young men, Buddy Nelson among them, met to plan and form the Navajo Invitational Tournament (NIT). The NIT held its first men's tournament in December that year, hosting teams from across the reservation at the Navajo capital, Window Rock, Arizona.[2] The next year the NIT added a women's division. From 1961 through 1965 the *Navajo Times* lists a Shiprock women's team, the Bankerettes, in all NIT tournaments and in scores of community, state, and regional tournaments. Georgia and Cecilia Nelson were regularly in the lineup; other players included Mami Jim, Ineth and Beverly Diswood, Ida Henderson, Barbara Yellowhorse, Linda Izatt, Emma Lou Begay, Sharon Goodluck, June Curley, Joyce Ford, Annabelle Charley, and Ruby Keams. The team never called themselves the Bankerettes, however. They called themselves the Bankers because they were sponsored by the First National Bank in Shiprock. In the *Navajo Times* all of the women's teams listed during those years had the suffix "ette" attached to their names. Neither Georgia nor Cecilia knows who decided to attach "ette." The teams weren't consulted. In the mid-1960s the Bankers changed their name to the Cardinals.

The Cardinals, a champion team that collected over a thousand trophies in state, regional, and national tournaments, had a twenty-five-year history spanning the early 1960s through the mid-1980s. Membership was always in flux, as most team members were working women with families. Cecilia played throughout the team's history; Georgia was there through the early 1980s. For the most part the Cardinals coached themselves. There were no team captains in the traditional sense; the captain changed from game to game depending on who was hot, who had energy, and who had an interesting game strategy. The Cardinals were flexible and spontaneous, good at assessing situations and adapting to the challenge of the moment. They recognized and valued individual players' strengths. They were, above all, good friends. And they were obsessed with playing.

When Cecilia, Georgia, and I first began talking about writing the Cardinals' story, we had no models in mind. We started simply by trying to remember the details from those early years, they as players, I as a fan. We'd meet whenever we could at my mother's house in Farmington, New Mexico, and put a tape recorder in the middle of the table. Once Cecilia brought her friend, Gwendolyn Charles. Halfway through the session, Gwen, her eyes wide, suddenly said, "I remember you!" to Georgia with such emphasis it was as if the memory were alive. She remembered watching the Cardinals from the stands when she was a child and being so inspired that she hit the court herself and became good enough in her teenage years to get picked up by the older women's team. Gwen's memories added dimension, both filling in details from the 1970s and describing how membership on the team shaped her life. It occurred to us that ideally, the story of the Cardinals would be a blend of individual voices, an assortment of players telling a story not simply of this team but of generations. We began trying to find other team members and to hold public storytelling sessions.

Telling a story, though, is not writing a story. I teach creative writing at Northern Arizona University (NAU). In my experience, authorship and ownership are synonymous, the author usually singular. I come from a tradition where writers toil over sentences, shaping them to create something called a voice; in my profession the reader wants to know not simply what the story is, but who's telling it—who the narrator is. But we wanted this to be a multivoiced narrative featuring each writer's unique voice. We feel that collaborative authorship presents an exciting dimension, placing collective expression—perhaps we could say tribal expression; in this case the tribe would be a loose organization of basketball players, family, and friends—next to Western paradigms that privilege singular authorial ownership. The ideal, though, was logistically impossible. We live hundreds of miles from each other. Our jobs (Georgia is a fifth-grade teacher on the Ute Reservation; Cecilia is a health professional on the Navajo Reservation) consume our time. To simplify (and meet deadlines), I took on the task of transcribing, synthesizing, and editing material from the taped sessions at my mother's house and the public storytelling sessions. The role troubled me. Any writer's innate ethnocentrism gives particular shape to a narrative that betrays cultural bias. As a creative writer I'm always trying to figure out how to feature the dramatic moment. In our taped sessions I found myself asking questions like this: "Sure there were decades when the Cardinals played and won, but was there one period that was the high point in the team's history?" I love a good hero story where one defining moment sets us all free. I had read and appreciated books that celebrated and highlighted heroic moments for Native basketball players and their teams (Larry Colton's *Counting Coup: A True Story of Basketball and Honor on the Little Big Horn*[3] and Ian Frazier's *On the Rez*[4]). Left to my own inclinations, I would write in the same vein and turn the Cardinals' story into a hero story with dramatic peaks and valleys. But every time I asked to hear the story of the Cardinal renaissance period, somebody would dismiss my question. For the women on the team, they were all high points.

I was also uncomfortable with analyzing or trying to categorize the stories primarily because I'm hypersensitive to the hazards of misrepresentation. (In projects such as ours, the group is the authority over the material and in the best position to extract meaning. We were still in the process of collecting stories and had not yet begun to write collaboratively, so I felt I was at a disadvantage.) The dangers of misrepresentation became evident during the public storytelling session held at NAU featured later in this essay. In this session each storyteller recounted how other members of the group influenced or inspired her. For these women, at this particular time, to speak about basketball was to speak about friendship and relationships among sisters. But in other sessions other themes emerged. Each session we've held has been unique in tone and content.

At the end of the NAU session, a man in the audience—a graduate student—asked a question: "I'm wondering how you feel about winning and losing."

Georgia said, "Winning is most important."

Cecilia followed up. "It's so heartbreaking when you lose by one point, especially if it was you who didn't make that point, or if you miss a lay-up, and you know how easy lay-ups are."

The audience member said, "That dispels a myth. I had heard it was hard to teach Navajos to be competitive."

Georgia leaned closer to the microphone and eyed the man. She said emphatically: "We wanted to win."

The graduate student in the audience didn't say how he encountered the myth that "it was hard to teach Navajos to be competitive," but in my research for this project I discovered a book—the only book in NAU's library dealing exclusively with Navajo basketball—that could lead someone to this conclusion. In her dissertation, "A Structural Analysis of Navajo Basketball," Maria Allison, employing Levi-Strauss's methods, set up detailed case studies where she observed Navajo and Anglo basketball teams in the Window Rock area. Allison's purpose was to describe and analyze the differences between Navajo and Anglo approaches to the game. She concluded: "If there was a single resounding theme which emerged throughout the data, it was that the Navajo game content was guided and influenced by the Navajo's concern for maintenance of group solidarity. . . . The idea of being a single winner without being able to transfer and share that recognition with the group system is perhaps again inconsistent with the individual-group harmony principle." An Anglo coach interviewed by Allison described the Navajo players as noncompetitive. "In regard to the competitiveness of the Navajo, the lack of 'killer instinct' and physical aggressiveness was frequently pointed out as a characteristic."[5]

Academic research is rife with studies that have contributed to misrepresentations of human cultures; these studies leave impressions that don't always disappear when research models become outmoded. This is not to say that Allison's study has no merit. Many of her observations could certainly be applied to aspects of the Cardinals' group dynamic. The team built game strategies collaboratively; they excelled in large part because they valued friendship and interdependence. But group harmony was not the "single resounding theme" that defined the group. The Cardinals also had a burning, competitive desire to win. In fact each speaker at the NAU session addressed the importance of competition; these comments preceded the audience member's question. The Cardinals may not have competed within the group, but the team certainly competed against every team it met on the court. If Allison had broadened her study—if she had talked to the players she observed, or if she had studied linguistic cultural differences (perhaps the use of "killer instinct" in reference to competition says more about the Anglo coach than it does about Navajo athletes)—she may have found other equally important "defining themes" for the groups she observed.

But any representation is misrepresentation, and it is certainly better to engage in conversations about difference than to keep silent. Still, out of fear of "getting it wrong" my first attempts at shaping this work were minimalist. Colleagues who read early drafts felt that something was missing. They wondered where they might place the narratives. Could the stories be considered oral histories? Ethnographies? One reader wanted to know how they connected to Native American autobiography—to expressions of Indianness?

When I mentioned this term to Georgia and Cecilia, they responded in unison: "Indianness?" I have since learned that some historians, ethnographers, and anthropologists use the word when speaking of shared sensibilities among diverse tribes, but at the time the term was new to all of us. Terms like this that develop within academic disciplines can act as catalysts for suspicion among those outside academia whose identities are somehow connected to the term. We wondered what the "ness" in Indianness meant. Who put it there? Perhaps a teacher seeking to help educate students by categorizing ethnic ways of being and thinking? We dribbled the word around for a while. Then Georgia said, "Hey, remember that time Leonard found out he was an Indian?" And she launched into the story about her nephew and his cheíí. I have known Georgia for thirty-eight years. She likes to find humor in language, to tell jokes that restore buoyancy to language, especially to terms that can be catalytic. I don't see this trait as specifically "Indian," evidence of "Indianness." I see this as specifically Georgia.

She followed the story about Leonard with another about her own grandfather who hid from Kit Carson in the mountains by Cortez, Colorado, and never went on the Long Walk. He escaped, victoriously, the hardship of the Long Walk. "That's your Indianness for you," she said. But she did not say what she meant by that. Did she mean that the Indian heart defies and eludes capture? She told another story. Back then, she said, one boy in every family was required to go to school. Her uncle went to Shiprock Boarding School long enough to learn some English, but when World War I came along, he decided to go into the army. Decided. The verb is important. His choice. The second boy, her father, got to go to school in his place. Got to. Georgia emphasizes the fact that for her father, the opportunity for education was just that—an opportunity. He didn't know that he would be sent away from the reservation to a boarding school in Riverside, California, instead of to Shiprock, and he didn't know that he wouldn't be allowed to return home for a long while. But he wanted to go to school, and later he wanted his children and their children to go to school.

At Riverside Woodrow met his future wife, Lillian. Lillian had first gone to Shiprock Boarding School, where she had been taught domestic skills. When she had mastered all they had to teach and had graduated to the laundry room, she was sent to Riverside. She and other Native American girls had been groomed as domestic servants for white residents of the Riverside community. Lillian told Georgia and Cecilia that in her spare time at Riverside she played basketball.

If we look at the sequence of these stories, we might be inclined to think that Indianness, as defined by Georgia Briggs, is about taking the opportunity to choose, no matter what the circumstances. To choose against walking to Fort Sumner during a hard, cold winter. To choose school even if it meant boarding school. To choose basketball whenever possible. But Georgia never goes so far as to say how we should understand her stories. This may be distaste for categorization, for pinning things down. Or perhaps the connections are more in my head than they are in hers and reflect my need to understand the complex story. I don't ask Georgia if we should find meaning in the sequence of stories, partly because I know she'll tell me what she thinks is important, and partly because past experience has shown me that if I ask Georgia a direct question, she will answer me with one word: dáát si, which means maybe.

In the end I abandoned attempts to synthesize our sessions and returned to the original idea of telling the story with a multivoiced perspective, not through the time-consuming process of collaborative writing but by featuring transcripts from the oral storytelling session at NAU. What follows are stories told by Georgia Briggs, Cecilia Anderson, Gwendolyn Charles, and Leigh Chase during a session held on 30 November 2000. This session was more formal than those we'd held at my mother's house. I took on the role of moderator; the others, arranging themselves behind a table sequentially in order of age, took on the role of panelists.

Ideally a videocassette would accompany this text. It is impossible to capture in writing the audience interactions via laughter, applause, and exclamations, just as it's impossible to capture exactly the storytellers' nonverbal interactions—gestures, facial expressions, intonations. The presentation was unique in that the speakers didn't know the audience. The majority of the audience came from the academic community around Flagstaff. There was the pressure to try to anticipate an unknown audience's expectations. Georgia's suggestion to the group in the hotel room before the session was to keep it light. In fact, she and Cecilia fell into a spontaneous comedy routine, alternating roles, one playing the "straight guy" while the other delivered the joke, and they had the audience laughing through the first forty-five minutes. The audience shaped the performance in other ways. Some of the stories were muted—cleaned up. In one instance Cecilia told the story of how the team was humiliated at a tournament in St. Joseph's, Missouri, but she didn't specify who humiliated them. I had heard the full story before, and I asked Cecilia if I could elaborate in the endnotes of this essay. She agreed that I could fill in some of the details, but she preferred that I use initials rather than full names. We all—writers, storytellers, scholars—negotiate the terrain between private and public in our own ways and for our own reasons. Sometimes the reasons may be located in family or tribal custom—rules for how to talk to strangers—and sometimes they are purely individual. Cecilia didn't say why she didn't want me to name names, simply that she didn't.

Other factors shaped the Flagstaff performance. The group wanted the stories to be spontaneous, so they didn't script the session or rehearse, though Cecilia and Gwen both brought notes. The Arizona Humanities Council (AHC) sponsored the session. The notes filled in details that would address AHC goals: The session must not be merely anecdotal but educational; the stories should contribute to our understanding of the history of women's basketball on the Navajo Nation. In her narration Cecilia took care to place the Cardinals' history within the larger context of American history.

The story of women's basketball on the Navajo Nation that follows is an hour-and-a-half-long story—a small part of a much larger story. It is the story about how forty years ago individual athletes found teams, teams of talented friends who traveled together to tournaments and brought home trophies, self-motivated, self-directing teams; teams that intersected with institutions like banks and churches, churches with their own motives for sponsorship, church teams coached by white men employed by uranium mills making money in the Navajo homeland. Now the story includes memory fragments, fragments born not simply in the words each storyteller finds to tell what's remembered, nor in the sequence of memories, nor in the questions a listener asks, but in what each listener hears, each reader reads—each reader keyed to find meaning by the circumstances that have brought him or her to the page.

Ann Cummins

The Stories

The transcript: After an introduction by historian Jennifer Denetdale, I opened the session with comments about the group's history and storytelling process. In consideration of length and so as not to repeat information given above, I've omitted those here. I have reproduced the text as I heard it on the video recording of the session, though I have made minor edits where I thought the narrative was too difficult to follow, and I have added brief descriptions of a speaker's gestures to try and give "the flavor" of the performance.

The setting: The Liberal Arts Auditorium at NAU seats eighty in tiered rows facing a stage. The room was packed, and several people stood in the aisles and at the back of the room. The speakers sat behind a rectangular table that had been draped with a Pendleton blanket. The speakers had arranged several trophies at their feet in front of the table, and against one of the trophies they propped a photograph of the Cardinals in gold and red basketball uniforms. They were seated from right to left according to age, with Georgia, the eldest, next to Cecilia, then Leigh Chase, and Gwen Charles. A table microphone sat in front of each woman.

Georgia Briggs begins the session. "I was just going to say that maybe I should start with a joke, but I might just end with one. I started playing ball when I was about eleven, but I already knew by that time that that was going to be my life. I was born in 1939. By the time I started school in Albuquerque, my folks were already working with the war effort. Cecilia and I would have to be taken care of by our two older brothers. We had an early start throwing the football and playing basketball. When you're raised by two older brothers, you become tomboys. We're both tomboys."

"Actually," Cecilia interrupts, "you were first, and then you dragged me into it."

Georgia nods. "We were in the process of learning how to get into shape by running away from the dogs when we stole pears and . . ."

"Don't tell that story," Cecilia says.

"No, no. I'll quit there." Georgia pauses. Her expression is neutral. "But yeah, we played basketball. . . ."

"I still have the scars to prove it," Cecilia says.

Georgia smiles. "The dogs caught her. Anyway . . ."

Cecilia is not smiling. "It's a good thing I had my diaper on," she says.

Georgia hunches over her mike and whispers, "She continues to ask, 'Why did you abandon me?'"

"Everybody went running for the fence!" Cecilia says. "I was only, what, four years old? And they left me!"

Georgia, smiling, nods. "Anyway, we got in shape."

"I started when I was two," Cecilia says.

Georgia begins again. "We would play ball with boarding school boys," she says. "Our father was boys' attendant and because of that we would have access to basketballs and the outside dirt court. We always used boys' rules. Being the elder here—not the *eldest*, but the *Elder*— I started when the basketball court was divided into three sections. You had six people on your team, two here [she draws a rectangle on the table and places the two players on one end] two in the middle section, two in the other section. You had to stay in your own section. I started playing ball using those rules. I can't imagine how I tolerated that because when we practiced, we'd use boys' rules. After a few years they divided the court in half courts, three on this side [she draws on the table], three on this side, and after that, two rovers on each team who could go either way. Finally, we got to play by boys' rules,[6] but we already knew how; we were at home with boys' rules. I was playing ball when the three-point age came into being. And Cecilia. She was a good player. She could shoot from—"

"Was?" Cecilia says. "Was?"

"Oh. Sorry," Georgia says. She motions with her thumb toward the women next to her. "These three are still playing ball. I'm not. Oh, I'm a fifth-grade teacher, and I go out and play ball with my kids. Fortunately I'm about a foot taller and they try not to trample over their fifth-grade teacher. Being sixty-one years old, I decided, well, I'm going to confine myself to fifteen minutes at recess, but I remember the days. I had a good time. I played softball, volleyball, did other things, but the basketball years were the best. We started out with a bang. We had uniforms. We had knee-high socks. We had gold shoestrings in our Converse—"

"Canvas," Cecilia says.

Georgia looks at her. She smiles. "Your turn," she says.

"I didn't mean to interrupt all the time," Cecilia says.

"No, no," Georgia says. She smiles at the audience.

Cecilia leans forward. "My name is Cecilia, her younger sister, and I was born in 1942, you guys do the math. As I was growing up, I would follow Georgia all over the place and when she started playing I was always sitting on the sidelines watching—"

"That's why she was behind me when the dogs caught her," Georgia says.

"I don't know what year it was," Cecilia says. "We were in Albuquerque, and my brothers were supposed to be taking care of me, but they decided to go over the fence into this orchard. The dogs came. They went running. Georgia went running, too."

Georgia motions toward Cecilia. "She was *trying* to run."

"Georgia was going, 'Hurry, run, hurry, run.' There I was in my diapers. As I was going through the fence, they caught me, right on the butt. And I used to have the scars. I don't know if they're still there. I can't see back there. But anyway, I think my diaper saved my life. It's a good thing in those days you had cloth diapers, not the disposable ones you have now. But anyway, that's my story. There may have been good things to eat in there. Anyway, I was always following Georgia. I was on the sidelines, saying, 'Coach put me in, I'm ready to play.'

"I started actually playing, going on court, when they had half court rules and we had one rover, two guards, two forwards—no it was still six, wasn't it?" she asks Georgia. Georgia nods. "Anyway I was a rover. I thought I was a very important person being the rover on the team. We used to travel all over the reservation. I don't know how many of you are familiar with the reservation, but at St. Michaels, Arizona, the Catholic nuns were running a school, and they would have gold medal tournaments over there. We would make every one of those tournaments, plus other tournaments throughout the Navajo Reservation. We never forfeited. We would go through—"

"Wind, rain, snow," Georgia and Cecilia say in unison.

"Just like the postal service," Cecilia says. "We went to St. Michaels one year, I don't even remember what year that was. That was the year of the big snow on the reservation. Nobody was on the highway. But we knew the road, so we knew where the road was even though it was covered with snow. By the time we got to St. Michaels nobody was there. They had cancelled the tournament, but nobody bothered to tell us."

"We made it," Georgia says.

"It was over a hundred miles that we traveled," Cecilia says.

Georgia says, "We had to try to get money. We'd each pitch in about twelve dollars to earn the entry fee. Sometimes we would be entered in two tournaments—"

"At the same time," Cecilia says.

"So we'd have to split the team. During some tournaments we'd play two to three games a day. We just loved it. We had a great time."

"I think I started when I was about fifteen," Cecilia says. "As always, I was going after Georgia, following her around. Eventually I graduated from high school, and I went to Fort Lewis College [in Durango, Colorado]. I was hardly ever there on weekends. Every weekend I was gone because I was in tournaments, and my mother would drive, also through snow, [eighty miles] to come get me, pick me up, and take me back to the reservation to the tournaments. And there were a lot. We would go to tournaments not only on the reservation but in other states. We traveled all over Utah, Colorado, New Mexico, Arizona. One year I remember going to Council Bluffs, Iowa, to play in the nationals. We also went to St. Joseph's, Missouri. In Council Bluffs we were sitting there waiting for our game to begin. These ladies back east, they grew them tall. I was, at five-foot-seven, considered tall on the reservation, but when we went over there—she comes walking through the entrance. You know how you are on the basketball team. You scope the enemy out. You watch them, plan your strategy, we're saying, 'Georgia, that one's yours. Cecilia, that's yours.' And this lady comes in. She actually had to bend down. She must've been seven feet tall. I swear, that was the largest or the tallest—well, large, too. That's when everyone said, Cee: That's yours."

"Her legs were as big around as my waist," Georgia says.

"She was *huge*," Cecilia says. "Naturally I don't have to tell you we lost. All she had to do? They'd throw her the ball, she'd grab it, hold it over her head, turn around, do a pivot, shoot. And there we were, us little Navajos; the highest we ever got in guarding her was hitting her elbows. I think I boxed her knees a couple of times. I'm not exaggerating."

Georgia says, "She was that tall. She never missed."

"Well, you couldn't really miss," Cecilia says, "if you were like three or four feet from the rim. Those were good old days, and once when we went to St. Joseph's, Missouri, to play, we went with this other team, they asked us to play with them. Myself, Georgia, and another girl. When we were there at halftime, we had to give this demonstration."

"Yeah," Georgia says softly.

"I didn't want to do it because I felt very embarrassed because what they[7] wanted us to do—you've seen these Indians in the Western movies?

Georgia says, "You're not an Indian unless you wear feathers."

Cecilia says, "They wanted us to wear feathers, paint our faces, and you know how you whoop? We were told if we didn't do that we wouldn't be able to go home. We did it reluctantly. We don't have to tell you that we lost that tournament. That's the last time I remember not liking to play basketball. That was an experience I'll never forget."

After a long pause, Cecilia continues. "We would travel all over the place. This one time we went to Salt Lake City. When we got there we lost half of our team members because the other teams recruited them. So we had like three players. We'd driven all the way to Salt Lake from Shiprock. That's a good eight-hour drive. We weren't ready to go back, so we picked up some other women. We ended up playing our own team."

"Who won?" an audience member calls.

"We did!" Georgia and Cecilia said in unison.

"We went into the semi-finals," Cecilia said. "They gave us a gym to practice in. One morning we were scrimmaging against another team. There was a particular girl we had picked up from Shiprock. She had always been heavy. Five-five, she was out there playing. She'd go in for a rebound, she'd get knocked down, and we'd see her go flying across the court on her butt. She'd get right up and start playing again. I'd say, Hey, Ida. Doesn't so and so look like she's pregnant? Ida said, I don't know. She does look like it. That was all we said about it. Oh, by the way, we took third place with what team we had recruited. We had just gotten organized. We had never played together. Anyway we went home. Drove home through a snowstorm. Then the next day, Ida called me, she said, Cee, did you hear about so and so? I said, No, what happened. She delivered a healthy baby boy. She was pregnant. We didn't even know that. There she was. Everybody was knocking her down, and she went flying around the court. Believe it. Navajo women are strong."

"In more ways than one," Georgia says.

"When we were older, some of us married and had families. Once we went to Utah. Two ladies were nursing, only one took her baby. You know how nursing mothers get? You get so full of milk, it begins to hurt and it's really painful. She didn't have a pump, either that or we didn't know how to work it. She ended up nursing this other lady's baby during halftime or time out. Needless to say, she felt a lot better after that. Things like that happen.

"We were diehards. You could always depend on us. Whether it was snowing or not. Once we had to go to Albuquerque, our windshield wipers didn't work, we were out there wiping the windshields with a rag. When we got there we didn't play because the other team didn't show. They had to forfeit. But you know what? That other team was from Shiprock. We were saying, why couldn't we have played in Shiprock and phoned in the results? They wouldn't let us do that."

"They had rules," Georgia says.

"They stuck by the rules," Cecilia says. "And while we were in our own little world playing basketball, other things were going on in the world. Woodstock. Kennedy was assassinated. Martin Luther King was assassinated. Robert Kennedy was also assassinated in the sixties, wasn't he?"

Georgia says, "The Beatles."

"Yeah, the Beatles," Cecilia says. "And the Vietnam War was on. You remember that? I remember my friends going to Vietnam. After Kennedy was assassinated, Johnson became president. He indicated he'd get us out of the war, but it wasn't for another four or five years before we finally got out of Vietnam.

"The hippie movement," she says. "Remember that? You're not that old," she tells the audience. Many audience members assure her they are. "Woodstock. Joan Baez, the Doors, Janis Joplin."

"We listened to the radio on the rez," Georgia says. "Going back and forth."

"Barbara Streisand," Cecilia says. "Remember her song? 'People'? I'm telling you my age now. Free love was in the atmosphere. The emancipation of women. Although I think that had been going on for hundreds of years."

"Especially on the rez," Georgia says.

"The Cuba invasion," Cecilia says. "That was the sixties. *Laugh-In*. Remember Roland and Martin? In the seventies—"

"Women were wearing blue jeans," Georgia says.

"Georgia and I had already started that trend in the sixties," Cecilia says. "Jim Morrison, sadly to say, died of an overdose; Mama Cass died; Janis Joplin died. Jimi Hendrix. All those good people. Carter became our president. The invasion of Iran. Then the eighties. Reagan got us into an eight-hundred-billion-dollar deficit."

"A Republican," Georgia says.

"Linda Ronstadt. *Drugstore Cowboy*. Remember that movie? But we had fun. Those were good times. I'm still playing. We have a basketball league where I work. We've got nine hundred employees. Physicians, doctors. We have a coed league. The older we get, we're still competitive. We have our own little intramurals. We had our first league last year, and you'd be surprised how the older we get, we're still competitive. We only established the league to have fun and get to know each other—but I still have it.

"I do want to mention in 1971 we went to Albuquerque and played in the state AAU tournament, and we took first. I'll always remember that. Those were the days when they would introduce you at the beginning of the tournament, and as we were going in—I remember it was packed. On the rez women's tournaments were always packed. On the Navajo Reservation in Window Rock, Arizona, they'd always have the Navajo Tribal Band there, so basketball was a big thing. So when we were in Albuquerque they had just about the same amount of people there, and as we were going through the crowd, Georgia was in front of me, and she quickly turned around, and said, 'Who did that?' And I looked at her, and I said, 'Did what?' She said, 'Somebody pinched me on my butt.'"

Georgia says, "Yeah, there were a whole bunch of high school boarding school boys there. But we had fun."

"Oh," Cecilia says, "and I asked Leigh if I could tell this, and she said, go ahead, but Leigh spells her name L-e-i-g-h, so [in Albuquerque] when they were introducing us, the fellow that introduced her couldn't pronounce her name. Ever since then she's been known to us as Le Guy. There we have Le Guy Garcia, he said. We looked around, we looked at each other; we said, who's the guy? Does anybody know who the guy is?"

Leigh says, "It sounded French."

"But, that's it," Cecilia says. "I don't want to take any more time. Like I said, we had fun. We're still having fun, though right now it's without Georgia. I don't have anybody to follow now. People would always say, who's the oldest, and I would say, she is. Georgia's more outspoken. I was a little bit shy."

Leigh, smiling, says, "Hi. I'm Le Guy Chase. Georgia and I sat in on an interview this afternoon, and we were asked, when was the first time you picked up a basketball, and I told my story. Well this happened in junior high when I was in the seventh grade. I picked up the ball and dribbled. Stopped. Dribbled again, and the PE teacher said, 'You're walking.' I said, 'Walking?' I improved slowly. My sister Nona was a natural talent. [8] She was supposed to be here today but couldn't make it. Nona was my role model. I wanted to be like her. You know how the sister thing goes. She was always chosen. I improved.

"How I got started? I'm a Catholic. Back in the sixties, we had CYO, the Catholic Youth Organization. Ann's father was the youth director. He was to get all the young boys and girls active. They knew Georgia, and he knew Georgia knew all about basketball, so he asked her if she'd coach the girls, and that's how I met Georgia. So we'd go to St. Michaels, Fort Defiance, and the other parishes, and we'd play the girls' team. There were boys' teams, too, and the boys would play them. When I was in high school the Cardinals were in a tournament and Georgia said, 'We're short a player.' That year they came and asked my parents if they could take me and Nona to Utah, and my parents knew what good people Georgia and Cecilia were, so they let us go. They became my role models. A lot of what I know about basketball I learned through them. But that tournament I didn't go as Le Guy. I went as

Kathryn George, and she's right here [she points to one of the players in the team photograph]. I was an illegal player in that tournament. Because Kathryn George couldn't make it."

"We kept telling her, 'Remember your name. You're Kathryn George,'" Cecilia says.

"We never broke the rules," Georgia says. "We just bent."

"Their team back then was *the team*," Leigh says. "They had the uniforms, the full uniforms, right down to the shoelaces. There was no girls' high school basketball. We had a PE class. The teacher chose the best players and took them to other high schools where they played against other PE teams. Like Cee was saying, we still have it in our hearts, we love it so much. I don't play that often anymore. I work at a school. We have health and wellness, and I play with the students and teachers."

Georgia says, "Leigh's the school librarian."

"What shall I say next. Oh, it's an honor to be here, and thank you for having me. I'll let Gwen speak now. She's the youngest."

"Yatahee, everybody. My name is Gwendolyn Charles. [Gwen introduces herself by naming her clan on her mother's side and on her father's side.] I make Shiprock my home. I work there; recently I moved to Farmington, but I still call Shiprock home. I'd like to say thank you to everybody who's here. I know it's late. I'd like to thank the two ladies, Georgia and Cecilia, who invited me. I was a fluke. Cecilia says, come with me, we're having a meeting about basketball, and I said, what am I going to do? And here they started talking. They were talking about the old times, about basketball. I was just sitting there. And I said, 'I remember!' And I remember Georgia. I'm forty years old. When I was in seventh grade we had basketball in Newcomb Junior High School. I had a PE teacher who brought us girls together. We wore bloomers and, what do you call them?—pennants. Yeah. He'd make us play for five minutes at halftime in the basketball tournaments. Everybody would be laughing at us. We'd be running around, probably looked like ants. I was telling her [looks down the table at Georgia], I remember you, and you're the person who inspired me to play basketball, and she just looked at me, and she said, 'You need to come with us!' So Cee said, 'Don't you remember me?'"

"Me?" Cecilia says. "I followed Georgia?"

Gwen says, "I was in seventh grade, 1972. We were at the AAU tournament in Gallup. And I saw these ladies. We were just young. I'd never seen an organized basketball team. So organized. They looked like ladies. They played like ladies. Well, they played like boys but they looked like ladies. I was telling Georgia, she was so ladylike on the court. She never yelled. She didn't get frustrated when she got pushed and whatever. You could just see that sportsmanship in her, and I decided right then, I'm going to be like her. I'm going to be like that lady. I'm going to continue playing. I didn't know you could continue playing until you were old. I was thinking, she's still playing! That's when I decided, I'm going to stick to basketball. I knew they were an older team. I didn't know them then.

"Our coach was Ronnie Rowe, and he'd take us to Naschitti to play tournaments. Naschitti and Newcomb were always rivals. Pretty soon it came to Tohatchi. We played our own tournaments.

"I'd like to bring this up since we're talking about Navajo women on the reservation. This is kind of personal, real personal, but I'd like to bring it out because I think it's time to feel better about everything. For myself, I was raised by grandmother, she's my Naąlí. My mom gave me away when I was small, so I got all that ridicule at school that I wasn't good enough to have a mother. So basketball changed that. For my self-esteem. For everything in my life. It has changed. I grew up with alcoholics and I went through a lot of hardships. The only reason why I'm here and I survived everything is through sports.

"For the Navajo women, everybody kept that quiet. About how you were raised, how you were treated. My Naąlí raised me so good, in a loving way, but she had alcohol in her. That was really awful to grow up with. I remember going to a basketball game. Talk about love. I was so ashamed of my grandmother who raised me to come and watch me play basketball. I used to play basketball and, I'm going to tell you this, it was so good to be out there, to play, just to get away from them, but they would follow me to the game and see that's where the mixed feelings came. You were happy they were there, but you were ashamed of them. And as time went by, oh man, it didn't matter whether they were drunk. My grandmother was the main one, she'd be drunk out there, and she'd be yelling, she'd yell "ALL RIGHT," and she used to embarrass me, everybody knew she was alcoholic, kids who didn't know would laugh at me. As years went by, even until high school, oh, man, just seeing her up there. I did the best I could, and we took Basin League and we beat Shiprock! Not only that, like I said, my mom gave me away to my grandmother, my Na̜álí, and I never knew my dad. At that time he came back from the Vietnam War. What he did, he came back and he was a stranger. I knew he was my father. But I was raised by my grandmother's husband, and my dad came back, and it was so different. He was real mean to me. He'd tell me how spoiled I was and what a big baby I was, and I looked at him, and I said, He's my father? He's supposed to love me? And one day I looked at him—this was my freshman year—I told him, I said, 'Dad, how come you don't come to any of my games?' He never did. He looked at me, and he said, 'You're going to have to be good enough for me to go to your games,' and that's it. 'The only time I'm going to go is if you're playing for championship.' That's it. 'Other than that, I'm not going to go.' You wouldn't believe how hard I tried. I really wanted him to love me. I wanted to be the best just for him, just that year, and I did. And I told him the day that the basketball game was going to be on. We were playing for championship. And I said, 'Dad, are you going to come?' I said, 'We're playing for championship.' He didn't seem interested but he reluctantly came to the game. And I made the winning point.

"That was my freshman year. It was 1974. No '75. 1975. Newcomb only went to ninth grade so I had to go to Aztec. My whole family went to Aztec. That year the girls we beat for championship and the ones we played against at Aztec came together. They knew how I played and I knew how they played. We made a real good team. That year we went to state. We lost to the first-place team, which was El Dorado. We lost by five points. I was named by *Albuquerque Journal* the outside lady, and this other lady, Donna Reed, was named the inside lady. In the *Albuquerque Journal* in 1976 it says our game was the championship game because El Dorado beat the second-place team by twenty points. We didn't place but we gave them a good game. So I'd like to brag about that.

"Not only that, but talking about women and basketball—With me growing up the way I did, with the type of family and all the different feelings, I ended up having a baby and losing my four-year scholarship to go to Eastern. But forget about that and let me tell you about how I met Cecilia and her team.

"That year in '76, I was going to Aztec, which is a border town school so you had to stay in the dorm. Her team was playing the intramural game. I was on the high school team so I couldn't play, but they came without half their team, so they picked me up. Ever since then, Cecilia would pick me up. Talk about role models. After I stopped playing basketball in high school, I had my daughter, who is now twenty-three years old. Cecilia has a twenty-three-year-old son; they grew up together. She inspired me as a woman because she took her whole family, she took her two sons and her mom, and herself, and she would pick me up and haul me all over the place, and I didn't have any money. I was just trying to struggle myself, and I would feel real bad because I didn't want anybody to pay anything for me, but she would say, 'Just come!' She just wanted to win."

"And we won!" Cecilia says.

"I thought it was me," Gwen says. "It was the game, it wasn't me. She did that and really inspired me; basketball made my life. Cecilia encouraged me, because like I said, my family background and growing up with alcoholics, I ended up in a bad marriage. Cecilia would say, 'Come on, let's go play basketball,' and I'd say, 'No, I can't go.' She'd say, 'Forget it! Just come play. Play with us.' Stupid me. I'd play basketball, and I'd come home, and I'd get beat up. I never told Cecilia that. What would come out, and I think about it: Navajo men that don't know about being jealous about having somebody have their own life, they want to keep their wife right here, and if you do anything different, you get it. Later on she found out that was hard for me, but back then, she'd say, 'Come on, let's go, let's go.' And I'd come home, and I couldn't stay because he'd follow me to the tournaments and pick me up, not even to watch my game but just to pick me up, bring me back. Cecilia would come back with my trophies because I couldn't pick them up. She would pick them up for me because I couldn't stay, and see, it didn't matter what it was, even though I was going to get beat up, and I knew I was, I would still go to the games because that helped me. It made my life better. Everybody was watching, and the exercise, and everything. That really helped me, and I found out later in life. Going through all this, I had a breakdown, a nervous breakdown, but basketball always brought me back. Even though your husband would say, 'You just like to play basketball because you like those men to watch your legs. They see your legs, that's what you like, you're going over there, you're not going to play.' You know. Here you are, you're having fun with your friends, your ladies. Of course there're men out there. You're just a human being and you want to have fun. I don't know. The men in those days, I don't know. It was just something I had to go through, something I learned. And another thing: I'm not with him anymore because I learned I can do things, I can accomplish things, even though I struggle with children, and I raised and helped raise seven kids. And every time I had a basketball game, every time I did things, I would follow what Cecilia did: She took her kids, she took her family. I did the same thing. Now, I'm the one who picks up the younger good players. I'd pick them up, take them with me, feed them, tell them, 'You know, let's go,' they'd say, 'No, I don't have money,' I'd say, 'Don't worry about it, just come.' I did the same thing Cecilia did—to pay back, and to make myself feel good, and the same thing with my kids. Now two of my kids, two of my girls, they play basketball. And they're good at it. We all play together. We played together two years for the tournaments for the leagues they have down there, and my daughter was fourteen, my oldest nineteen, and everybody couldn't believe I was still playing with them, and now talking about the ways things have changed. It really has changed. The teams on the reservation don't dress like this anymore [she holds up the team photograph]. That's the thing that really inspired me when I first started watching these guys play and have uniforms, that was the neatest thing I saw, and I wish every team on the reservation would have the rules of having this type of uniform because this makes basketball basketball. Nowadays they just wear those tops over them—everybody throws them around. Those days, you took care of your uniform. I came at the end, like they said, but I really enjoyed playing with them, and they are the people I learned from. From Georgia, I learned how to be a woman on the court. Not one time have I ever gotten a technical. I never cussed, I never did anything, because in my head when I was young that was the first thing that I saw. I saw the beauty in those ladies out there, and I saw her, the way she was being a leader on the team, and so now when the younger players are playing—and it's competitive now, too, because you go out there, and you're my age, and these guys are just now coming out of high school, they played on high school basketball teams, but they didn't make it to the college to play. But they play real good, and they just look at me like who's this old lady coming out, but I showed them. Maybe they can stuff me and everything, but I showed them I can play offense, pass the ball, get assists, show them that there's experience."

Cecilia says, "And Gwen is a real good three-point shooter."

"Oh, I miss that," Gwen says. "The only time I can make a good three-pointer—because these young girls are so good—is if I'm by myself. But that's true in high school, that they didn't have three points then, and I told her [motions toward Cecilia], those were my 98 percent times for three-pointers.

"Some things I wanted to mention, oh, not only that. Talk about Navajo women not knowing anything on the reservation. Where I grew up we didn't have a car, we didn't have hamburgers, we ate mutton and potatoes everyday. The first time I ever had hamburger was going to school and going on a basketball trip. Oh man, I said, there's really food like this! The first time I ever went to Deezy—that's between Bloomfield and Cuba—it was eating hamburger for the first time, the first time I went a lot of places on the reservation, Ganado—it freaked me out because it was my first time, and I wouldn't tell anybody this is my first time seeing this place, I wouldn't tell because I was ashamed. I shouldn't have been. Let me tell you something. I don't know if Cee wants me to tell this. [Cecilia puts her fingers in her ears.] One time they picked me up for a basketball tournament, at Durango—Ft. Lewis. We went up there, her and Ida and I—I was probably sixteen or seventeen. They came down and they drove up to get some drinks, and Cee said, 'Gwen, what do you want?' and see, the only time I went to a drive-up was with my grandmother to a drive-up liquor store, and she would tell me, 'Do you want a boiled egg?' I used to get boiled eggs. So we went up to a drive-up and Cecilia said, 'What do you want? Do you want anything?' and I said, 'Ask for a boiled egg.' She was asking me if I wanted a coke or something, and I asked for a boiled egg.

"That's one thing I wanted to say, and another thing? We both played when we were pregnant. We played until our seventh month—"

"And the doctor said to quit playing, quit playing," Cecilia says.

"—and we had our kids a month apart."

"She had a daughter, I had a son," Cecilia says.

Georgia says, "And I have a son, too, and he's right over there." [She points to her son Ryan in the audience.]

Gwen says, "A lot of things that happened in my life were shameful for me, and I kept them to myself, but like I said, when it came to the trial to find out who I am, the first thing that comes to my mind is that I'm a basketball player. Like Cecilia said, I'm not ready to hang up my tennis shoes."

To finish the session, I ask Georgia if she wants to end with her joke.

"Do we have time?" she says.

"I don't know," I say. "How long is this joke?"

"Navajo jokes are kind of long," she says.

"Tell the bilegana [white] version," I say.

"Oh. OK," she says. "This young Navajo boy was going home from elementary school, and he had to find a quick way to earn a dollar or two for the next day's trip—his class was going to go on a trip—and he knew his mom and dad didn't have any money. So he told them he was going to the trader to ask if he could do some work for them so he could earn a quick dollar. So he did. Mr. Trader man, could I work for you, I need to earn some money for my trip, and the trader said, Yes, you can, I have some jobs for you, but you have to know how to count, can you count? He says, I can count. The trader says, that's good. Show me. The boy says, ťááłá'í, ťáa' ii; naaki; táá; dįį'; ashdla. The trader says, That's good. Now some of the things I need you to do out in the corral, I need you to count higher. Can you count any higher? The little boy says, Yes I can. The trader says, Show me. [Georgia stands up.] He says, ťááłá'í, ťáa' ii; naaki; táá; dįį'; ashdla.

Notes

1. Maria Allison, "A Structural Analysis of Navajo Basketball" (Ph.D. diss., University of Illinois at Urbana-Champaign, 1980), 11, citing research by K. Blanchard, "Basketball and Cultural Transmission: The Continuities and Dis-

continuities of American Indigina" (paper presented at the Pacific Sociological Association Meetings, Phoenix, May 1973).

2. *Navajo Times* (Window Rock AZ), October 1960.

3. Larry Colton, *Counting Coup: A True Story of Basketball and Honor on the Little Big Horn* (New York: Warner Books, 2000).

4. Frazier, *On the Rez.*

5. Allison, "A Structural Analysis of Navajo Basketball," 114, 116, 119.

6. Father D., for many years a key organizer and coach in the Window Rock area community-league tournaments, informed the Cardinals of the rule change just moments before they were to play his team in a tournament game.

7. Father D. recruited Georgia and Cecilia as part of a handpicked team to take to nationals. He brought headdresses and face makeup with him. He had paid for transportation and told the women he would not pay their way home if they did not perform the halftime demonstration.

8. The Cardinals recruited Winona Chase when she was a sophomore in high school (1968), and she was a key player throughout the rest of the team's history.

8. An Examination of Sport for Aboriginal Females on the Six Nations Reserve, 1968–1980

Sport can be defined as a social practice, where human expression occurs within "structured possibilities."[1] As a social practice sport creates and confirms a particular subjective reality in keeping with the dominant cultural form.[2] In Euro-American society female participation in sport is trivialized, or devalued, maintaining the masculinized connotations associated with sport.[3] This takes shape, for instance, through the limited sport opportunities available to women in relation to men, and the lack of recognition given to women compared with men. Thus, sport operates as a significant symbolic force in women's subordination to men, reinforcing patriarchal values.

Sport is also, however, an area in which values, ideologies, and meanings may be contested.[4] Resistance to the dominant subjective reality may arise, and cultural practices emerge and exist alongside the dominant cultural form, offering alternatives to it. Emergent sport practices need to be examined to see if they reproduce or challenge the power relations that exist in society,[5] since these practices can support—or at least not contradict—other elements within the dominant culture.[6]

Reviews of gender and sport, and race relations theories and sport, have noted the dearth of information on women of color.[7] An examination of the literature on Aboriginal women's sport supports this statement. This volume notwithstanding, there has been scant research on Aboriginal athletes and sport in North America. However, when the issue of gender is considered, the record shows an even greater absence of information on Aboriginal women athletes. Thus, little is written about the "structured possibilities" that exist for Aboriginal

The Mohawks team, 1971. Back, left to right: Brenda Davis, Sandy (Hill) Jamieson, Kathy Hillis, Bev Beaver, Carolyn Martin, Terry (Porter) Frazer, Charlotte Jacobs. Front, left to right: Kathy (Porter) Hill, Ruby Jacobs, Marcia (Douglas) Hill, Winnie Thomas. Courtesy of the author.

women in sport, and/or how closely the power relations underlying these practices mirror those of the dominant sport system.

The absence of women in the literature on Aboriginal sport seems to demonstrate their insignificance within the sport realm. This perception is reinforced by existing Aboriginal awards for sport achievement, which have in the past failed to recognize female athletes. There are two very different explanations as to why female athletes are largely absent in the literature on Aboriginal sport, and from Aboriginal awards for sport excellence. Perhaps women are not involved in sport. Or perhaps there is a systematic bias at work in the reporting and recognition given to Aboriginal women within the sport realm comparable to that for Euro-American women.

The Mohawks team, 1982. *Back, left to right*: Winnie Thomas, Audrey McDonald, Bev Beaver, Tammy Skye, Linda Hill, Jackie Bomberry, George Beaver. *Front, left to right*: Sandy Jamieson, Virginia Duxtadur, Beth Martin, Julie Martin, Helen Lickers, Debbie Aaron. Courtesy of the author.

In this chapter I begin to address these issues. I present an initial review of the literature on Aboriginal sport, along with an examination of Aboriginal awards for sport achievement, to support the premise that Aboriginal females *appear* to have an insignificant involvement in sport. I then present a case study of women's sport on the Six Nations Reserve that examines the nature and extent of female involvement in sport from 1968 to 1980. I also include recommendations for further study that would more fully illuminate the nature of Aboriginal women's sport.

I chose the Six Nations Reserve in Ontario as a case study since previous work on their organized sport system (1964–89) had indicated the ongoing presence of women's sport. The data that I gleaned through their community newspaper, the *Tekawennake Reporter*, for the period 1968–80 clearly indicates extensive involvement by women in a variety of sports.[8] Sport biographies that could be composed from newspaper accounts also suggest that some of these athletes have had outstanding sport careers. These data lend support to my hypothesis that a systematic negative bias in terms of recognition may be at work in Aboriginal women's sport.

Aboriginal Women Athletes:
An Insignificant Presence?

An overview of sport history conferences and journal articles on Aboriginal sport suggests that Aboriginal athletes within mainstream sport, and at times the literature recording Aboriginal sport involvement, have been marked by racism, exploitation, and ethnocentric distortion.[9] This record may also have been marked by sexism: in the mid-1990s when this paper was originally written, only one of the thirty-two articles available on this subject pertained to Aboriginal female athletes.

This pattern of omission is reflected in seminal overviews on Aboriginal sport by Ward Churchill, Norbert Hill, and Mary Jo Barlow, Brenda Zeman, and Joseph Oxendine.[10] The historical overview of twentieth-century Native American athletics by Churchill and his colleagues focuses primarily on male athletes attending the Carlisle or Haskell Indian schools, without mentioning what Aboriginal girls were playing in those institutions. The minimal coverage of female athletes in this review includes a note on Angelita Rosal, who was an international-caliber table-tennis player, and a mention of three "promising" women in track and field.[11] This overview was slightly improved upon by Zeman in her docufiction on famous Canadian Native athletes, in that one of the twelve chapters deals with Aboriginal females.[12]

A three-hundred-page overview by Oxendine strongly reinforces this pattern of omission. Oxendine's book, which purports to examine the Native American sport heritage from before European contact to the present day, includes a section titled "Sports for Women and Girls," but it is a mere five pages.[13] Oxendine briefly mentions female involvement in horse racing, double ball, lacrosse, fastball, and basketball, then includes an entire section on sport programs at the Carlisle and Haskell Indian schools with no mention of female sport involvement.[14] The fifty-one biographies of famous Aboriginal athletes he provides in his text, from 1890 to the present, are all of men. Women were clearly notable in his book by their absence. After reading these overviews, one is left with the impression that Aboriginal females have not been active or noteworthy in sport.

The few articles that have been written specifically on Aboriginal women in sport dispute this. Scholars like Susan Craig and Alyce

Cheska note the traditional involvement of women in ancient tribal games and their particular affinity toward ball games such as double ball.[15] They also recognize Aboriginal women's current involvement in the popular sports of basketball, softball, track, and rodeo.[16]

Craig disputes the fact that Aboriginal women are not notable as athletes when she outlines four successful individuals involved in trick riding, cross-country running, and international-caliber basketball and table tennis. She also provides support for the idea that sports involvement is not at odds with an Aboriginal girl's gender identity. As examples of this, she notes that family and friends are very supportive of and interested in female athletes, that female athletes are considered leaders at the Albuquerque Indian School, and that "femininity" does not seem to be an issue for Native female athletes.[17] These claims support the idea that Aboriginal girls have considered sport to be an attractive and worthwhile activity.

Zeman includes the Firth twins, Sharon and Shirley, among her twelve accounts of Canadian Aboriginal athletes. They participated in four Olympics before retiring from World Cup competition in 1984.[18] They received early support from their mother, who encouraged them to get involved with the cross-country ski program in Inuvik even though doing so took them far from their home for extended periods of time.[19]

When we examine Aboriginal sport awards, we immediately notice that Aboriginal women are largely absent. The Tom Longboat Award, for example, has been given annually in Canada since 1951 to Indian athletes who display outstanding examples of character, leadership, and "sportsmanship." However, in the first twenty-three years of its existence, only one Aboriginal woman was a recipient: Phyllis Bomberry in 1968.[20] Similarly, there was only one woman, Angelita Rosal, out of fifty-seven inductees into the American Indian Hall of Fame from its inception in 1972 until 1985.[21] The American Indian Hall of Fame honors those who have brought distinction through sports to themselves and the Indian community.[22]

Several writers have stressed the need for Aboriginal role models in sport.[23] The failure of Aboriginal people to identify outstanding female athletes through established awards either supports the hypothesis that Aboriginal females are not active and/or competent in sport or points to a systematic bias by Aboriginal people themselves against women in sport. In either case, the lack of recognizable female role models in sport does a disservice to Aboriginal girls who might aspire to be athletes.

The presence of a systematic bias against Indian women has been seen in another realm of Aboriginal life. Research on Aboriginal women in Canada has tended to focus on Section 12(i)(b) of the Indian Act, which discriminated against Indian women on the grounds of race, sex, and marital status.[24] In 1985 Bill C-31 was passed, which "provide[s] either first-line instatement or reinstatement to persons who either lost or were denied status as a result of discriminatory elements of the *Indian Act*."[25]

Even within an account of this struggle, there is evidence of the importance of sport in the lives of Aboriginal women. Janet Silman provides several accounts by Aboriginal women of their lives growing up on the reserve.[26] Games and sports were often mentioned as a positive aspect of their upbringing.[27] Perhaps the most telling story is by Mavis Goeres, who became concerned about the loss of status Indian women faced upon marrying non-Indian men. She stated:

[A]nother thing that hurt me regards my youngest daughter, Susan. She is very, very active in sport, very good in teams. When it came to Indian Summer Games, they said, "You can't play because you're non-status. You're not an Indian." I said, "My God, she's got as much Indian in her as a lot of them here." That's when I really got mad. I think the anger and hurt is what pushed us on, too. It wasn't only happening to my daughter, but to other women's daughters and sons. I protested and the Toronto Star *did a story on my Susan and on Mary (Two-Axe) Early, showing how 12(i)(b) affected both their generations.*[28]

This account indicates that both sport and sexism have been significant aspects in the lives of some Aboriginal women.

Female Involvement in Organized Sport on the Six Nations Reserve, 1968–80

When we examine organized sport on the Six Nations Reserve, we see that Aboriginal women are indeed actively involved. The Six Nations Reserve, located in southwestern Ontario, is the largest Indian community in Canada with a population of approximately seven thousand Indians from six different Iroquoian tribes.[29] Women account for slightly more than half (52.3 percent) of the total Aboriginal population in Ontario. Accordingly, there would be a fairly large number of women on the reserve from which to draw potential athletes.[30]

An analysis of their involvement during 1968–80 indicates an ongoing presence of Aboriginal women as participants in and organizers of a variety of sports. These athletes participated in an extensive sport system that included both Euro-American and all-Indian competitions. In this case study I examine the nature of that participation in terms of the variety of sports played, the extent of the sport system, and the sport roles adopted by the women. I then provide some examples of women who have been active in sport on the reserve during this period; specifically, I give brief biographies of women who have had outstanding sport careers.

Data for this case study have been collected primarily from the *Tekawennake Reporter*, a reserve-based newspaper that began circulation in 1968 and was published twice a month during the time I examined it.[31] Accounts of women's participation in sport are consistently included, and there are no derogatory or sexist comments. This pattern is not consistent with newspaper and magazine coverage of mainstream women's sport, which is known to be both scarce and sexist in nature.[32]

I examined 248 issues of the *Tekawennake Reporter*. Seventy-eight percent of them (193 issues) included information on women's sport. The yearly percentage of issues including women's sport ranged from 100 percent (for 1977–80) to 50 percent in 1972 (the first year the paper had a sports editor). Coaches usually provided information for the sports section. The newspaper database was supplemented with information previously gleaned from community Recreation Committee files.

VARIETY OF SPORTS PLAYED

Women's involvement in sport on the Six Nations Reserve during the time I studied it was far broader than the existing literature might indicate. In keeping with this literature, women were involved in basketball, softball/fastball, horseback riding, cross-country running, and lacrosse on the reserve. However, additional sports, mentioned in newspaper accounts, included badminton, baton twirling, bowling (both five- and ten-pin), broomball, figure skating, golf, hockey, karate, billiards, track and field, speed skating, tennis, and volleyball. Some sports lasted longer than others. Women participated in softball/fastball, hockey, bowling, and track and field throughout the period under consideration, and figure skating maintained a broad participation base from its inception as a reserve-based club in 1975. Other sports—including karate, speed skating, baton twirling, and badminton—were linked to specific competitors and did not appear to have an ongoing participation base on the reserve. Meanwhile, school sports, including basketball, cross-country running, track and field, and volleyball, maintained an ongoing though transient participation base among the school population.

Informal interviews with members on the reserve have shown the presence of other women's sports, too, although not necessarily in the period under consideration. Archery was a popular sport for both men and women before I began this study. More recently individual women have been active in professional wrestling, roller derby, barrel racing, harness racing, and professional ballet. There is also a dance studio on the reserve, which has been active for several years, in which both men and women are active. Clearly the variety of sports undertaken by the women of this reserve is much greater than has been suggested in the literature.

EXTENT OF THE SPORTS SYSTEM

Existing literature has paid little attention to the sports settings within which Aboriginal women participate, which can be either all-Indian or Euro-American in nature. Susan B. Craig briefly notes the involvement of women athletes at all-Indian schools. [33] And Oxendine indirectly refers to the existence of all-Indian organizations when he notes that the National Indian Activities Association (NIAA) was founded in 1974 to conduct national championships in women's and men's basketball. He also notes the formation of the Iroquois national women's lacrosse team in 1984. [34]

Both of these examples represent a sport setting restricted to Indian participants. This participation base is enforced through membership rules. For example, the letter of invitation for the Open Women's Fast

Pitch National Championship of the NIAA in 1980 states: "You must be at least one-quarter degree of Indian blood in order to compete in this tournament. In registering, each applicant must provide positive proof of Indian ancestry and submit documentation."[35] Restrictive membership criteria are found in most all-Indian tournaments, including some competitions that allow a certain number of non-Indian players to participate on each team.

The majority of accounts in the literature on Aboriginal women's sport note athletes who participate in mainstream sport systems, such as the Firth twins or Angelita Rosal. This may reflect a bias in the literature on Aboriginal sport generally in that the athletes who are deemed to be "successful" are those who have "made it" in Euro-American sport competitions at an international or professional level. This pattern is also evident in Aboriginal sport awards—the two women who had awards, Phyllis Bomberry and Angelita Rosal, both achieved their success solely within the Euro-American sport system.

My examination of the newspaper accounts of 1968–80 revealed a broad system of sport for Aboriginal women on the Six Nations Reserve. Competitive environments were both all-Indian and Euro-American. All-Indian settings included intrareserve leagues and tournaments at the interreserve, provincial, national, and international levels; Euro-American settings included leagues at the interschool and regional levels, and tournaments or league championships at the provincial, national, and international levels. Individual athletes and sports teams often played simultaneously in Euro-American leagues and all-Indian tournaments.

School teams competed against other schools on the reserve and entered into leagues involving the surrounding communities. In two of these sports—basketball and cross-country running—there were also competitions against all-Indian teams that were not in the immediate vicinity. Only one competitor was mentioned at the university level—Kathy Porter, who played badminton for McMaster University.

Athletes who played club sports on the reserve participated in both intraclub and interclub competitions—two examples of such clubs are the Six Nations Figure Skating Club and the Saddle Club. Athletes who were involved in clubs off the reserve participated in Euro-American events such as baton twirling, speed skating, and figure skating.[36] A karate club, which had both male and female members, existed for only a short while on the reserve.

A number of sports teams were formed on the reserve and then competed as a team in regional Euro-American leagues. Examples of this are the Ohsweken Women Warriors in broomball, several teams in softball/fastball ranging in level from Lassies through Senior B Fastball, junior and senior hockey teams competing in three regional leagues, and both bantam and juvenile girls' lacrosse teams. Six Nations teams consistently won both regional and provincial league championships. During the period under consideration, the lacrosse teams won three regional and two provincial titles, the hockey teams won four regional league titles, and the softball/fastball teams won nine league titles, nine separate provincial titles, and several league Most Valuable Player (MVP) awards. These teams clearly established a winning tradition.

Softball/fastball teams formed on the reserve also entered all-Indian tournaments, where they excelled. For example, the Ohsweken Mohawks, a fastball team, not only won the Senior B championship in a Euro-American league but had members on the winning Canadian Native ladies softball team and the North American Native fastball championship team in 1979. They subsequently hosted the Canadian Native fastball tournament in 1980. It is interesting to note that softball was the only sport mentioned that was also played at longhouse gatherings and at Indian gatherings celebrating their heritage—both of which are traditional Indian settings.

Individuals from the reserve would often play on other teams in their preferred sports where, as Aboriginal athletes, they were in the minority. Such athletes included Bev Beaver and Helen Lickers, who played on championship hockey teams off the reserve, and Phyllis Bomberry, who played fastball for the Canadian championship team in 1967 and 1968.

Leagues were also set up for reserve members in bowling, billiards, and golf, even though these leagues usually utilized facilities off the reserve. Bowling was by far the most popular league; the newspaper consistently reported the weekly high single and high triple winners, as well as the year-end club champions. Besides the bowling league championships, there was a well-developed all-Indian bowling tournament, as there was for golf, both of which began in the 1960s. Competitions in these sports were developed between reserves throughout Ontario, and across Canada and the United States. Billiards, on the other hand, remained a local league, and it attracted interested women to the sponsoring bar on a regular basis.

It is clear that a broad system for sport existed. Aboriginal athletes could choose to enter only all-Indian tournaments and local leagues, but more often they participated in non-Indian competitions. Teams from the reserve tended to enter Euro-American regional leagues, while individual Aboriginal athletes tended to join a Euro-American team or club to compete in the mainstream sport system.

SPORT ROLES

The literature on Aboriginal women and sport deals with them almost exclusively in the role of athlete. There is a passing reference in Craig's article to two Aboriginal athletes who returned to coach other Aboriginal women: Pauline Pino, who majored in physical education; and Dixie Woodall, who gained international fame as a basketball player. [37] An examination of the Six Nations Reserve, however, shows that women were involved in a variety of roles, including that of athlete, coach, supporter, Recreation Committee member, and executive board member for voluntary sports organizations. Women apparently did not take on the role of referee, which is true for both men and women on the reserve. For example, the only umpire clinic ever held on the reserve, in April 1987, attracted only two individuals. [38]

Although most of the newspaper articles mentioned Aboriginal women as athletes, female coaches were mentioned for basketball, softball, lacrosse, and figure skating. All of these coaches had first participated in their sport, and several were still doing so while they coached.

The *Tekawennake Reporter* contains many references to community support for minor or youth sport. One notable example is the Mothers' Auxiliary for Minor Athletics (MAMAs), which was established to provide support for minor sports. This group of mothers accepted responsibility for hosting officials and visiting teams as early as 1969. They also donated trophies to both boys' and girls' teams, including the two trophies donated in 1978 to the girls' lacrosse team. [39]

The Recreation Committee, which was established in 1964 to coor-

dinate and financially support existing sport organizations on the reserve, also included women members during the period of my study.[40]
Some of the members were local female athletes, such as Sandra (Hill)
Jamieson (on the committee in 1972 and 1975) and Winnie Thomas
(1980). Other female members included Claudine VanEvery (1970) and
Carolyn Beaver (1979). Though female members were in the minority
(usually one or two members per eight people on the committee),
they remained an ongoing presence on the committee. It eventually
became a committee policy that one of the six members elected from
the community must be a woman, suggesting a sensitivity to the need
for both male and female representation.[41]

There is also evidence of frequent women's involvement on the executive boards of both male and female sports organizations. Women
served in various capacities, including president, treasurer, and secretary, on several different sport organizations. Executive members were
often mothers of athletes, although there is also evidence of athletes
who accepted administrative roles in their own sports, such as Doris
Henhawk, who was secretary for the Bowling Association while still
playing in the 1960s.

Sport Biographies of Some Prominent Female Athletes

The career highlights of five female athletes from the reserve help sub-
stantiate the premise that Aboriginal women not only played but also
excelled in sport. Each was at one time nominated by the reserve for
the Tom Longboat Award. They were active in sport during the period
of my study, although these biographies are not restricted to that time
frame.

Bev Beaver was an outstanding athlete in three sports (fastball,
hockey, and bowling) in both all-Indian and Euro-American sport systems. In fastball she won the MVP award eight times between 1962 and
1980. In 1979 she was named best pitcher, top batter, and MVP at the
Canadian Native championship, as well as all-star pitcher at the North
American Native Ladies Championship. In hockey she competed only
in the Euro-American sport system. She won five MVP awards from

1966 to 1980 and was the top scorer in the league in five different years. In bowling she maintained "high female average" and had "high triple score" for the Six Nations Bowling League in all but one year between 1969 and 1974. She also competed in all-Indian tournaments, and had "high triple score" in the Ontario Indian Bowling Championship in 1973. She was awarded the regional Tom Longboat medal[42] as the outstanding Indian athlete of southern Ontario in 1967.[43]

Ruth Hill was involved in only one sport, fastball, but is notable because of her longevity as a successful pitcher. She began her career as a teenager, competing as a member of the Ohsweken Mohawks fastball team. In 1964 she was asked to go with the Euro-American Toronto Carpetland team to the world championship in Florida, where she was named the best pitcher of the tournament. She later pitched for the Syracuse all-Indian Red Jackets in another world championship, and her eighteen strikeouts in twenty-one innings was one short of the women's world record. In 1969 after twenty years of pitching, she still had an average of fourteen strikeouts per game, and her career continued into 1979, when she pitched at the Canadian Native Fastball Championship.[44] She was nominated for the Tom Longboat Award by the Recreation Committee in 1965.[45]

Phyllis Bomberry is notable as the first female recipient of the Tom Longboat Award, which she won in 1968. She was a fastball catcher on the Euro-American Canadian senior women's softball championship team in 1967 and 1968 (the Toronto Carpetland Senior A team). She was also the top batter at the 1967 championships and the all-star catcher for Canada in 1967 and 1968. She was on the Ontario senior women's championship team in 1967 and 1968 and played with that team when they won the gold medal at the Canada Games in 1969.[46]

Helen Lickers is notable for her successful careers in fastball and hockey. She began playing as a catcher for the Ohsweken Mohawks in 1972. In 1973 after winning the rookie of the year award, she was recognized as the best catcher in the regional Euro-American league. In 1979 she was named best catcher, had the most RBIS at the Canadian Native Championship, and was named the all-star catcher at the North American Native championship.[47] She was a member of the Ohsweken Mohawks, a senior tier-2 women's softball team, when they won the Canadian Native women's softball tournament from 1982 to 1985.[48] Her involvement in hockey took place within the Euro-American sport system. She was named the league MVP in 1975 and 1976,[49] and while playing with the Hamilton Golden Hawks Senior A team in 1987 she won the Canadian championship and was involved in an international tournament. That same team won the Ontario championship in 1983 and 1984 and came in third, then second, in the Canadian senior women's hockey championship in those years. She also played to a Canadian championship in 1983 with the Burlington senior women's team.

Helen Lickers has contributed to sport in other capacities as well. She has served as treasurer for the Ohsweken Mohawks since 1985 and was described as a willing volunteer for organizing minor sports tournaments on the reserve.[50] She was nominated by the Recreation Committee for the Tom Longboat Award in 1985.

Doris Henhawk began her sports career playing second base for the Ohsweken Mohawks, but her notable contributions were made in the years after her playing days were over, when she coached numerous girls in softball. During her playing career for the Mohawks from 1952 to 1962, the team won three Ontario championships in Euro-American intermediate women's competitions. She was also successful as an athlete in the reserve bowling league in 1969 and 1970. In 1976 she had the women's low net score in golf at the North American Indian golf tournament.[51]

Doris Henhawk's coaching career has taken place within the Euro-American sport system. She began coaching the bantam girls team in 1973. In 1974 she, her husband, and another man started minor softball for both boys and girls on the reserve. While serving on the minor softball executive committee from 1974 to 1983, she coached bantam, midget, and junior girls' teams and won the Ontario rural softball A championships four times. The teams she coached also won their division in the Haldimand women's league for three of those years, and they won the bronze medal at the Ontario Summer Games in 1976. She was assistant coach for the all-star Ontario junior women's softball team, which won a gold medal in the 1985 Canada Summer Games, and an assistant coach for the Ontario team, which competed at the Canada Games in 1989.[52] She was awarded the Tom Longboat regional medal in 1985.

These five women have had outstanding careers in sport. As athletes, they have competed in both Euro-American leagues and all-Indian tournaments, in many cases over an extended period. They have been successful in a variety of sports. As well, some of these athletes have chosen to contribute to sport as volunteers in other ways, such as coaching or serving in an administrative capacity. Their careers lay to rest the myth that Aboriginal female athletes are not worthy of recognition.

Recommendations for Further Study

My examination of organized sport on the Six Nations Reserve from 1968 to 1980 shows an ongoing presence of Aboriginal women as participants and organizers in a broad variety of sports. Aboriginal women athletes are both active in and worthy of recognition in the realm of sport. The data support the hypothesis that, as for women in the non-Aboriginal context, there may be systematic biases at work against Aboriginal women in sport that lead to a lack of recognition in sport literature and award structures.

As several other essays in this volume underscore, further research on Aboriginal female athletes is clearly warranted. It would not only contribute to the existing literature on Aboriginal female athletes but enhance the study of women in sport generally, which has focused primarily on the experiences of young, white, middle-class women.

In Euro-American society generally, women's participation in sport is trivialized and devalued, in accordance with the patriarchal underpinnings of sport.[53] It is not clear yet if the same is true for Aboriginal women. We need to examine further the effect of colonization and the perceptions about "sport" that came with colonization to better understand the power structure that exists in Aboriginal sport, and this needs to be done within the context of the broader Aboriginal cultural system.

The next step should be formal interviews with female athletes on the reserve. Several issues arose in informal interviews during my study, which hold promise for a better understanding of the Aboriginal female sport experience. For example, I found that in the past, Indian girls who came from a traditional longhouse background were supported in their sport participation, while Christianized girls were dissuaded from participating. It would be illuminating to examine the relationship between religion and sport.

I was also told that some Aboriginal people believe they are supposed to be "natural" athletes and competent in sport without the training and strategy that are integral to Euro-American sport. One coach shared how she was ridiculed for using signals in softball; she was told that "Natives don't do that." The degree to which this ideology shapes the performance and expectations of Aboriginal female athletes needs to be examined.

Finally, Aboriginal athletes are participating in two seemingly different sport environments—Euro-American and all-Indian. It would be illuminating to examine these two systems in more detail, to assess the degree to which Aboriginal people, through the creation of the emergent all-Indian system, have transformed sport through resistance and/or have been co-opted into the dominant concept of sport. It is interesting at the outset to note that Indians have often and perhaps unconsciously adopted the definition of an Indian created by the government and incorporated it into their membership criteria at all-Indian tournaments. Each of these avenues for research should prove fruitful in the ongoing challenge to understand not only mainstream women's sport but also the experiences of those "invisible" girls and women whose stories have not yet been told.

Notes

1. Richard Gruneau, *Class, Sport, and Social Development* (Amherst: University of Massachusetts Press, 1983).

2. Clifford Geertz, "Deep Play: Notes on the Balinese Cockfight," in *Play, Games and Sport in Cultural Contexts*, ed. Janet C. Harris and Robert Park (Champaign IL: Human Kinetics, 1983).

3. Susan J. Birrell, "Discourses on the Gender/Sport Relationship," *Exercise and Sport Sciences Reviews* 16 (1988): 459–502.

4. Peter Donnelly, "Sport as a Site for Popular Resistance," in *Popular Cultures and Political Practices*, ed. Richard Gruneau (Toronto: Garamond, 1988).

5. Delia Douglas, "Discourses on Black Women—A History of Science: A Review of Relational Analyses in Education and Sport Literatures" (paper pre-

sented at North American Society for Sport Sociology Conference, Cincinnati, 1988).

6. Raymond Williams cited in Donnelly, "Sport as a Site for Popular Resistance," 69.

7. Birrell, "Discourses on the Gender/Sport Relationship," and Susan Birrell, "Racial Relations Theories and Sport: Suggestions for a More Critical Analysis," *Sociology of Sport Journal* 6:3 (1989): 212–27.

8. The timeline for this paper was shaped by the restrictions of the newspaper database, beginning with the inception of the *Tekawennake Reporter* in 1968 and continuing until 1980, when the long-term editor of the paper retired. This study is premised on the assumption that the newspaper coverage of women's sport was indicative of actual sport behavior on the reserve.

9. Vicky Paraschak, "Native Sport History: Pitfalls and Promises," *Canadian Journal of History of Sport* 20:1 (1989): 58.

10. Churchill, Hill, and Barlow, "An Historical Overview of Twentieth-Century Native American Athletics"; Zeman, *To Run with Longboat*; and Oxendine, *American Indian Sports Heritage*.

11. Churchill, Hill, and Barlow, "An Historical Overview of Twentieth-Century Native American Athletics," 32.

12. Zeman, *To Run with Longboat*.

13. Oxendine, *American Indian Sports Heritage*, 22–26.

14. Oxendine, *American Indian Sports Heritage*, 22, 295–99.

15. Susan B. Craig, "Indian Sportswomen," *The Sportswoman* 1:4 (1973): 10–13; and Alyce Cheska, "Ball Game Participation of North American Indian Women," *Proceedings from the Third Canadian Symposium on the History of Sport and Physical Education* (Halifax: Dalhousie University Press, 1974).

16. Cheska, "Ball Game Participation," 23; Craig, "Indian Sportswomen," 12.

17. Craig, "Indian Sportswomen," 10–11.

18. Zeman, *To Run with Longboat*, 105–6.

19. Zeman, *To Run with Longboat*, 102.

20. Wilton Littlechild, "Tom Longboat: Canada's Outstanding Indian Athlete" (Masters thesis, University of Alberta, 1975), appendix F.

21. Oxendine, *American Indian Sports Heritage*, table 14.1.

22. Oxendine, *American Indian Sports Heritage*, 282.

23. Charles Ballem, "Missing from the Canadian Sport Scene: Native Athletes," *Canadian Journal of History of Sport* 14:2 (1983): 33–43; Littlechild, "Tom Longboat"; Zeman, *To Run with Longboat*; Oxendine, *American Indian Sports Heritage*.

24. Kathleen Jamieson, *Indian Women and the Law in Canada: Citizens Minus*, study sponsored by Advisory Council on the Status of Women, Indian

Rights for Indian Women (Ottawa: Ministry of Supply and Services, 1978), 1.

25. Ontario Women's Directorate, *Economic Status of Native Women in Ontario* (report prepared by J. Phillip Nicholson, Policy and Management Consultants, Inc., for the Government of Ontario, 1987), appendix on terminology, p. 1.

26. Janet Silman, ed., *Enough Is Enough: Aboriginal Women Speak Out* (Toronto: Women's Press, 1987).

27. Silman, *Enough Is Enough*, 39, 70, 88.

28. Silman, *Enough Is Enough*, 219.

29. Ontario Native Women's Association, "Doctor, Lawyer, Indian Chief," *Newsletter* 9:3 (1988): 24.

30. Ontario Women's Directorate, *Economic Status of Native Women in Ontario*, 6. Ohsweken is a small village located in the center of the reserve, home to approximately four hundred people. All of the businesses and several of the recreation facilities are located in Ohsweken. The reserve has an arena (opened in 1974), two ball diamonds, a school gymnasium, and a community hall available for various recreational activities. Cheryl Henhawk, "Recreation on the Six Nations Reserve" (speech presented at Faculty of Human Kinetics Speaker Series, University of Windsor, October 1987).

31. In 1971 a woman from the reserve, Carolyn Beaver, bought the newspaper from the Jamiesons, another local couple. She became editor in 1972 and, although she sold the paper to the Woodland Cultural Centre in 1975, she agreed to stay on as editor, eventually resigning in October 1980. The paper did not usually publish in August, and some of the issues were not available for examination (for example, issues from May to December 1977 were not accessible during my study).

32. Jay Coakley, *Sport and Society: Issues and Controversies*, 4th ed. (Toronto: Mosby College Publishing, 1990), 289-92.

33. Craig, "Indian Sportswomen."

34. Oxendine, *American Indian Sports Heritage*, 299, 298.

35. J. Kays, letter to the Six Nations Band Council, 4 June 1980, Six Nations Reserve Recreation Files, Ohsweken, Ontario.

36. In baton twirling and speed skating, athletes reported in the newspaper were not currently living on the reserve, although they were related to members on the reserve. Figure skaters who joined outside clubs were mentioned during the summer of 1980 (the Six Nations arena did not operate during the summer months).

37. Craig, "Indian Sportswomen," 12.

38. Six Nations Recreation Committee File, Recreation/Fairgrounds M–Z, Six Nations Reserve Recreation Files, Ohsweken, Ontario.

39. It would be interesting to assess the uniqueness of this organization by

examining the extent to which other community women's groups have chosen to adopt this support role.

40. Six Nations Recreation Committee Minutes, 29 December 1964.

41. Six Nations Council, 19 July 1978.

42. The Tom Longboat Award winner is chosen nationally; regional Tom Longboat medals are awarded each year.

43. *Tekawennake Reporter*, 20 June 1980, p. 8.

44. *Tekawennake Reporter*, 20 June 1980, p. 9.

45. Six Nations Recreation Committee Minutes, 12 July 1965.

46. *Tekawennake Reporter*, 17 September 1968.

47. *Tekawennake Reporter*, 20 June 1980, p. 8.

48. Six Nations Recreation Committee Minutes, 21 November 1985.

49. *Tekawennake Reporter*, 20 June 1987, p. 8.

50. Six Nations Recreation Committee Minutes, 21 November 1985.

51. *Tekawennake Reporter*, 8 July 1976.

52. Six Nations Recreation Committee Minutes, 21 November 1985.

53. Birrell, "Discourses on the Gender/Sport Relationship," 487.

ELLEN J. STAUROWSKY

9. SuAnne Big Crow
Her Legend and Legacy

She showed us a way to live on the earth. —Warfield Moose, Sr.

While conducting background research in anticipation of writing about SuAnne Big Crow, I soon realized that within sport sciences literature and mainstream sport media, studies about American Indian women in sport appear intermittently while individual biographies of American Indian women athletes are rare. [1] Even in recent biographical compendiums designed to address shortfalls in the reporting of women's sport history, American Indian women athletes are essentially not mentioned. [2] Whereas American Indian organizations in the 1990s sought to highlight the accomplishments of Indian athletes, both female and male, as evidenced by the publication of *Give It Your Best! Profiles of Native American Athletes*, a pamphlet produced by the United National Indian Tribal Youth, there is a relative vacuum with regard to substantive biographies about American Indian women athletes. [3]

Apart from a children's reader that features three biographical sketches of American Indian women athletes, including Kitty O'Neill, Ryneldi Becenti, and SuAnne Big Crow, I found myself contemplating the implications of this apparent inattention from a historical perspective. [4] As Jennifer Hargreaves writes, "A culture is remembered for its heroes and heroines, and sport constructs them and influences our perceptions of them continuously. . . . But heroes are more easily defined than heroines and there is greater social importance attributed to the production and celebration of male heroism." [5]

The concerted efforts of sport sciences scholars and journalists during the last three decades to uncover and recover women's sport history has led to a greater awareness of women's place in sport and an ever-growing commitment to ensuring that the lives of women athletes will be documented for future generations. Through the identification of generational connections, significant gains have been made in our collective understanding and appreciation of who our foremothers are and what their experience was like. This body of work, by linking one generation to the other, serves as a profound reminder that women athletes today stand on the shoulders of those who came before them and will provide the foundation for the accomplishments of those who will follow. However, as a greater awareness of women's sport history and women athletes develops, it becomes patently obvious that there are significant gaps that must be addressed. For me, the question of why American Indian women like SuAnne Big Crow are missing from the discussion and non-Native consciousness has become as much a part of this story as SuAnne herself.

This chapter begins with an exploration of the reasons why American Indian women athletes are largely omitted from mainstream sport publications. The second part of the chapter elaborates on the complexity of the racialized gender hierarchy within which American Indian women, like SuAnne, participate. The purpose of this exploration is to situate SuAnne Big Crow's story within a broader historical and cultural context. The third and fourth sections concentrate on developing the legend and legacy that have come to be associated with SuAnne Big Crow.

American Indian Women Athletes—Visible But Invisible

To observe that there is a vacuum in the sport sciences literature with regard to Native American female athlete biographies does not mean that these women's lives occurred in a vacuum. The story of SuAnne Big Crow is one that has already been told and continues to be retold. Most assuredly, her family and community on the Pine Ridge Reservation are keenly aware of SuAnne's life and accomplishments. Certain sectors of the national American Indian community are also familiar with SuAnne's story. Regionally, SuAnne's prowess as an athlete generated a measure of notoriety for her within South Dakota and among a circumscribed group of college basketball coaches who had an interest in SuAnne as a player. But in most parts of the country, and within mainstream sport media, her story never surfaced. It is telling that a biography about SuAnne does not emanate out of sport media or sport science scholarly circles but acquires accessibility through a literary effort written by Ian Frazier titled *On the Rez*. [6] Three-quarters of the way through Frazier's chronicle of life on the Pine Ridge Reservation, he happens upon a sign marking the "SuAnne Big Crow Health and Recreation Center." Perhaps one may then be inspired, as Frazier was, by the story of the woman for whom the center is named. [7]

Frazier's seemingly accidental "discovery" of SuAnne Big Crow is accidental by design from the standpoint that SuAnne grew up within a racialized gender hierarchy where American Indians, and American Indian women in particular, are largely invisible to the dominant culture. As Elsie Meeks, an Oglala Sioux from Pine Ridge who was the first American Indian to be appointed to the U.S. Commission on Civil Rights, observed, "Indians just aren't on anyone's radar screen." [8] Indian writer Michael Dorris and recent past president of the Native American Bar Association Lawrence Baca have commented generally on the invisibility of Indians. Sioux anthropologist Bea Medicine argues that scholars typically misread or misunderstand the role of women within their tribal communities.

The tendency of the dominant culture to render Indians invisible presents a partial answer to the question of why SuAnne Big Crow's story and others like it do not appear on our radar screens. The matter, however, is far more complex. In a critique of Frazier's *On the Rez*, American Indian author Sherman Alexie points out that one of the shortcomings of the book is Frazier's failure to realize that some American Indians are reluctant or resistant to whites' writing about certain aspects of their lives. Alexie further observes that Frazier displayed at times a lack of "self-consciousness" in writing about Indians. [9] In effect, for reasons that emanate out of self-protection, self-preservation, and racial distrust born out of a long history of white betrayal, Alexie argues that American Indians do not want certain stories to be shared with a larger audience or to be told at all by whites. [10] In turn whites who write about American Indian subjects need to cultivate an awareness that we have our own cultural blind spots that affect how we experience and understand the events and circumstances that shape not only American Indian lives but our own.

To these dynamics is then added one more. The minimal and marginal sport media coverage of women's athletics contributes to this invisibility as well. Despite an assertion of positive female athleticism, as seen in the obvious displays of "GRRL Power" that accompanied the emergence of the popular U.S. women's soccer team in 1999, a study released by the Amateur Athletic Foundation in September 2000 documented that little progress has been made in the quantity and quality of television coverage of women's sports. According to the report, "the percentage of stories and airtime devoted to women's sports on local news programs remains as low as it was a decade ago [approximately 5–8 percent of all coverage]." Katherine Kinnick reported the existence of rampant gender bias in the reporting and photography associated with coverage of female athletes during the 1996 Summer Olympic Games.[11] Thus, for SuAnne as a young woman from the reservation who was an athlete and a member of the Oglala Lakota, getting on the radar screen may be a testament to the power of her story, the willingness of her family to have SuAnne's story told, and a symbol of shifting cultural perspectives that recognize her story is an important one to be told.

Situating SuAnne Big Crow's Story within a Racialized Gender Hierarchy

As a cultural space, sport serves as a nexus where race and gender intersect. Locating SuAnne's story within that nexus recognizes what Susan Birrell and Mary McDonald call the race and gender "power lines" that shape individual lives and stories.[12] Victoria Paraschak, a researcher who has spent a great deal of time studying Native women in sport, points out that the reproduction of racialized gender relations is affected depending on the kind of sport in which Native women participate. Thus, "while athletes competing in all-Native environments (re)produce gender relations specific to their culture, Native men and women often encounter racism as an integral part of their experience in mainstream sport. Historically, a racial hierarchy was constructed, with 'civilized' (i.e., non-Native) forms of gender behavior as the preferred choice. Native behavior was monitored and reshaped, even eliminated in order to realign it with mainstream, non-Native values."[13]

When understood within the context of women's sport history overall, the racialized gender hierarchy created a substantial obstacle for Native American women within non-Native settings. Sport historian Susan Cahn provides some insight in this regard when she notes that for "Native American women, Latinas, and Asian American women, the lack of resources or well-traveled avenues into athletic culture has made the sports world even less accessible."[14] In a similar vein Paraschak notes, "Although both Native men and women play sport, there has often been a gender imbalance in the recognition of their accomplishments."[15]

The historian John Bloom, in his work on sports at Native American boarding schools, confirms this. Prevailing attitudes regarding women's essential frailty and inferiority as they were translated into guiding principles for physical activity were very much in evidence within the boarding school curriculum for girls. This contrasted markedly with the highly competitive and visible male sport team system that produced a cadre of teams, most notably the Carlisle Indians and the Haskell Indians, and athletes who would become prominent figures, including Jim Thorpe, Louis Tewanima, Charles Bender, and William "Lone Star" Dietz, among others. During the years 1880–1940, Indian girls were discouraged from participating in "competitive athletics" or "strenuous physical activity." Most often dance, gymnastics exercises, and calisthenics were preferred because they "promoted passivity, sexual restraint, and domestic femininity by emphasizing indoor activity and light exercise."[16]

The surveillance of the female body—and by extension the monitoring and attempted "control" of female sexuality—was a feature of women's physical education, whether the curriculum was delivered at all-white Smith College or the all-Indian Carlisle school. However, sexuality as it was interpreted through the lens of socially constructed racial categories produced an even more watchful and strict application of rules governing the lives of Indian girls, whose physical strength and adaptability to outdoor settings were viewed as signs of the "abuse" from which the assimilation process, referred to as "civilizing them with a stick," would purportedly spare them.[17]

Today this kind of monitoring would seem to be a thing of the past. However, during a 1995 YMCA-sponsored tournament in Rapid City, South Dakota, the team from Loneman School, which is operated by the Oglala Sioux tribe, wholly comprised of Native American girls between the ages of nine and twelve, received a complaint, alleging that the team had boys on it. Prior to participating in the final game, the Loneman girls were accompanied into a restroom by female volunteers from the YMCA to visually inspect the girls to verify that they were in fact girls.

In an article about the gender verification check, the mother of one of the team members, Pansey Weasel Bear, noted, "My daughter looks up to SuAnne Big Crow. Those are good high goals, but when she was checked and questioned about her gender, well, I hope it doesn't stop her from doing that."[18] In effect Ms. Weasel Bear was pointing out that the presence of an inspiring female role model may not be enough to counteract the negative forces Indian girls encounter in a racially hostile world. Although the girls' parents attempted to seek redress in the courts for the embarrassment and emotional distress their children experienced following the incident, the case was dismissed at the federal trial court level on the grounds that the plaintiffs had failed to show proof of racial and sexual bias despite the fact that no white teams, and certainly no boys' teams, were subjected to this kind of scrutiny. In subsequent appeals, the 8th Circuit Court upheld the dismissal in November 1999 and the U.S. Supreme Court refused to hear the case without comment during the summer of 2000.

This heightened scrutiny of American Indian women primarily by whites in power positions takes on a different form when American Indian women seek to play college basketball. In a 1999 program about Native American sport experience aired on ESPN, a segment featured LeAnn Montes, a Chippewa Cree from Montana. Because of the excellence of her basketball career at Box Elder High School, LeAnn was recruited by coaches from several colleges and universities. Electing to play for the University of Montana, LeAnn was told by the coaching staff, according to assistant coach Shannon Schweyen, that she would not be given an athletic scholarship until she had completed her first year at the university because "It was a high risk situation. We told LeAnn 'we want you to come here and prove to us that you can make it.'" When the interviewer asked, "Is LeAnn a high risk because she is a Native American woman?" Schweyen initially agreed and then qualified the remark by noting that "it is difficult for them to leave their sur-roundings."[19] Two factors converge here to create an obstacle for LeAnn as a minority woman encountering and being encountered by a non-Native sport system. As a woman she shares the difficulties all women face in dealing with a system that has traditionally supported men at substantially higher and more visible levels than women. Because there are fewer athletic scholarships available for women, competition for them is fierce. Positioning oneself athletically and academically to in-spire a scholarship offer presents a gauntlet in and of itself. The message from the coaches at the University of Montana signals a stance that the non-Native "college sport culture" is not convinced that an Indian can assimilate into its value system and customs. This message is a white challenge to American Indian athletes: "Prove to us that you can make it in our world and we'll give you the scholarship." Confronted with what amounts to a modern-day assimilationist mandate, it is not surprising that American Indian athletes like LeAnn have difficulty making the transition from the reservation to non-Indian college and university athletic programs.

The divide between the corporate value system of non-Native high school or college sport programs and Native sport programs can be vast. Joy Griffin, an American Indian sport scientist, offers insight in this regard: "For Native American women, there is a strong connection between sport and physical activity and social, spiritual, and economic aspects of daily life." [20] The development of bonds of kinship, both familial and tribal, is the central purpose of sport for Native American women. Within prevailing notions of North American sport, the rigid hierarchical structure based on Darwinian survival of the fittest mores is not replicated in Native American sport although, in a profound way, these mores have unmistakably shaped white-Indian relations. As a consequence, competition is not viewed by Native American women as a win-loss proposition that emphasizes individual domination of an opponent. [21] Competition is instead self- and group-oriented for the purpose of expanding one's understanding of self-limits and self-knowledge. To be overly focused on competition with the intent of dominating an opponent violates a guiding principle of balance that is at the core of Native sacred traditions. One plays to maintain balance, not to create conflict.

This gulf between the Indian and non-Indian world is developed further by Nathan Aaseng in his brief work on American Indian athletes and their experiences. He notes that "even those Native Americans who could function under such alien values were often frustrated by the white culture's style of coaching." The intractability of the white view can be seen in the observations of one college coach who recruited Indian athletes. This coach observed that Native Americans do not respond to "normal motivational coaching. They never develop their potential because they don't want to dedicate themselves to the white man's ways." The assertion of race privilege in this statement is revealing from the standpoint that Indians are expected to change, not whites.[22]

By defining normalcy as a white construct, there is an assumption that Indian athletes' failure to develop to their full potential is due to lack of dedication to the "white man's ways." This assumes, of course, that the only way for a human being to fulfill her/his potential is by employing white ways and success is measured according to a white value system. This white notion of "normalcy" becomes a factor in (de)valuing the differences found or seen in American Indian athletes. For American Indian athletes, however, dominating opponents to humiliate them, encouraging blatant individualism, and equating authoritarian leadership with effectiveness may well exceed the bounds of civility and common courtesy (that is, violate norms) within their culture. As an athlete who played on a team from the reservation but was also engaged with the broader white sport environment, SuAnne Big Crow was subjected to the tensions created within this racialized gender hierarchy.

The Legend of SuAnne Big Crow

Sherman Alexie writes about SuAnne Big Crow, "On and off the court, Big Crow engaged in acts of heroism . . . it is enough to say she enjoys a mythic status among the Oglala."[23] This description takes on more meaning when considered within the overall context of Alexie's writings about basketball on the reservation as a modern way for athletes to become warriors and for Indian communities to generate new legends. These otherwise familiar words—hero, legend, warrior—that appear frequently in mainstream sport media, popular culture, and sport history take on a significantly different meaning when considered from the perspective of the reservation. In his fictional work *The Lone Ranger and Tonto Fistfight in Heaven,* Alexie elaborates on how athletic heroes are viewed within the Indian community. In an admiring reminiscence about the basketball hero Silus Sirius, who achieved fame when he seemed to literally take flight in one moment of an otherwise forgettable game, a young Indian character named Junior observes, "In the outside world a person can be a hero one second and a nobody the next. . . . A reservation hero is remembered. A reservation hero is a hero forever. In fact, their status grows over the years as the stories are told and retold."[24]

Just as it is important to grasp the nuances that differentiate the concept of the hero within American Indian culture so as to better appreciate the life and legend of SuAnne Big Crow, it is also important to cultivate an understanding of the meaning of the "warrior" concept within the context of basketball as it is played on the reservation. In Peter Donahue's "New Warriors, New Legends: Basketball in Three Native American Works of Fiction," he considers these differences. Whereas a "warrior" in mainstream American conceptualizations of athleticism is infused with the value system of the dominant culture, as seen in the reliance on quantitative, statistical measures that are brought to bear in the calculation and determination of who is a "warrior," American Indian athletes and their communities tend to define the term in accordance with an Indian value system, what Donahue refers to as an "insider" value system. Thus, a reservation basketball "warrior" plays for family and community recognition as an affirmation and assertion of Indian identity and cultural values. As a consequence the Indian athlete warrior symbolically engages in acts of resistance directed toward the "outside" world, the non-Indian world, while perpetuating and reinforcing Indian family and cultural connections to sport. As will become clear later in this chapter, SuAnne Big Crow became a quintessential Indian warrior athlete and hero on the Pine Ridge Reservation.[25]

SuAnne was born in 1974. Her childhood coincided with arguably one of the most turbulent times in the reservation's history. Within a year of her birth, a struggle over tribal leadership erupted into a standoff between FBI agents and members of the American Indian Movement at Wounded Knee. The fate of so many involved in that conflict would be the substance of investigation, prosecution, and widespread speculation for years to come.[26] Beyond the deep-seated disputes among the Lakota over the best way to advance their collective interests as Indian people locked into a struggle for cultural and economic survival is the shared fight in which they engage for their sovereignty as a nation and their land. Since 1875 residents of the Pine Ridge Reservation have participated on a daily basis in a dispute, what some consider an act of war, with the U.S. government.

Within a world shaped by these profound racial, political, cultural, religious, and economic realities, SuAnne became a symbol of hope and validation. Through her accomplishments and actions she emerged as a transcendent figure, someone who was capable of healing tribal divisions. It is difficult to determine, however, the precise moment when SuAnne started to become a hero on the reservation. The daughter of a watchful and ever-present mother, SuAnne and her sisters were kept close to home, a home that by all indications provided a nurturing and loving environment.

Active, strong, and coordinated from an early age, SuAnne enjoyed participating in physical activities. She insinuated her way onto the tribe's Tiny Tots drill team, a group too old for her, by the age of three. Her mother, Chick, tells a vivid story of arriving home to witness four-year-old SuAnne riding a ten-speed bike, balanced on the crossbar and holding onto the handlebars. As a little sister aching to play in the games her older sister Pigeon played, she became a basketball defender by necessity as Pigeon practiced her offensive moves. SuAnne's first "big break" in a tournament would come while she was in kindergarten. The defense she had learned while practicing with Pigeon came in handy when a March snowstorm prevented a full team of second through fifth graders from taking the floor. The coach, desperate to field a squad, asked SuAnne to play. In remembering the event, SuAnne related, "All I really knew was how to play defense. I not only took the ball away from our opponents, but also from my own teammates."[27]

While learning basketball in elementary school from her own role model, Pine Ridge basketball star Lolley Steele, SuAnne exhibited talent of notable proportions. By eighth grade she had already made the high school team, which had been named in honor of the legendary Jim

Thorpe. SuAnne certainly seemed to have the same kinds of qualities for which Thorpe is famous. By ninth grade she had already developed her basketball game to a mature level. She averaged twenty-two points per game, was praised for her defensive play, could shoot well from the outside, and had quick moves to the basket. Like Thorpe, she excelled in a variety of sports. She ran cross-country in eighth and ninth grades, qualified for the state meet as an eighth-grade jumper and sprinter in track, played softball in the summers, volleyball in the winters, and even played pickup football games with the boys. As a high school cheerleader, her squad would gain national recognition when they were selected to participate in the Aloha and Fiesta Bowls.[28]

The high goals SuAnne established for her athletic life were replicated in both her academic and social life. She aspired to graduate first in her class in high school and, in time, go on to earn an athletic scholarship to a Division I institution and play on the U.S. Olympic team. At a social level, she responded to her mother's encouragement to become a role model for her fellow classmates and teammates. SuAnne eventually used her status as an accomplished student and successful athlete to publicly advocate anti-drug and anti-alcohol messages. When Rol Bradford, a Pine Ridge teacher and coach, was asked about whether SuAnne experienced peer pressure as a result of her stance on these matters, he said, "You have to understand. SuAnne didn't *respond* to peer pressure, SuAnne *was* peer pressure."[29]

These themes of courage, character, and conviction are consistent across renderings of SuAnne Big Crow's story. They have been highlighted in two particular events that seem to have solidified her status as a bona fide hero. During her second year playing for the Lady Thorpes, the team traveled to nearby Lead, South Dakota. Longstanding racial animosities often surfaced in contests between the Pine Ridge and Lead teams. As the Thorpes readied themselves in the locker room, the sounds of a hostile crowd could be heard. The home team fans had already begun mock chanting and yelling war whoops. As the team began lining up in the corridor outside the gym, forming their usual line with their tallest player, Doni DeCory, in front followed by SuAnne as the second tallest, the anti-Indian chants became louder. Racial slurs, such as "squaws" and "gut-eaters," were accompanied by the school band pounding out fake Indian music and drumming. When the team was signaled to go out onto the floor, Doni hesitated, turning to SuAnne saying, "I don't think I can handle this."[30]

SuAnne then stepped forward and proceeded to run onto the court. However, rather than starting the warm-up as planned, she stepped into the jump ball circle at center court. Taking off her warm-up jacket, she draped it over her shoulders and began what is called the Lakota shawl dance, a traditional dance.

[T]he dance she chose was a young woman's dance, graceful and modest and show-offy all at the same time. "I couldn't believe it—she was powwowin", like, "get down!" Doni DeCory recalled. "And then she started to sing." SuAnne began to sing in Lakota, swaying back and forth in the jump ball circle, doing the shawl dance, using her warm-up jacket for a shawl. The crowd went completely silent. "All that stuff the Lead fans were yelling—it was like she reversed it somehow," a teammate said. In the sudden quiet, all you could hear was her Lakota song. [31]

Chick Big Crow has said that her heart would fill with pride when she watched SuAnne play and witnessed the kind of role model she became. In 1989 when the Lady Thorpes won the state basketball tournament for the first time in the school's history, it was clear that this achievement symbolized something far more than an athletic win. As a community, Indians in the region avidly followed the team, renewed and revitalized by the pride their daughters showed in being Indian, in being strong, in being powerful. En route to the championship, SuAnne set a South Dakota state high school record by scoring 67 points in one game (she hit 26 of 44 shots and made 15 of 20 free throws) against Lemmon High School. At the conclusion of her sophomore year, she averaged more than 30 points a game and finished the season with another state record, 763 points in a season. [32]

After enduring the physical and emotional roller coaster of an intense basketball season, the team knew the final game against rival Milbank would not be easy either. With the score tied at 40–40 with eleven seconds remaining, the ball changed hands three times, first in the possession of Pine Ridge, then Milbank. A scramble for the ball resulted in SuAnne's being positioned to take the last shot. She squared her shoulders to the basket, released the ball, and it went through the net as the buzzer sounded. [33]

The Lady Thorpes returned home to a hero's welcome. Accompanied by a police escort across the Rosebud Sioux Reservation, the bus was joined fifty miles from Pine Ridge at the Bennett County line by carloads of fans. The entourage grew to hundreds of cars as it got closer to home. Parents, children, and grandparents stood on the side of the road to wave and cheer.

At the approach to Pine Ridge Village, people had parked their cars so as to make an illuminated path right into the heart of the community, leading to Billy Mills Hall, named in honor of another Lakota athletic hero. There, speeches were made and an honoring ceremony was held. Indian leader Dennis Banks recalled, "Those girls *owned* that town." People who had otherwise been deeply divided for years over tribal politics reunited, celebrating the accomplishments of their team. SuAnne would emerge from the season at the age of fifteen as an All-American according to *USA Today* and a college prospect.[34]

The triumph of the season was juxtaposed with a frustrating incident that SuAnne had commented on earlier in the season. The week the team won regionals, which also happened to be Thanksgiving week, NBC *Nightly News* presented a two-part report titled "Tragedy at Pine Ridge." Anchor Tom Brokaw's lead read as follows: "This is Thanksgiving week, of course, but on the Pine Ridge Indian Reservation in South Dakota it's hard to find reason to give thanks, when tragedy is never out of season." Despite shooting extensive footage and interviewing numerous people, the NBC crew wholly missed that during the time of their visit the Lady Thorpes and SuAnne Big Crow were offering a joyful and exciting display of hope on the reservation. The characterization of her people on national news as hopeless and a people whose only prospect of success was to live elsewhere to avoid the trappings of "idleness and alcohol" was an affront that fueled SuAnne's play in the weeks ahead. Even after the team won the championship, there was almost nothing in the national news about the story of the magnificent season of the Lady Thorpes or the impressive feats of SuAnne Big Crow.[35]

The Legacy of SuAnne Big Crow

SuAnne's remaining high school years were marked by similar triumphs. Although another championship was not in the offing, she was selected to play on the National American Indian Women's Team to participate in a European tour, the first time this kind of event had been organized. SuAnne played in Finland and Lithuania with the team. While in Lithuania SuAnne contracted a stomach virus that prevented her from playing on her high school team for about half of her junior year. Despite missing that much time, SuAnne was still voted a member of the all-state team. By her senior year SuAnne seemed to have recovered her strength and her game. She averaged nearly 40 points per game and was elected homecoming queen. SuAnne finished her high school career with 2,541 points, earning all-state honors for a third year in a row. Her accomplishment prompted her nomination as a finalist for the South Dakota "Miss Basketball" title.

In February 1992 on a trip to attend a banquet where she would learn whether she had been named "Miss Basketball," SuAnne apparently fell asleep behind the wheel and died in the resulting car accident. Her mother was in the car with her, asleep in the passenger seat. Upon learning of SuAnne's death, throngs of people attended her memorial service and funeral. As a tribal hero, beloved young woman, and basketball player who inspired respect around the state, people paid homage in a variety of ways. Lakota memorial songs were composed for her. The radio station on the reservation, KILI, played five hundred requests in her honor. High school teams from around the state sent representatives to her funeral. The state legislature observed a moment of silence in her honor, and business on the reservation ceased the day of her funeral.[36]

In the wake of the grief surrounding SuAnne's death, her mother began to envision a way of keeping SuAnne's dreams alive through the creation of a boys and girls club that would be built on the principles SuAnne had so often espoused. The result of Chick's work, and that of her sisters and others in the community, has been the founding of the SuAnne Big Crow Boys and Girls Club Youth Wellness and Opportunity Center. The project began at her dining room table, where Chick thought about SuAnne's dream of an ideal place she called "Happy-town, USA" where children could come, participate in activities, and have fun. Chick then sketched out a preliminary plan for a recreation center. After an appeal to tribal councilman G. Wayne Tapio for space, the tribe agreed to lease Chick a 6,000-square-foot building that had formerly served as a doll manufacturing plant. The yearly rental was established at $1.00. By 1992 the project had grown to include a restaurant and later evolved into a partnership with the Boys and Girls Clubs of America.[37]

Since then this modest idea for a community recreation center has garnered support from a coalition of Pine Ridge organizations, such as the youth coalition and several federal agencies. In June 2002 the SuAnne Big Crow Boys and Girls Club Youth Wellness and Opportunity Center, a 30,000 square foot facility, which includes a soccer field, regulation swimming pool, and a library/technology center, was opened.[38] As a project that coincided with President Clinton's designation of the Pine Ridge Reservation as an economic "Empowerment Zone," the center was described in *News from Indian Country* as "A young girl's dream and the promise of a president." In his remarks during the "blessing of the ground" ceremony for the SuAnne Big Crow Center in August 2000, then HUD secretary Andrew Cuomo said, "SuAnne is in many ways with us today, I think. Because her vision, her dream is alive. And it's not alive in a building. This Center will be the monument to her vision and her memory. But her inspiration is beyond that. Because it says what we can do when we remember that there is a brighter future, when we look at hope instead of despair, when we focus on those things that unite us rather than those things that divide us."[39]

A shrine to SuAnne, referred to as the "incentive room," with pictures, trophies, and video from her playing days, serves as a focal point for the center. It is her memory that serves to inspire the continued development and growth of the center. In an August 2000 report the impetus for the center is described this way: "The inspiration of the SuAnne Big Crow Boys and Girls Club comes from the memory of an energetic, good-hearted, and extraordinarily gifted girl named SuAnne Big Crow. The star of her high school basketball team, SuAnne led the Pine Ridge High School team to the state championships and inspired her people with great excitement and joy. She was a leader for her peers as well as a leader for her people."[40]

SuAnne's legacy has been taken up by her community and perpetuated. Bessie Vitalis, a teen volunteer at the center, said, "People always want to leave the reservation, but SuAnne wanted to change things instead of leaving. She was a positive role model for everybody."[41]

By Sherman Alexie's definition of an Indian hero as someone whose status grows as the stories are told and retold, there is little doubt that SuAnne is an Indian hero. The reach of her story has been expanding exponentially during the past decade not only with regard to the development of the SuAnne Big Crow Center but through the awards named in her honor. Each year at the South Dakota High School Basketball Championships, the Spirit of Su Award is given. One of the winners of the award, Jodi Schroeder, who plays for the University of South Dakota, said, "When I received the award I was very honored. It was the perfect ending to my senior year. I knew that the award was based on more than athletic honors."[42]

SuAnne's legacy has slowly been taken up by legislative and educational organizations. In 1997 the State House of South Dakota passed a commemoration honoring SuAnne Big Crow, "who lived her life as an example for young people everywhere." In the early 1990s the National Education Association created the SuAnne Big Crow Memorial Award, which is presented to an "individual who promotes leadership, improves the self-esteem of minorities, and contributes to the elimination of social injustice and prejudice." Tatewin Means, the daughter of Indian activist and actor Russell Means and Peggy Phelps, a school counselor, who was the 1996 recipient of the award, remarked, "When you know your culture, you know who you are, and you're not ashamed of it. Because of this, you are not afraid to stand up for yourself and your people and confront racism when you see it."[43]

Several years ago sport studies scholar Lawrence Wenner wrote that sport fans were "just generally big on history." As enamored as the mainstream sport community has been with the biographies of athletes and the subsequent memorialization of athletes in the collective consciousness of the nation, the representation of athletes within accessible histories has been selective, often reproducing the prejudices and preferences of a racialized gender hierarchy. In coming to terms with that reality, significant progress has been made in generating a more inclusive body of knowledge that considers the stories of racial minorities and women. However, there is a lesson to be acknowledged in the slowness with which American Indian sport and American Indian athletes have been incorporated into this wider discussion. SuAnne Big Crow's story is important not just because of who she was and the legacy she left behind. She is important because she provides an entry point for becoming more aware of the other American Indian women athletes whose histories contribute to the richness of their own communities and to the broader athletic community. She is important because in order to glimpse and grasp the reality of her life and the significance of her legacy, one must subscribe to a history that, as Jennifer Hargreaves notes, breaks with "the history of cultural imperialism, Eurocentric discourses, and the universalized accounts of 'women in sport.'"[44]

In order to appreciate SuAnne's heroism, it should be assessed within the context of how it was conferred, not within the confines of the dominant culture's popular conceptions of athletic heroism. What signals SuAnne's status as a hero is not her prowess as a basketball player as validated by statistics, but the strength of her identity as an Indian woman who would not allow the dominant culture to impose its will on her sense of possibility for herself and her people. Whereas in mainstream sport, conferring the status of hero means ultimate conformity, SuAnne Big Crow's heroism emanates from an ultimate embrace of her people and the history of the Lakota Sioux and an ultimate rejection of the American status quo. A failure to recognize this crucial point only serves to homogenize the accomplishments of SuAnne Big Crow, to make her just like any other "All-American hero." And this she is not and should not ever be. To reduce her to that would be to reinforce the very racialized gender hierarchy that she labored against and to render her virtually invisible within it. The lesson of SuAnne Big Crow's life and legacy is to acknowledge that she is a Lakota woman, a Lakota athlete warrior, and a Lakota hero.

Notes

1. Examples of work that feature studies of Native American women in sport include Colton, *Counting Coup*; Joy Griffin, "Native American Women

in Sport," in *Encyclopedia of Women and Sport in America*, ed. Carole A. Oglesby (Phoenix AZ: Oryx Press, 1998), 220–22; Susan Keith, "Native American Women in Sport," *Journal of Physical Education, Recreation & Dance* 47:3 (April 1999): 70; Oxendine, *American Indian Sports Heritage*, 2–26, 55–58, 63; Victoria Paraschak, "Doing Race, Doing Gender: First Nations, 'Sport,' and Gender Relations," in *Sport and Gender in Canada*, ed. Philip White and Kevin Young (Oxford: Oxford University Press, 1999), 153–69; J. Schroeder, "Developing Self-esteem and Leadership Skills in Native American Women: The Role of Sports and Play," *Journal of Physical Education, Recreation & Dance* 66 (1995): 48–51. Works that include biographies of American Indian women athletes include Frazier, *On the Rez*; Victoria Paraschak, "Ryneldi Becenti: A Role Model for Her People," in *International Encyclopedia of Women & Sport*, ed. Karen Christensen, Allen Guttman, and Gertrude Pfister (Great Barrington MA: Berkshire Reference Works, 1999); and Gary Smith, "A Woman of the People," *Winds of Change* 8 (fall 1993): 192–204.

2. Anne Janette Johnson, *Great Women in Sports* (Detroit: Visible Ink Press, 1996); Janet Woolum, *Women Athletes: Who They Are and How They Influenced Sports in America* (Phoenix AZ: Oryx Press, 1998).

3. Nathan Aaseng, *American Indian Lives Series: Athletes* (New York: Facts on File, 1995). Russell Coker and Sherry Kast, *Give It Your Best! Profiles of Native American Athletes* (Oklahoma City: United National Tribal Youth, 1996); Sonja Weisel, "Indians in Sports: Looking for New Legends," *American Indian Report* 14 (September 1998): 12–15.

4. Aaseng, *American Indian Lives Series: Athletes*.

5. Jennifer Hargreaves, *Heroines of Sport: The Politics of Difference and Identity* (New York: Routledge, 2000), 1.

6. Frazier, *On the Rez*.

7. Frazier, *On the Rez*, 197.

8. P. Hammel, "Giving Indians a Voice: New Civil Rights Panel Member Elsie Meeks, an Oglala Sioux, Vows to Bring Federal Attention to Indian Concerns," *Omaha World-Herald*, 27 December 1999, p. 1.

9. Sherman Alexie, "Some of My Best Friends," *Los Angeles Times*, 23 January 2000.

10. For in-depth reading relative to the source of this distrust, see Helen Hunt Jackson, *A Century of Dishonor: A Sketch of the United States Government's Dealings with Some of the Indian Tribes* (New York: Harper, 1881; reprint, Norman: University of Oklahoma Press, 1995).

11. Findings from a study conducted by Margaret Carlisle Duncan, Michael Messner, and Cheryl Cooky titled "Gender in Televised Sports," which was done at the behest of the Amateur Athletic Federation, were disseminated on

SuAnne Big Crow's Legend and Legacy

5 September 2000 through a press release. The citation for the release is as follows: Margaret Carlisle Duncan, "Women's Sports Go Unreported in Television News" (Los Angeles: Amateur Athletic Foundation, 5 September 2000); Katherine Kinnick, "Gender Bias in Newspaper Profiles of 1996 Olympic Athletes: A Content Analysis of Five Major Dailies," *Women's Studies in Communication* 21 (fall 1998): 212–17; Joli Sandoz, "Victory? New Language for Sportswomen," *Women and Language* 23 (spring 2000): 33–43.

12. Susan Birrell and Mary McDonald, eds., *Reading Sport: Critical Essays on Power and Representation* (Boston: Northeastern University Press, 2000).

13. Paraschak, "Doing Race, Doing Gender," 164.

14. Susan Cahn, *Coming on Strong: Gender and Sexuality in Twentieth-Century Women's Sport* (New York: Free Press, 1993), 167.

15. Paraschak, "Doing Race, Doing Gender," 154.

16. Bloom, *To Show What an Indian Can Do*.

17. More information regarding the moderate forms of physical activity prescribed for women that adhered to Victorian notions of female frailty can be found in Cahn, *Coming on Strong*; Allen L. Sack and Ellen J. Staurowsky, *College Athletes for Hire: The Evolution and Legacy of the NCAA Amateur Myth* (Westport CT: Praeger, 1998). The application of these principles as they were infused into the curriculum at American Indian boarding schools is developed in Bloom, *To Show What an Indian Can Do*, 77–96. The expression "civilizing them with a stick" is taken from Mary Crow Dog, *Lakota Woman* (New York: Harper Perennial, 1990), 28–43.

18. Tara Davenport, by her legal guardian and natural mother, Jean Belt, et al., Plaintiffs, Appellants v. Young Men's Christian Association, et al., Defendants—Appellees, 205 F.3d 1345, 1999 WL 1059829, 8th Cir. S.D. The court's decision is referenced in a "Table of Decisions without Reported Opinions" that appears in the *Federal Reporter*. An account of what happened at the tournament was written by David Melmer, "Girls' Team Put through Gender Check: Parent Says Racism Root of the Problem," *Indian Country Today (The Lakota Times*, 15 (14 December 1995): A1. The practice of gender verification started in the early 1960s when suspicions arose that men were masquerading and competing as female athletes. Riddled with problems, the mandatory gender verification testing the International Olympic Committee began in 1968 was finally abandoned in 2000. The American Medical Association and other medical associations around the world had advocated for such testing to be abolished as early as 1985. See commentary by Joe Leigh Simpson, Arne Ljunqvist, Malcolm A. Ferguson-Smith, Albert de la Chapelle, Louis L. Elsas II, A. A. Ehrhardt, Myron Genel, Elizabeth Ferris, and Alison Carlson, "Gender Verification in the Olympics," *Journal of the American Medical Association* 284 (27 September 2000): 1568.

207

19. Bob Ley, *Native Americans Sports Experience* (Bristol CT: ESPN, 16 November 1999). This program was aired as part of the network's ongoing *Outside the Lines* program. According to the University of Montana's Web site, LeAnn Montes was on the women's basketball roster for the academic year 2000–2001. The University of Montana was one of the schools recruiting SuAnne Big Crow at the time of her death.

20. Griffin, "Native American Women in Sport." In the spring of 2001, Dr. Griffin was elected president of the National Association for Girls and Women in Sport.

21. A discussion regarding the prevailing values of success and competition that form the basis of the U.S. sport system can be found in D. Stanley Eitzen and George Sage, *Sociology of North American Sport* (Madison WI: Brown and Benchmark, 1997), chap. 3.

22. Aaseng, *American Indian Lives Series: Athletes*, xix.

23. Alexie, "Some of My Best Friends."

24. Sherman Alexie, *The Lone Ranger and Tonto Fistfight in Heaven* (New York: HarperCollins, 1994), 46.

25. Peter Donahue, "New Warriors, New Legends: Basketball in Three Native American Works of Fiction," *American Indian Culture and Research Journal* 21:3 (1997): 43–60.

26. Peter Matthiessen, *In the Spirit of Crazy Horse* (New York: Penguin, 1991); S. Stern, *Loud Hawk: The United States versus the American Indian Movement* (Norman: University of Oklahoma Press, 1994).

27. Discussions regarding SuAnne's childhood can be found in Aaseng, *American Indian Lives Series: Athletes*; Frazier, *On the Rez*; and Jean Roach, "SuAnne's Memory Lives On," *Indian Country Today (The Lakota Times)* 16 (11 November 1996): B1.

28. Aaseng, *American Indian Lives Series: Athletes*; Frazier, *On the Rez*; Roach, "SuAnne's Memory Lives On."

29. Rol Bradford quoted in Frazier, *On the Rez*, 204.

30. Accounts of this appear in both Aaseng, *American Indian Lives Series: Athletes*, and Frazier, *On the Rez*. Specific information regarding racial slurs is found in Frazier, *On the Rez*, 208–9. Aaseng reports another incident in which the team emerged from a game to discover that the word "Thorpes" had been altered to spell "hores." According to Aaseng's sources, SuAnne figured out a way to ridicule the message, breaking the tension created by the range of emotions experienced by the other players when they saw it (some cried, others rested on the pavement recovering from the affront). By the time her teammates got on the bus, they were laughing. "Again, Big Crow had broken the spell

of racism by refusing to give in to it" (Aaseng, *American Indian Lives Series: Athletes*, 104).

31. Frazier, *On the Rez*, 209.

32. Aaseng, *American Indian Lives Series: Athletes*, 103.

33. Frazier, *On the Rez*, 232–36.

34. Aaseng, *American Indian Lives Series: Athletes*; Frazier, *On the Rez*.

35. Barbara Bad Wound, "Author Praises Emergency Work: Says He Tells Story of SuAnne Big Crow," *Indian Country Today (The Lakota Times)* 20 (4 October 2000): D1. David Rooks, "Keeping the Dream: Oglala Lakota Mother Carries on with Her Daughter's Hope," *Indian Country Today (The Lakota Times)* (16 August 2000): D1. There are several things to note regarding NBC's two-part series titled "Tragedy at Pine Ridge." NBC *Nightly News* with Tom Brokaw received the Silver Baton in 1989–90 from the DuPont-Columbia Awards for that program. (See *http://www.jrn.columbia.edu/events/dupont/searchresults.asp*.) However, as Ardy Bowker Soxkiller Clark writes in chapter 8 of *Sisters in the Blood: The Education of Women in Native America* (Newton MA: Education Development Center, 1995; the introduction to this book can be accessed at *http://www.sixkiller.com/publications.htm*), the reading of life on the reservation by non-Indians results in a misreading and misunderstanding of what the real issues are. She cites a failure on the part of most Americans, particularly educators and television producers, to come to terms with the "poverty, the extremely high unemployment rates, and the lack of economic incentives on the part of the federal government as the root of the problems" on Pine Ridge. Instead, "the reservation-specific culture and the pathological behaviors of alcohol abuse became the basis of the news special."

36. Jerry Reynolds, "A Salute of Love," *Indian Country Today (The Lakota Times)* 12 (19 February 1992): A1.

37. "SuAnne Big Crow Boys and Girls Youth Wellness and Opportunity Center Report," 3 August 2000. This was found on the U.S. Department of Housing and Urban Development Web site (March 2000).

38. "SuAnne Big Crow Boys and Girls Club Grand Opening in Pine Ridge, South Dakota Marks Major Milestone," 28 May 2002. *Canku Ota* (an on-line newsletter celebrating Native America), 1 June 2002, issue 62: *http://www.turtletrack.org/Issues02/Co06012002/CO_06012002_Boys_Girls_Club.htm*.

39. Jim Kent, "HUD Secretary Andrew Cuomo Visits the Pine Ridge Reservation: Promises Support for SuAnne Big Crow Center," *News from Indian Country* 14 (31 August 2000): A4; David Rooks, "SuAnne Big Crow Center to Become a Reality," *Indian Country Today (The Lakota Times)* 20 (16 August 2000): D1; "Cuomo, Rominger Join Pine Ridge Tribal Leaders for Wellness

Center Ground Blessing," press release produced by the U.S. Department of Housing and Urban Development, 3 August 2000.

40. "SuAnne Big Crow Boys and Girls," 14.

41. Roach, "SuAnne's Memory Lives On."

42. Jodi Schroeder, e-mail correspondence with the author, 12 March 2001.

43. Representatives Hagen and Lucas and Senator Valandra, House Commemoration No. 1010, State of South Dakota, 72nd Sess., Legislative Assembly, 1997, *http://www.state.sd.us/state/legis/lrc/lawstat/https/72/bills/bil1798.htm*. The description of the National Education Association Award named in honor of SuAnne Big Crow can be found at *http://www.nea.org/nr/nr990619.html*. The award reads as follows: "SuAnne Big Crow (1974–1992) was an American Indian student in Pine Ridge, South Dakota. An outstanding athlete, student leader, and role model, she spent her high school years working to give her peers on the reservation a greater sense of self-worth and dignity. Big Crow died in an automobile accident at the age of 17." Rosemary White Shield, "Women to Get National Awards," *Indian Country Today (The Lakota Times)* 16 (2 July 1996): C1.

44. Jennifer Hargreaves, *Heroines of Sport: The Politics of Difference and Identity* (New York: Routledge, 2001), 4.

10. A Notable Exception
Notes on Notah Begay,
Race, and Sports

In September 2000 the *Des Moines Register* ran a brief feature on Drake University's starting quarterback, Ira Vandever. The account of the young Navajo player was both touching and strange. It rendered a rather intimate and approachable portrait of the indigenous athlete but did so through topics and tropes relatively uncommon in mainstream sport. Indeed, the sketch of Vandever and the "Navajo lessons" he brings to the football field references familiar themes—character, family, dedication, class, and material disadvantage. At the same time, when read against other stories on the sport page it remains odd, focusing as it does on Vandever's spirituality (his reverence for what the report dubbed Mother Earth), his knowledge of traditional culture ("I learned the stories . . . I learned about herbs and the earth, I learned to hunt, to fish, to ride horses"), his ethnic pride, his Americanness (evidenced by his grandfather's role as a code talker in World War II), his early years on the reservation (a happy childhood, despite the lack of running water or electricity), and his endurance of racist stereotypes upon moving to St. Louis with his mother ("Kids would ask me things like, 'Hey, where's your bow and arrows? Where's your horse? Where's your long hair?'").[1]

For all of its brevity, the article says much about popular perceptions of Native Americans within (and beyond) sports. The overt racism and hostile stereotypes pervasive throughout much of the twentieth century have softened, even faded from common usage. In post–civil rights America, certain clichés, discussed in greater detail by other contributors to this volume as well as scholars in sport studies and Native American studies, have all but disappeared from interpretations of indigenous athletes, including the reduction of Indian athletes to a collection of physical traits, the use of "Chief" as a nickname for Indian players, especially in baseball, the prevalence of the savage metaphors (whether noble or ignoble), and the presentation of indigenous athletic participation in terms of racial dramas that replay the struggles to subjugate or "civilize" indigenous peoples.[2] Nonetheless, even as sport is celebrated as a path to racial equality and an arena for cultural understanding, racial ideologies continue to shape the ways in which individuals and institutions play, watch, describe, organize, and imagine sports.[3] The resiliency of race and racism has profound implications for the representation and reception of Native American athletes. Indeed, within the context of sports, as the personality piece on Vandever suggests, formulations of Indianness, in contrast with formulations of whiteness or blackness for instance, now turn on questions of heritage, culture, tradition, spirituality, deprivation, the reservation, nation, character, and discrimination. In addition, Ellen Staurowsky has recently argued, popular accounts of indigenous athletes at the turn of the millennium tend to tell decontextualized, tragic tales about talented athletes, living in desperate, disadvantaged conditions, who ultimately spin out of control.[4] In the process they not only regularly resurrect the vanishing Indian but also often use Indian athletes and their lives to present object lessons, rather than present nuanced lives of fully embodied social agents.[5] To fully account for these reconfigurations of race and representation, as well as their implications, it is necessary to unpack images of Native Americans while recognizing their agency as fans and athletes.

In what follows I begin to clarify the themes and techniques through which authors, audiences, and athletes make indigenous athletes legible, that is, how they make their achievements within and beyond sport meaningful and readable, by examining the career of Navajo (Diné) golfer Notah Begay. I concentrate on Begay because of his successes and failures, his celebrity, and his efforts to serve as a representative and role model for indigenous people, all of which arguably make him the most discussed Native American athlete of the last quarter century. The volume and variety of public conversations about Begay, moreover, afford a unique opportunity to inquire into both the production of Indianness at the dawn of the twenty-first century and the racial politics of sport in post–civil rights America. After offering a brief biographical sketch of Begay, I examine a series of themes in succession: the versions of Indianness and Americanness produced by individuals and institutions to mark difference and formulate identity; the accentuation of Begay's character and its elaboration in the social drama following his arrest for drunk driving; and the semiotic and structural relations between Begay and Tiger Woods. The closing discussion integrates these themes to comment on the significance of the Indian athlete and to complicate ongoing discussions of race and sports.

A Golfer's Life

Notah Ryan Begay III has followed an unlikely path to athletic prominence. In fact, his life clashes in most ways with the popular image of golf and those who watch or play it. Born on 14 September 1972 to a Navajo father and a Pueblo mother (of San Felipe and Isleta descent), he is one of the few non-white players in professional golf and the only full-blood Native American currently on the Professional Golf Association (PGA) Tour. In addition, he enjoyed neither the luxuries of suburban life so often associated with golf, nor the class, racial, or instructional privileges central to the country club. He spent much of his youth on a reservation in New Mexico, moving to the state capital only after scoring well enough on an entrance exam to attend Albuquerque Academy. Throughout, his family was lower middle class at best, struggling initially against the underdevelopment of the reservation and then later to pay the tuition to the prestigious private school. Begay refuses to describe his childhood in terms of poverty and deprivation, but does admit that his family's economic circumstances were difficult at times, including periods during which they depended on public assistance.[6]

Like many of his peers he began playing golf at an early age, perhaps as young as six. He refined his game on municipal courses and largely without elite assistance. Throughout his youth he displayed passion, sneaking onto courses to play and to be in the presence of golf. He exhibited commitment, working not for money but for playing time and making personal sacrifices to afford basic equipment, and he possessed great talent, winning more than a dozen junior and amateur titles during his teens. Begay also played soccer and basketball in high school, leading his high school to state championships in the latter sport in 1989 and 1990. And he was named New Mexico Athlete of the Year in 1990.[7]

After graduating high school, Begay attended Stanford University, earning a degree in economics. During his four years there his teammates included Tiger Woods and Casey Martin. Together they won the national championship in 1994. Begay distinguished himself among such illustrious peers, earning All-American honors three times and shooting 62, a record for a single round in the NCAA Championship.[8]

In 1995 Begay turned professional. Initially he struggled, reworking his stroke and relearning fundamentals, even as he questioned the wisdom of pursuing a career in golf. After three years he began to hit his stride on the Nike/Buy.Com Tour. He was runner-up on four separate occasions, and at the Dominion Open he shot a 59, a record 13 under par. Combined, these achievements granted him entry to the PGA Tour in 1999. In the first two years he won four events: the Reno-Tahoe Open (1999), the Michelob Championship at Kingsmill (1999), the FedEx St. Jude Classic (2000), and the Canon Greater Hartford Open (2000). Due in part to his two major victories in 1999, he was nominated for rookie of the year honors and offered a lucrative endorsement contract with Nike. Given his success on the links, Begay has attracted much attention, enjoying great popularity among Native Americans.[9]

In spite of his excellence and exploits, many know Begay only because he was arrested for drunk driving in January 2000 after backing into a parked car outside of a bar. His blood alcohol level was .21, more than twice the legal limit. In a move that surprised many and heartened others, he took responsibility for his actions and even informed prosecutors of a drunk-driving conviction he had received in Arizona five years earlier: "I made a big mistake, and I want to be held responsible." Begay was given a 364-day sentence with all but seven days suspended, a $1,000 fine, and 48 hours of community service, and was ordered not to consume alcohol for a year. Although some have criticized the terms of the plea, namely the work-release during his brief incarceration that enabled him to spend up to half of the day outside of prison, training and playing golf, Begay has retained endorsement contracts and arguably polished the luster of his celebrity.[10]

Begay's brief career, his status as the only American Indian on the tour, and his recent transgression facilitate a rereading of the place and significance of indigenous athletes and athletics and the articulations of race and sport in North America.

Indianness

Not surprisingly, most accounts of Begay pivot around questions of Indianness. Indigenity does not unfold in any sort of flat or simple fashion but emerges as a fairly ambivalent and conflicted ideological space. Indianness emerges largely through unstated contrasts with whiteness or the values, practices, institutions, and experiences associated with Euro-America, "modernity," and "civilization." Such readings, of course, have become the foundational tropes of North American identities, cultures, and nations, but discussions of Begay twist them slightly. In many interpretations of Begay, Indianness takes shape through an association between tradition and deprivation fostered on reservations. During an installment of espn's *Outside the Lines* devoted to the Native American sport experience, Tom Farrey gave clear expression to this common pattern, asking, "what cosmic set of circumstances could have conspired to lift Begay above the despair, alcoholism, and lack of education that have claimed other Native American youth, but place him in an orbit . . . that is so far removed from the consciousness of the reservation that Begay may as well be an alien to his own people?"[11]

Here, as elsewhere, indigenity emerges as a notable lack; poverty, isolation, foreclosed opportunity, and underdevelopment lay at the heart of Indianness and its significance. At the same time radical, even incommensurable difference distinguishes Indianness as a kind of dead end, an alien, historical artifact.

Furthermore, the indigenous name fascinates commentators on Notah Ryan Begay III. Notah, they routinely remind readers, translated from Navajo means "almost there," and then they comment on the development and trajectory of Begay's life and career. Such translations direct attention to the impulses and institutions of American imperialism and surely would be unthinkable in accounts of Irish American, German American, or even African American athletes.

A similar effort to make indigenity legible crystallizes around spiritu-ality. Authors regularly use Begay's attendance to traditional ritual prac-tices and religious doctrine to materialize his Indianness, making tangi-ble his ethnicity and difference. Kelli Anderson, for instance, begins her biographical piece on Begay at a Pueblo religious ceremony where the then six-year-old Begay danced all night, displaying both endurance and courage. [12] Moreover, Begay's approach to golf, according to Michael D'Antonio, "is consistent with a spiritual approach to life that Begay learned from his family and the Native American community. 'There are prayers that are said when you are going out to meet a challenge,' explains his mother, Laura Ansera. 'You draw upon spirits to bring you strength to succeed if it is for you. If you don't prevail, then you must learn from the experience.'" [13]

It is not that Begay is not sincere in his practices and beliefs, nor that indigenous spirituality did not profoundly shape Begay, leaving an indelible imprint upon his life and outlook. Rather, such snippets almost invariably take indigenous spirituality out of context, forcing it to operate as a synecdoche of cultural identity and difference. In most narratives completing the exaggerated symbolic work performed by indigenous beliefs and rituals is a failure to offer a complete picture of how Begay practices spirituality, namely the role Catholicism has or plays, and how and why indigenous peoples in the Southwest have come to incorporate it in their lives. It is highly unlikely, even inconceiv-able, that mainstream sport journalism would attend to the ritual pre-occupations or spiritual preconceptions of Jack Nicklaus, Tiger Woods, or David Duval with the same consistency, content, or tone it brings to Begay. Such decontextualized emphases and differential erasures surely reinforce superficial understandings of Native Americans.

Against Stereotypes

Whereas much of the discussion of Begay reinscribes colonial clichés, it also facilitates conversations about, and arguably contestations of, more overt stereotypes. Indeed, as one might anticipate, the Navajo golfer has a keen awareness of popular ideas about Indianness. For instance, while Begay formerly marked his face with clay to prepare himself for competition, connect himself with the natural world, and intimidate his opponents, he ceased doing so when he feared it perpetuated negative notions of Indianness, underscoring for whites the savagery and bellicosity too often projected onto indigenous peoples.[14] More recently he has expressed deep regret for the way his drunk-driving arrest confirms ugly stereotypes about Indians and alcohol. In interviews Begay routinely celebrates his Indianness.

Native Americans represent less than 2 percent of the population, but more than 80 percent of the diversity. There are more than 500 nations. I think the thing I am most proud of is that I'm out there, flying the flag for all Native Americans, for the Sioux, the Chippewas, the Seminoles, for everyone.[15]

Begay does more than speak proudly about being an Indian; he also pairs his awareness of stereotypes with interrogation, questioning assumptions and imagery. Begay, who finds, "lifestyle on reservations . . . [and] broken English in movies" to be the worst stereotypes about Native Americans, repeatedly reminds readers, "We're real people. . . . We're not the romanticized stereotyped characters you see in cartoons and movies."[16] In 2001 Begay even suggested that Native American mascots were problematic, hoping that fans and owners "would be a little more respectful of other people's feelings and concerns. Whether there is a portrayal of you as a black, white, Native American or Asian that was somehow giving you a negative self-perception, obviously it's not what a logo is supposed to do." In fact, he continued, "A logo is something you're proud of. . . . It should not be something that is indirectly demeaning to somebody else. . . . I would not support the type of logos that would degrade any race." And despite his reserved position, Begay voiced support for nonviolent protest as a way to create "awareness."[17]

The fact that popular publications and the mass media linger on racial stereotypes and that Begay pauses to highlight the persistence and power of stereotypes should be read as an interruption of the racial imaginary. They clear a space in which to challenge anti-Indian sentiments and to work to reclaim Indianness.

Indian Audiences

Begay also facilitates alternate renderings of Indianness. During an electronic discussion coinciding with ESPN's discussion of Indianness and sport, a group of American Indian schoolchildren asked Begay to identify his clan.

5th graders from the Navajo Reservation: Aaron in our class asked, "What are your clans?" Notah Begay: On my mother's side, I am of the Fox Clan. On my Navajo side, I am born of the Folded Arm People. And my paternal grandfather is of the Salt Clan . . . that is who I am.[18]

Here, kinship, heritage, and tribal connections not visible to most sport fans reconfigure the Navajo/Pueblo golfer, making him more complex as they localize and reclaim him.

For other Native Americans, Begay fosters ethnic pride. Bruce Belone, a Navajo, remarked, "He is an honor to Native Americans. I'm very proud of him."[19] A resident of the Isleta Reservation goes further: "He is like a god to us."[20]

The indigenous media has celebrated Begay as well. Contrasting himself with the mainstream media, which "publicizes and promotes negative issues," George Tiger writing in the *Oklahoma Indian Times* lauds Begay for "his athletic skills and warrior spirit," which have had "a very positive impact on the young. . . . He should look forward to each tournament knowing Indian people are proud of him and the warrior spirit he displays."[21]

Begay has not only attracted an array of fans across Native America, he has also taken a leading role in promoting golf. He has secured a $250,000 grant from the United States Golf Association and more than $500,000 in equipment from Nike. Consequently, he has inspired younger Indian golfers. Cody Quetone and Nick Fixin, for instance, point to Begay as their motivation on and off the links.[22] At the same time he has reenergized and expanded existing networks of golfers in Indian Country, who participate in events sponsored by the Native American Golf Association or are part of tribal tournament circuits in the Dakotas and the Southwest. Older golfers find in Begay both validation and a connection to the past. Derek Burshiem, four-time winner of the Oglala Nation Open, echoes the sentiments of many

Native Americans when he says, "We're proud of him." And Joe Blue Horse "swelled with pride" upon hearing of Begay's record-setting 59 on the Nike Tour: "When he shot 59 . . . all Indian golfers shot 59." Begay reminds Blue Horse of Rod Curl, a Wintu Indian who won the Colonial National Invitational in 1974.[23]

On polished Web pages and reservation golf courses, in television rooms and bedrooms, at local coffee shops and community events across Native America, fans, golfers, and everyday citizens reimagine their sense of what it means to be Indian in America. Indeed, through practices largely hidden to the majority of Americans, participants in this emergent fan-sporting culture have repossessed Begay from Nike, the PGA, and other corporate interests, making him once again one of their own.

Oddly Absent

While many narratives foreground, romanticize, and even celebrate Begay's Indianness, other accounts all but omit it. They reduce Begay to a series of demographic features and athletic accomplishments. ESPN, for instance, renders Begay's biography as follows:

> Notah Begay III
> Height: 5'11"
> Weight: 195
> Birthdate: 14 September 1972
> Birthplace: Albuquerque, New Mexico
> Residence: Albuquerque, New Mexico
> Year turned professional: 1995
> College: Stanford University
> 4 PGA Tour victories
> 2000: St. Jude Classic; Greater Hartford Open
> 1999: Reno-Tahoe Open; Michelob Championship

Against this background, it presents series of "career highlights" including

Finished 2000 season 20th on the money list with more than $1.8 million in earnings.

Birdied three of final holes in regulation to force a playoff, then beat

Tom Byrum on second hole of sudden death to win 1999 Michelob Championship.

Earned PGA Tour card by finishing 10th on Nike Tour money list in 1998 thanks to four runner-up finishes.

Winner of 15 major junior and amateur titles.[24] There is no mention of the fact that Begay is a Navajo/Pueblo Indian or that he is the first Native American golfer on the tour since Rod Curl. Similarly, the PGA concentrates on details and accomplishments. After offering essentially the same vital statistics and noting his PGA victories, it lists his noteworthy accomplishments:

Four top-10s and 10 top-25s doubled rookie year totals. Also eclipsed first-year earnings with $1,819,323, good for 20th ranking on PGA TOUR official money list. . . . Rebounded from five missed cuts in 10 starts with third career victory, one-stroke win at the FedEx St. Jude Classic. Nominated for Rookie of the Year honors after not only winning his first PGA TOUR title but adding his second. . . . Became the first Native American to win TOUR event since Rod Curl at 1974 Colonial. . . . Member of United States Walker Cup team. Member of Stanford's 1994 NCAA Championship team, along with Casey Martin.

Next, breaking with other statistical and demographic portraits, the biography encapsulates his personal history.

Began playing golf at age 6. Father played in a business league while working for the Bureau of Indian Affairs. Notah would tag along for the twilight, nine-hole competition. . . . Most successful Native American golfer. . . . Half Navajo, one-quarter San Felipe and one-quarter Isleta. . . . Putts left- and right-handed, depending upon direction the putt breaks. . . . Brother Clint caddied in his two 2000 victories.

The piece concludes by noting his playoff record on the PGA and Buy.Com Tours (1–0 and 0–1 respectively) and his membership on national teams—Walker Cup (1995) and Presidents Cup (2000).[25] The PGA opts to mention his Indian heritage but trivializes it. It becomes a demographic marker or, worse, a curiosity, akin to being an ambidextrous putter or having his brother caddie for him.

In both of these cases, what is noteworthy is how Indianness is flattened or forgotten. These Web sites (and others like them) might be better understood as spaces of memory that prompt fans to remember or even relive key facts, spectacular moments, and great accomplishments. They work at the same to time to erase or undermine race. They literally enact a form of whiting-out, "a process of eliminating some approaches in favor of others. . . . Whiting-out is a routine activity . . . and thus largely remains invisible."[26] In sport, as Charles Springwood and I have argued, spaces of memory often work to exclude race, either by de-emphasizing and backgrounding race and power or by eliminating race altogether as a variable.[27] Summaries such as those at ESPN.com or PGA.com have similar effects, turning attention away from, covering over, and ultimately dismissing the significance of Indianness to understanding Begay and his achievements.

Americanness

Begay matters not simply because he attracts multiple interpretations of Indianness but because he promotes particular versions of Americanness. "America's son" or "an American original" both recode his aboriginality in national terms. If this were not enough, on occasion longer pieces linger on his genealogy. They do not reckon his kinship as the indigenous students did but locate him in a national narrative. Moreover, he is named after his grandfather, Notah Begay I, who rebelled against Euro-American policies and prejudices by running way from and eventually dropping out of school before serving as a code talker during World War II. His grandfather's life thusly rendered captures the ambivalence of colonial situations while highlighting the triumph and greatness of America. Notah Begay I proved himself to be a real American. By extension, as his heritage attests, the Navajo golfer is a real American. And much like his grandfather, he displays ambivalence about the United States. For instance, Begay discusses alcohol use among Native Americans in broad terms that reference the American experience: "If you were marched off your land at gunpoint and stripped of your language and culture, I think you would have some sort of inferiority complex. . . . Thrown in unemployment equivalent to that in Third World countries, no economic activity. . . . To build character, independence, pride, you have to be able to support your family and those around you. If you couldn't do that . . . wouldn't you be pretty discouraged?"[28] Finally, the rhetoric of individualism and the American dream secure his Americanness.[29]

Character

Accounts of Begay do not merely render his Indianness in largely familiar and approachable terms or confirm his Americanness, but they celebrate his triumph over class. He emerges as an individual overcoming circumstances through determination and character. He secures a spot at Stanford not because of his status but because he worked hard to improve his test scores, committing himself to extracurricular tutoring and preparation to achieve his goal. He becomes a great golfer not because of inborn traits, technological advantage, or mentoring but because he made sacrifices and dedicated himself to the game he loved.

Having achieved greatness, he embraces his role and status, understanding that he is a role model for youth and a representative of Indians: "I'm not an activist. . . . I'm not going to go out and raise hell and tell people that they're wrong and they need to change their beliefs. I'm an advocate—an advocate of positive American Indian issues. I just want to break down stereotypes and educate people."[30] For Begay, being an athlete means more than accomplishing great feats on the course: "It goes beyond trophies. The legacy that I want is that I made a difference in the lives of kids."[31]

As odd as it may sound, his arrest for drunk driving confirmed his character for many. He did not, as so many athletes do, endeavor to evade the consequences, avoid punishment, or hide past transgressions. Rather, he took responsibility, displaying his maturity. In an interview in April 2000 Begay noted that none was more disappointed than he by his DUI: "I try to handle it as best as possible and show them that not everyone is perfect . . . if you do make a mistake, own up to it and move on. . . . I've done everything I could to take care of it properly and in the right fashion, and I'm back playing good golf."[32]

Speaking before the annual United National Indian Tribal Youth in December 2000, Begay spoke of his DUI and its implications, enjoining those in attendance, "The sole responsibility [for your actions] lies on your shoulders, whether good or bad."[33]

His public stance won praise from fans, pundits, and sportswriters, who almost universally celebrate his candor and character. Begay also received praise from policy analysts. Joan Kirby, director of Government and Media Affairs at the National Center for Policy Analysis, pointed to Begay as a model of responsibility in an era of media hype and liberalism that have left "a nation hungry to develop ways to keep its youth accountable in the aftermath of Columbine." Kirby turned to Begay to advance a position on juvenile justice, namely that consequences deter crime.[34] Even President Clinton took note of his character: "And there was one young man who meant to come with me today, who could not come—a man I admire very much, not only for his success, but for the way he has handled adversity, Notah Begay. And I think we ought to give him a hand."[35]

The stark conditions of the reservation, the hardships of class away from it, and his commitment to the public and his personal struggles frame Begay as "America's son" and an "American original," marking his as a quintessential America story.

Supplement

Nearly every piece on Begay also mentions Tiger Woods. They underscore the talent and achievements of the multiracial golfer, soliciting Begay's assessment. They regularly linger on the historic relationship between the two athletes, dwelling on their experiences at Stanford, noting the differential developments of their careers, and asking Begay to draw comparisons. A GolfWeb interview exemplifies this pattern. A series of questions direct attention to Woods and Begay:

Q: When you guys were at Stanford, did you envision having a reunion out here [on the tour]. . . .

Q: As we all know, Tiger started with a little money in the bank. I see you are a Nike guy, too. Did he help you get endorsements. . . .

Q: Also, Tiger has his foundation. . . .

Q: As much as you may like Tiger and are friends with Tiger, respect Tiger. . . .[36]

Even though Woods is the junior player, he represents the emergent, if not crystallized, establishment of professional golf. Begay, in turn, draws his significance only with reference to or in contrast to Woods. His abilities and exploits have meaning only as read against Woods. Even his import as an ethnic athlete might be said to materialize only with reference to Woods.

Legibility

The legibility of Notah Begay, the aspects of his life made notable in media accounts, pose some important challenges to scholars concerned with race and sport in the contemporary United States. At the very least, representations of the Navajo golfer suggest that the play of racial signs animating sport spectacles is complex and conflicted, terribly resilient, and irreducible to black and white.

First, popular renderings of Begay underscore both the flexibility and limits of racialization. They highlight the recoding of often unspoken sentiments about Indians: the persistent negative evaluation of Indianness, the tendency to confine Indianness within the past or at least tradition, and the fascination with Native American spirituality and naming demonstrate the continued importance of imperial idioms. They also facilitate alternative and counterreadings as they question stereotyping and hail marginalized audiences.

Second, as one of the few nationally recognized Native American athletes of the past quarter century, Begay permits a rereading of the racial politics in post–civil rights America. Popular accounts endeavor to fit Begay within the dominant narrative of upward mobility and racial equality and propose that he balances the best of both worlds. While such renderings may have some validity, I think his career and its reception say something more complex. As an American Indian professional golfer, he lives and plays betwixt and between cultural categories. On the one hand, as a social agent, he actively poaches from both Euro-American and Native American traditions to fashion himself, while on the other hand, he symbolically mediates, encouraging diverse interpretations. Although his hybridity and the apparent popular receptivity to it would seem to confirm the rhetoric of colorblind or post-race America anchored in Tiger Woods and sports more generally, to my mind, Begay works against such happy endings. His presence routinely turns attention to historical inequities and abuses in a way that narratives about blackness and hybridity often avoid; and more, his ambivalence as a social actor and social sign problematize progressive, post–civil rights impulses. Begay reminds us that post–civil rights America crystallizes through multiple, overlapping, flexible, and contradictory readings and must be studied accordingly.

Notes

1. Nancy Clark, "Vandever Brings Navajo Lessons to Drake Football Field," *Des Moines Register*, 9 September 2000, C1.

2. See Churchill, Hill, and Barlow, "An Historical Overview of Twentieth-Century Native American Athletics"; Bloom, *To Show What an Indian Can Do*; Oriard, *Reading Football*; Powers-Beck, "Chief: The Indi-gration of Baseball."

3. King and Springwood, *Beyond the Cheers*.

4. Ellen Staurowsky, "Getting beyond Imagery: The Challenges of Reading Narratives about American Indian Athletes" unpublished manuscript in author's possession.

5. Kelli Anderson, "Notah Begay's Drive," *Stanford Magazine*, May/June 2001, http://www.stanfordalumni.org/news/magazine/2001/mayjun/features/begay.html; Tom Farrey, "Notah Begay's Long Walk," http://espn.go.com/otl/americans/begay1.html; John Garrity, "Dry Run," *Sports Illustrated* 93:1 (3 July 2000): 93; John Hawkins and Guy Yocom, "Getting to Notah," http://www.golfdigest.com/search/index.ssf?/features/getting_aguq53dc.html; John Strege, "An American Original on Tour," *Golf Digest* 50:7 (July 1999).

6. Anderson, "Notah Begay's Drive"; Farrey, "Notah Begay's Long Walk"; Hawkins and Yocom, "Getting to Notah"; Strege, "An American Original on Tour."

7. Anderson, "Notah Begay's Drive"; Farrey, "Notah Begay's Long Walk"; Hawkins and Yocom, "Getting to Notah"; Strege, "An American Original on Tour."

8. Anderson, "Notah Begay's Drive"; Farrey, "Notah Begay's Long Walk"; Hawkins and Yocom, "Getting to Notah"; Strege, "An American Original on Tour."

9. Anderson, "Notah Begay's Drive"; Farrey, "Notah Begay's Long Walk"; Hawkins and Yocom, "Getting to Notah"; Strege, "An American Original on Tour."

10. Anderson, "Notah Begay's Drive"; Farrey, "Notah Begay's Long Walk";

Hawkins and Yocom, "Getting to Notah"; Strege, "An American Original on Tour."

11. Farrey, "Notah Begay's Long Walk."

12. Anderson, "Notah Begay's Drive."

13. Michael D'Antonio, "Native Sun," *Golf Magazine*, May 2000, p. 67.

14. Farrey, "Notah Begay's Long Walk."

15. Strege, "An American Original on Tour," 143.

16. Hawkins and Yocom, "Getting to Notah," 127; Strege, "An American Original on Tour," 143.

17. Chris Tomasson, "Offensive Logos Have Run Their Course," *Akron Beacon Journal*, 28 August 2001.

18. *Http://espn.go.com/otl/americans/begaychat.html*

19. Brenda Norell, "Notah Begay III Takes Swing at Disease," *Indian Country Today*, 7 February 2001, p. 1.

20. Raul Dominguez, Jr., "Native Son," *San Antonio Express-News*, 6 August 2000, sec. C, p. 1.

21. George Tiger, "Beyond the Boundaries," *Native American Times*, author's files.

22. Dale Reeder, "Swingin for Sequoyah," *Canku Ota*, 6 May 2000, author's files.

23. Barry Lorge, "Native to the Game," *Golf Journal*, November/December 1999, pp. 43–47.

24. *Http://espn.go.com/golfonline/profiles/notah_begay.html*.

25. *Http://www.pgatour.com/players/bios/149683*.

26. Eileen M. Jackson, "Whiting-out Difference: Why Nursing Research Fails Black Families," *Medical Anthropology Quarterly* 7:4 (1993): 376.

27. King and Springwood, *Beyond the* Cheers, 17–40.

28. Garrity, "Dry Run," 58.

29. Farrey, "Notah Begay's Long Walk."

30. Farrey, "Notah Begay's Long Walk."

31. Brian Stokes, "Notah Begay Speaks from the Heart," *Indian Country Today*, 20 December 2000, p. 5.

32. John T. Alexander, "An Interview with Notah Begay," 15 April 2000, *http://www.asapsports.com/golf/2000mci/041500NB.html*.

33. Debra Utacia Krol, "Begay, Witherhill Inspire Youth at UNITY Benefit," *Canku Ota*, 30 December 2000, author's files.

34. Joan Kirby, "Teaching America's Youth to Play by the Rules," 28 April 2000, http://*www.ncpa.org*.

35. "Remarks by the President to the People of the Navajo Nation," 17 April 2000, *http://clinton4.nara.gov/WH/New/*.

36. James Cramer, Notah Begay preview interview, 27 October 1999, author's files.

11. No Fall from Grace
Grace Thorpe's Athlete of the Century Campaign for Her Father

Jim Thorpe is very much a living part of popular memory in the town of Carlisle, Pennsylvania. The wood-paneled walls of Wardecker's men's clothing store house a shrine to the athletic teams of the Carlisle Industrial School. Thorpe is prominently featured among the collection of photographs, old uniforms, and framed newspaper headlines. He was Carlisle's greatest star, earning worldwide fame as a football player and as a gold medal winner in the decathlon and pentathlon at the 1912 Stockholm Olympics while still enrolled at the Indian school. Thorpe would later play professional baseball, star as a professional football player, serve as the first president of the organization that would later become the National Football League, and become enshrined in the Pro Football Hall of Fame. Two blocks down the street from Wardecker's is a monument to Thorpe in the town square; a half mile away there is a three-dimensional image of Thorpe on a wall in one of the town's two decaying shopping malls; and, periodically, the local newspaper publishes a photo of a late middle-aged Thorpe sitting in a convertible, gleefully waving his hat at a local crowd during a parade down High Street held before the premiere of his cinematic biography, *Jim Thorpe: All American.*

Yet as much as Thorpe is remembered in Carlisle, until recently he had been forgotten around the rest of the nation. Despite the fact that the Associated Press voted Thorpe the greatest athlete of the first half of the twentieth century, some sports journalists less than fifty years later ignored him completely when compiling their own "best of the millennium" lists. As sportswriter Nicholas Lemann notes, becoming a superstar athlete is not only a measure of athletic ability, but it has

Jim Thorpe, with the New York Giants, ca. 1914. Courtesy National Baseball Hall of Fame Library, Cooperstown, New York.

also become increasingly indistinguishable from a "media-business apparatus." Because he lived in an era before multimillion-dollar endorsement contracts and cable television, Thorpe was consigned "to a rough marginal life that today would be unthinkable for an athlete one tenth as good as he was."[1]

Yet Jim Thorpe did have a passionate advocate: his daughter Grace. Grace Thorpe is the fourth of her father's eight children and has a long history of lending her famous name to causes on behalf of Native American people, most recently working as an anti-nuclear activist to persuade cash-starved reservation councils not to accept federal grants to store nuclear waste on tribal lands. Grace Thorpe was not going to let the intensity of the public spotlight on contemporary athletes blind people to the achievements of her father. In the 1990s she embarked on a campaign to have Jim Thorpe named the greatest athlete of the twentieth century. She posted an Internet site with a petition and circulated it through various contacts including archivists, biographers of her father, and members of the media. Her efforts were completely unaided by any professional marketing firm yet, ultimately, because of them, the very same consumer-driven media machine that had obscured the memory of Thorpe ended up providing a remarkable degree of recognition for his immeasurably well-rounded and triumphant athletic career in collegiate and professional football, professional baseball, and the Olympics. In 1999 ESPN's *Sportscentury* program placed Thorpe at number seven out of fifty top American athletes. And just a few weeks later, ABC Sports announced during halftime of Super Bowl XXXII that respondents to their Internet poll had selected Thorpe as the greatest athlete of the century.

Grace Thorpe's campaign for her father was remarkably successful. She evoked a tension between the ideals promoted within American sports and the histories of imperialism and injustice that are connected to Native American history and to her father's story.

Of course, it may seem odd to think of a campaign that ended in the celebration of a Native American athlete being broadcast by a division of the Walt Disney Corporation during the nation's premier corporate-sponsored media spectacle as one that confronts injustice and imperialism. But not even the media hype of the new century could hide the importance of Thorpe's quest for recognition, a fight that is not only about respect for an individual athlete but also about the importance of keeping Jim Thorpe's name alive. Grace Thorpe's campaign succeeded not only because it gained public recognition of her father's athletic achievements but also because it served to contest and reclaim who Jim Thorpe was, whom he served, and what his athletic career meant.

In 1999 ESPN released a companion book to their retrospective television series *Sportscentury*. Beginning in the first week of January 1999, the television show highlighted, in ascending order, the athletes that the network's own poll had voted the fifty greatest of the twentieth century.[2] The book, which devotes most of its chapter on the 1910s to Jim Thorpe, is not only a retrospective of great athletes but an important social document that reveals a great deal about the ideological functions of sports over the past century. In the foreword ESPN announcer Chris Berman clearly summarizes some of the utopian democratic ideals that are central to the culture surrounding sports in the United States. Noting that Jackie Robinson broke into baseball eight years ahead of Rosa Parks's Montgomery, Alabama, bus protest, and sixteen years ahead of

Martin Luther King's "I Have a Dream" speech (but not remembering that it came eighty-two years after the end of the Civil War), he writes, "Sports in this century have often been way ahead of society." Berman goes on to write,

[Y]ou could argue that when it came to civil rights, sports helped spur on social change, and certainly heightened public awareness.

One of America's beauties is that it is truly a melting pot. So, too, is sports. As we approach the 21st Century, where else can you find anything that knows no socioeconomic boundaries? Athletes, and certainly sports fans, are men and women, old and young, white and black. A millionaire and someone on welfare could have an intelligent discussion about yesterday's ballgame. Try that with any other subject.[3]

Berman presents a particularly utopian vision of American sports, one that reflects ideals associated with athletic virtue more than common lived experiences. During the hypothetical conversation Berman describes, the millionaire would surely keep careful guard of his wallet. Nevertheless, Berman articulates in these passages not only the association that many Americans make between sports and democratic values but the way that the success of minority athletes validates such a notion. "Three great black heavyweight champions—Jack Johnson, Joe Louis, and Muhammad Ali—are proof," according to Berman, that sports have helped pave the way toward a more democratic culture and society.[4]

To the examples of Johnson, Louis, and Ali Berman might just as well have added the name of Jim Thorpe. He, after all, represented his country on the international stage twelve years before Native Americans were even granted U.S. citizenship. Yet also like Johnson, Louis, and Ali, his athletic achievements were only realized after he and people like Grace Thorpe struggled against systemic racism and prejudice within institutions that governed sports—institutions designed to limit public recognition for athletic heroism to a privileged few. Such experiences demystify an understanding of "sports" as an entity that has its own rules and is governed by strict codes of honor, achievement, and merit. Instead, these experiences reveal how people organize and institution-alize athletic competition and entertainment. Not everything is decided on the field of play. People who occupy different positions of political power and who seek to defend their often divergent ideological interests and agendas have a large role in deciding who gets to play, who gets recognized, and who gets the money and resources to devote their lives to athletic achievement full time.

Jim Thorpe displayed an unmatched level of versatility on the field. Among his many accomplishments, he was a two-time Walter Camp All-American halfback selection while playing for Carlisle between 1907 and 1912, where he starred in both football and track; he played Major League and minor league baseball for over twenty years, often batting over .300; he was a premier professional football player, becoming the first president of the American Professional Football Association, the forerunner to the NFL; and, most famously, he set Olympic records and won gold medals in both the pentathlon and the decathlon in the 1912 Olympics in Stockholm.

Yet if it were not for the concerted efforts of his supporters, it would not be possible to make such an unqualified statement about Thorpe's Olympic performance. During the early twentieth century Olympic competition was guided by an amateur principle that strictly forbade all professionals from competition. Many contemporary sports fans lament that such standards have been widely compromised in recent decades, associating professionalization with corruption. But the amateur regulations were originally created to exclude all but white wealthy men of privilege from participation. The 1912 U.S. Olympic team, in fact, was the first to have been created from an open tryout that included athletes from outside an exclusive set of affluent athletic clubs.[5] After the 1912 Olympics the Amateur Athletic Union and the International Olympic Committee discovered that Thorpe had received money to play semi-professional baseball in North Carolina during the summer of 1909. Although the money that Thorpe received was in a sport entirely different from that in which he competed in the Olympics, these bodies ruled that he had received money as an athlete and should not have competed. They erased his Olympic records and awarded his gold medal in the pentathlon to Norway's Ferdinand Bie, and in the decathlon to Sweden's Hugo Wieslander. It was not until 1973, after a campaign led by Thorpe biographer Robert Wheeler and his wife, Florence Ridlon, that the AAU reinstated his amateur status; it was not until 1982 that Grace Thorpe was finally able to get his gold medals returned and the record books amended to name him "co-winner" of the 1912 pentathlon and decathlon.[6] As much as Thorpe's story is about his unparalleled athletic abilities and victories, it has also been about political struggles to gain recognition for his accomplishments from institutions that have governed sports. Grace Thorpe's campaign is a part of this larger struggle.

During a phone interview with Grace Thorpe, I asked her why it was important that her father be named Athlete of the Century. She answered simply, "Because he was." When she expanded on this answer, she focused entirely on his athletic achievements.

I mean there's just been nobody that's competed in so many different sports; not only competed, but actually excelled in them. I mean track and field, for example—the only person ever to win both the pentathlon and the decathlon. And then starting, you know, professional football, but then also being involved both as an amateur. Walter Camp just selected him as on the Team of the Century. That just happened last week. . . . And then he made his living playing professional baseball for twenty years. You know, so nobody else has been that versatile.[7]

Yet Grace Thorpe also acknowledges that it is not enough to simply perform better than everyone else to gain recognition for athletic accomplishment. Her father's history, his being stripped of his Olympic medals, and her own fight to get the medals returned vividly illustrate this. However, Grace Thorpe's campaign for her father at the end of the century would involve factors that were much more complex than her fight for the Olympic medals. Rather than coming from any organized governing body like the AAU, recognition for Athlete of the Century honors came from commercial media outlets like ESPN and the Associated Press.

ESPN's *Sportscentury* poll was the most well-publicized list and the one that likely evoked the greatest degree of public debate among sports fans. The cable sports network composed their list from the input of a "distinguished panel of 48 journalists, historians, observers, and administrators."[8] The program, which billed itself as the "definitive review of the people and events of sports in North America in the 1900s," won a great many accolades, including a George Foster Peabody Award. Nevertheless, the list did raise concerns over the criteria used to determine greatness (after all, horses were allowed on, but Pele was not). In an interview with the Web-based publication *Armchair* QB, sportswriter and historian Bert Sugar, who served on the ESPN panel, expressed dissatisfaction with the selection guidelines. According to *Armchair* QB, ESPN asked its panelists to base their votes on on-field performances. Sugar, who placed Thorpe second on his personal list, chose former Cleveland Brown running back Jim Brown as his top athlete because of his versatility and ability in both football and lacrosse in college. Such athleticism could not be measured, according to Sugar, by statistics alone.[9]

Some sports fans, however, felt that the panel looked at factors outside athletic performance when ranking athletes. A fan named Chuck Henderson, for example, posted on a sports e-mail discussion list, "The ESPN rankings seem to be a hodgepodge of all-around athletes and big-name/public-impact ones, trendsetters. How else, without the latter basis, to explain many of the names on the list (talking now about the full list of 100). How can Jack Nicklaus be in the top 100, let alone top 15?"[10]

Henderson's opinion may not be something that we can scientifically generalize as characteristic of most sports fans, but he does make a good point. The ESPN panel contained few who actually might have the best understanding of athletic performance: athletes and coaches. Instead, it was comprised almost entirely of sports journalists, celebrity sportscasters, and newspaper columnists. Since all of these groups play a role in publicizing athletic events within a commercial media structure, it is likely that image, connotations, and cultural ideals—factors that play a part in what Henderson terms an athlete's "public-impact"—played an important role in the selection criteria. In addition, media organizations like ESPN and ABC, in attempting to avoid controversy and provide a positive image with which advertisers could associate their products, tend to consider ideology as much as quantified performance when promoting particular athletes as representative of a particular time or place. Since the late nineteenth century athletes have attempted to carve out images that confirm the notion that athletic success is an affirmation of superior moral character.[11] Of course, great athletes are not always people who live lives characterized by pious and gracious behavior and, as we shall see, Jim Thorpe's own biography is one that sometimes digressed from such an image. Yet contemporary athletes work hard to bolster their images against negative reactions to the privileges of their celebrity and wealth.

In fact, ideologies surrounding athletic performance and moral character played a role in how Grace Thorpe characterized her own efforts to launch her campaign. When asked what prompted her to petition for her father, she responded, "Well, I think I probably did it when I heard that O. J. Simpson was going in for Athlete of the Century." Thus, she set her father up as superior in moral character to a more contemporary and famous athlete known today as much for his criminal record as for his athletic records. Yet she also notes that her father did not have the resources to create a positive image through charitable foundations and philanthropic activity that contemporary athletic superstars do. She stated, for example, that she believed ESPN's *Sportscentury* poll considered such charitable giving in its criteria.

I've talked to a couple of the guys that were on that. They had different ways that they marked people—not necessarily for their sports accomplishments, but for other things that they did . . . within the community, for example. Now, in Dad's particular case, Dad was so poor, you know, he was in sports before they became commercialized. So, he didn't have millions of dollars that he could put into a foundation. . . . He didn't have millions of dollars that he could have a staff like Muhammad Ali has, of nine people. As a matter of fact, he had trouble finding money to get food for the table, and to get shoes for the boys. . . . Life was a lot different than it is today. That's one thing that they graded people on. They graded the athletes on the work that they did aside from being an athlete. [12]

Not only was Jim Thorpe unable to buy himself a positive public image, but the most popular image people have of his life is that of the "tragic Indian" whose life was defined by a brief, fleeting moment of glory that was ruined by a combination of bad luck and prideful self-destruction. This story's framing of Jim Thorpe reveals as much about sports reporting during the twentieth century as it does about Thorpe himself. Lemann astutely writes that "the public's information about Thorpe's exploits came from ragtime-era sports reporters, a group with a flair for the dramatic and poetic, and from old-fashioned word of mouth." [13] Stories about Thorpe circulated in children's literature and, most prominently in the film *Jim Thorpe: All American*, show him as a great fallen hero. Narratives of his life tell how he went from Olympic glory, Major League baseball, and earning $500 a game playing professional football to digging ditches for five dollars a week during the Depression. They tell of his twin brother, Charlie, dying when Jim Thorpe was ten; of his first-born son, Jim Jr., dying of infantile paralysis. They tell of his divorces and his alleged drinking. And they tell of his being stripped of his Olympic titles. When such tales of misfortune are combined with the stories of his mythically heroic feats on the athletic field, Jim Thorpe's life becomes a modern parable framed within the classic narrative style of the tragedy.

The film *Jim Thorpe: All American* is perhaps most guilty of this. Starring Burt Lancaster as Thorpe, the great athlete is portrayed as a "natural," but emotionally immature man who craved the spotlight and indulged in self-pity whenever tragedy took it away. Early in the film, when Thorpe is denied a coaching job, he is quick to blame it on prejudice. His paternal coach, Glenn S. "Pop" Warner, admits that he does not know for sure why Thorpe was denied the job but offers the kind of inspirational pep talk that befits a legendary coach. [14] He argues in the film that even if Thorpe was denied the job because he was an Indian, "That's simply another hurdle for you to take. From what I've seen, that shouldn't be too difficult." This inspires the young Carlisle student to join the U.S. Olympic team. By the end of the film, however, Thorpe is shown as a pathetically defeated man broken by the stripping of his medals and the death of his son (who is portrayed as his only child—Grace Thorpe and her siblings are written out of this cinematic biography). In the final scenes Jim Thorpe has traded in on his fame to emcee a dance marathon in Los Angeles during the time of the 1932 Olympics. Warner comes to visit a sulky and moody Thorpe. When Warner offers him a ticket to the opening ceremonies, Thorpe tears it in half and throws it to the ground. This proves to be the last straw for Warner, who scolds his old star, "Somewhere along the line you've gone completely haywire. Picked up the idea the world owes you something. Well, it doesn't owe you a thing. So you've had some tough ones. Been kicked around. They took your medals away from you. So what. All I can say is when the real battle started, the great Jim Thorpe turned out to be a powder puff." [15]

Popular juvenile literature from the 1950s and reprinted through the

1960s also represent Jim Thorpe as a man who had natural abilities but knew little about self-discipline or sacrifice. This image is portrayed in an often repeated anecdote about the athlete's voyage across the Atlantic aboard the *Finland* to compete in the 1912 Stockholm Olympic Games. According to legend, Thorpe rested the entire trip while all of the other athletes trained for their competitions in the upcoming games. In his book *The Jim Thorpe Story: America's Greatest Athlete*, Gene Schoor provides one version. He writes,

If Jim Thorpe took any practice jumps, nobody saw him. If Jim ran around the deck once, there was no witness. He was the most relaxed athlete aboard the ship. He gave no sign of any pressure on him and couldn't understand why anyone should be tense about the Stockholm meet. . . . Certainly Jim didn't train the way a man who wins medals usually trains. He lounged in his steamer chair, found a hammock to swing in, looked out on the green water and the endless blue horizon. He liked to watch the big fish jumping over the surf.[16]

Later in the book Schoor describes a conversation between Warner and Thorpe regarding the New York Giants and their manager John McGraw, a coach who had developed the reputation for his hypercompetitive temperament and strict training regimen. Schoor uses this as another opportunity to portray Jim Thorpe as a lazy trainer.

"That's the team for me," [Thorpe] said to Coach Warner [about the Giants], and Warner nodded his head and said, "That's the team for you, Jim, but McGraw is a tougher man than I'll ever be. You'll have to work. You'll have to work hard."

Jim looked at his coach. He could never understand how anybody thought of a ball game as work. It was fun. It was always fun or else it wasn't worth the effort a man put into it.

"I like to play the game," he said.

"That's half of it Jim," said Pop Warner, trying hard to impress the Indian with the fact that professional ball meant a lot of sweating, a lot of training, and always sticking to the rules which made a good athlete. "The rest of it, Jim," he said, "is the grind, keeping yourself in condition. You've got to keep yourself in condition, good condition."

Jim was puzzled.

"But I'm always in good condition, Pop," he protested.
Warner shrugged his shoulders. There was no sense pressing the point. Jim
Thorpe would never be the ideal athlete as far as training was concerned.[17]

This kind of story helps perpetuate the image of Thorpe as the tragic hero. It portrays him as having a fatal flaw, one characterized by an undisciplined emotional immaturity and an unwillingness to sacrifice. Reading this, we are set up for his eventual fall from grace, as it seems as natural a part of his character as his athletic abilities.

More recent examples of juvenile literature about Thorpe actually address this myth and discount it. Bob Bernotas writes in his book *Jim Thorpe: Sac and Fox Athlete*, for example, "The story of Thorpe's life is entangled with legends and shrouded in myths. One of the most persistent and unfortunate of these unfounded anecdotes is the often repeated story that Thorpe refused to train aboard ship and instead spent the 10-day journey across the Atlantic Ocean drinking and sleeping."[18] Barbara Long, in *Jim Thorpe: Legendary Athlete*, similarly writes, "Stories that Thorpe did not train during the long trip have been repeated again and again. In fact, Thorpe trained for hours every day."[19] Bernotas even discusses how Ralph Craig (gold medal winner in the 100-meter and 200-meter dashes in Stockholm) derided stories of Thorpe's lack of training as a "'backhanded compliment.'"

It is always tempting for sportswriters and historians to overstate the level of such a person's natural ability. Although natural talent might carry a person through informal races on the playground or in gym class, no one can reach the Olympics, much less hope to win a gold medal, without having developed and honed these natural skills. That, of course, requires long, arduous hours of practices and training. Like all successful "natural" athletes, however, Thorpe knew that it took hard work to refine these gifts.[20]

The books mentioned above by Bernotas and Long were published in series created to honor Native Americans who have become recognized as important. Bernotas's book is part of the North American Indians of Achievement series published by Chelsea House; Long's is one of several in a Native American Biographies series by Enslow Publishers that includes books about Dennis Banks, Sitting Bull, Geronimo, Sacagawea, and Maria Tallchief. Given this fact, it is significant that each addresses the story about Jim Thorpe's training regimen. Both authors seem to understand how sports reporting often represents non-white athletes as "naturals" who do not work as hard as their Euro-American counterparts. Such representations feed into racist stereotyping of minorities as inherently physical, prone toward indulging their immediate desires, and lacking in moral character.

By contrast, the other texts that portray Thorpe as a tragic figure also claim Thorpe as a symbol of national patriotism, not Native American pride. This is reflected in the subtitles of these biographical accounts: *America's Greatest Athlete* (Schoor's book) and *All-American* (Thorpe's film biography). Within narratives of national patriotism, it is entirely acceptable to portray Native American heroes like Thorpe as tragic figures. Narratives that aim to teach children respect for Native American history, however, resist such characterizations of Thorpe. Yet even the authors of these texts struggle to reconcile ideals of moral virtue and Horatio Alger mobility with Thorpe's struggles and human weaknesses, things that he could not hide behind a lucrative charitable foundation. All of these biographies illustrate how Jim Thorpe has embodied dialogues over cultural values, ones not only about the veracity of accounts that describe key moments in the athlete's life but also about how one interprets the meaning of success, fame, and national identity.

Beginning with her quest to reclaim her father's medals and her *Sportscentury* campaign, and continuing with her most recent efforts to get her father on a Wheaties box and to have his trophies from the 1912 Olympics returned (they are in a museum in Switzerland), Grace Thorpe resists any clear understanding of her father as either a tragic figure or a metaphor for Native American history. In an article in *People* magazine in 1996, for example, she describes the last time she saw her father.

"I dropped him off at the corner to take a bus to New York City," she says. "He stood underneath the marquee of the theater there, and right above his head were the words 'Jim Thorpe—All American.' [Thorpe had signed away all rights to his name during the Depression and received no money from the movie.] I remember glancing over there and seeing him with the marquee and his scarred leather luggage. That was my last memory of him," says Thorpe. "He was kind of cool."[21]

This quote conveys sentiments that are often a part of texts that represent Thorpe's life. Indeed, Thorpe did endure tragedy, and there is a poignant and sad irony within the image that she provides of her father standing below the movie marquee. Yet Grace Thorpe's description of her father is not that of a "tragic Indian" but one of a father who was "kind of cool." Rather than seeing him as a broken man enduring the irony that audiences were paying to view only a few feet behind him, he is "cool"—a person who lived his own life and had no regrets regardless of what a Hollywood film might say. For some this statement might seem out of place, but it is appropriate because it frames Jim Thorpe as someone who persevered through tough times with dignity and grace.

In her interview with me, she similarly resisted having her father pigeonholed or labeled. When I asked her what her father's memories of the Carlisle school were, she provided a frank answer that she knew ran against the sentiments of most contemporary historians of Native American history.

Dad told me once that his happiest years were spent at Carlisle. . . . I'm thinking back on why he would say such a thing like that . . . that's where he first came of fame, . . . in Pennsylvania, at Carlisle. . . . And then that's where he met my mother, and he was very much in love with my mother. . . . So that's where they met, that's where they fell in love, and that's where they married, was at Carlisle. Mother was a student there, too. . . . She was very happy there, too. She liked Carlisle. I never heard one of them say anything against the Indian boarding schools, and both of them grew up in them. I know that there is a lot of talk today, and a lot of writing about how terrible the Indian boarding schools are, but my mother and father never had anything wrong to say about them, and I don't either. I went to them, too.

As someone who has written about "how terrible" the Indian boarding schools were, I nervously laughed when she said this to me over the phone. However, her statement about her father is an important one within the context of boarding school history. K. Tsianina Lomawaima found that many graduates of the Chilocco Indian school in Oklahoma (where Grace Thorpe attended school) also recalled that their boarding school experiences were happy ones, even if they also reported unhappy events that occurred while they were there. Instead of understanding these statements as endorsements of the federal government's policy of assimilation, however, Lomawaima interprets such sentiments as expressing a desire by former students to reclaim boarding schools as their own.[22] In her discussion of her father's memories of boarding school, Grace Thorpe does a similar thing. Rather than presenting Carlisle only as a place that shaped her father, she understands it as a school that provided him with the opportunity to, as she put it later in the interview, become one of the few Native Americans recognized and admired both nationally and internationally.

As with the memory of her father that she recalled in her interview with *People*, Grace Thorpe does not present her father as a tragic victim. Likewise, her campaign to get her father named Athlete of the Century does not accept the image of her father as a tragic hero whose accomplishments are, as many understand Native American history more generally, a part of a past that is no longer relevant. In fact, Grace Thorpe's campaign is audacious because she asserts that her father's athletic career, his records, and his accomplishments are relevant in the present. It is precisely this assertion of relevance that served as an important inspiration to launch her campaign. Besides her dismay over the prospect of losing out to O. J. Simpson, Grace Thorpe became involved in her Athlete of the Century campaign because she had heard a sportswriter speak dismissively of athletes who competed before the era of television. "I heard another sports commentator make the remark that they don't want to, you know, bring in all those old guys . . . that were [around] a hundred years ago; that they should just have something for the current athletes." Grace Thorpe not only made a case that her father's accomplishments were comparable, even superior, to those of Michael Jordan or Carl Lewis, but in the very act of doing this she brought his accomplishments into a contemporary debate, making them meaningful and alive in the present.

Such an understanding of Native American identity has been important to Grace Thorpe as she has been a long-time activist for recognition not only of her father's sports career but also for the rights of Native Americans. Along with her daughter, Dagmar Thorpe, she participated in the occupation of Alcatraz Federal Prison in the early 1970s by the American Indian Movement.[23] She has also been a leader in campaigns against the dumping of radioactive waste on Indian lands, an effort that in its structure very much resembled the petition on behalf of her father.

*It's exactly the same type of thing—making an awareness. Making the In-
dian tribes aware of the hazards and the dangers of nuclear waste; of what radioactivity will do to the body and do to the future generations of Indians. . . .
I'd go to these national Indian meetings—and I have literature about the
hazards and dangers of radioactivity—because . . . the Department of Energy was giving grants of $100,000 to anybody who would study the feasibility
of putting nuclear waste on their land. And so they sent this information
out to municipalities, states, cities, villages, and Indian tribes. Not one of the
states applied for the grant, but twenty-seven different Indian tribes did. My
tribe was one of them.*[24]

Grace Thorpe was able to get her tribe to listen to her ideas about
nuclear waste, a perspective that has its roots in her days in the Women's
Army Corps after World War II when she witnessed the devastation
in the aftermath of two nuclear bombs. She acknowledges that she
used her name as best she could to publicize her cause when she was
engaged in her lobbying efforts. During her fight to oppose nuclear
dumping, her identity as Jim Thorpe's daughter served as a lifeline that
connected her father's achievements to injustices that Native Americans
have endured as a result of European and U.S. imperialism.

In fact, Grace Thorpe's campaign is very connected to the legacy of
imperialism that indigenous people live with today. Her work to publicize her father's achievements has not only brought him the recognition
that he deserves as an athlete, but it has also publicly resisted the tragic
images that for so long dominated representations of her father's life.
As I have written elsewhere, stories about Native American athletes
are often framed within a tragic mode. Such narratives might tell sad
stories, but they also are comforting ones for white Americans, for they
suggest that problems faced by contemporary Native Americans are not
the result of historical events or political and economic interests but
are, instead, the product of cultural deficiencies of American Indians.
Stories about tragic Native athletes make it appear that Native people
alone are responsible for the poor conditions they face by portraying
them as lacking ambition, intellect, and strength of character.

One might logically form this kind of a conclusion about Native
American problems from watching *Jim Thorpe: All American*, but it
is not one that Grace Thorpe endorses. Instead she asserts a dignified

image of her father, one that does not let American society dismiss the problems of Native Americans as those of a tragic people. Likewise, her opposition to nuclear dumping calls on Americans to reflect on the ways that they are connected to a history of American imperialism, and it helps empower indigenous people to continue working on behalf of struggles that have resulted from this history.

Grace Thorpe's name is powerful, in part, because she has helped keep the name of her father alive—not as a tragic hero but as someone whose accomplishments are as relevant and meaningful as any found today, even if he was never a guest on an ESPN talk show. The victories that Grace Thorpe has won on her father's behalf have also helped her and other Native Americans who are wary of seeing their reservations and lands become nuclear dumping zones and who seek to have an understanding of their history. Grace Thorpe's campaign on behalf of her father may contain an element of pride, but it reflects her passion to simply have him recognized as a great athlete and illustrates how Jim Thorpe's heritage has served as an extremely valuable cultural resource.

Notes

1. Nicholas Lemann, "Jim Thorpe," in ESPN *SportsCentury*, ed. Michael Mac-Cambridge (New York: Hyperion, 1999), 70.

2. The ESPN *Sportscentury* series has continued since then with biographical sketches of the twentieth century's greatest sports stars, some of whom are not on the original list.

3. Chris Berman, foreword to ESPN *SportsCentury*, ed. MacCambridge, 17.

4. Berman, foreword, 17.

5. Allen Guttman, *The Olympics: A History of the Modern Game* (Urbana: University of Illinois Press, 1992), 12.

6. Barbara Long, *Jim Thorpe: Legendary Athlete* (Springfield, NJ: Enslow, 1997), 98–99.

7. Grace Thorpe, telephone interview by the author, 16 February 2001.

8. The ESPN *Sportscentury* panel consisted of Mitch Albom, Roone Arledge, Chris Berman, Steve Bornstein, Ray Cave, Bill Conlin, Bob Costas, Lucy Danzinger, Frank Deford, Anita DeFrantz, Mel Durslag, Harry Edwards, Dick Enberg, Roy Firestone, Curt Gowdy, Bud Greenspan, Bryant Gumbel, David Halberstam, Steve Hirdt, Keith Jackson, Sally Jenkins, Tony Kornheiser, Sam Lacy,

Richard Lapchick, Bob Ley, Robert Lipsyte, Donna Lopiano, Mike Lupica, Jim McKay, Al Michaels, Jim Murray, Jim Nantz, Dan Patrick, Shirley Povich, Robin Roberts, Harold Rosenthal, Bob Ryan, Dick Schaap, Vin Scully, Blackie Sherrod, Jim Simpson, Charley Steiner, Bert Sugar, Pat Summerall, Mike Tirico, Lesley Visser, Mike Wilbon, and George Will. See *http://espn.go.com/classic /biography*.

9. *Http://armchairqb.com/media_notes_sept17.html*.

10. "Where Is Minnesota Fats?" author's files.

11. Elliott Gorn and Warren Goldstein, *A Brief History of American Sports* (New York: Hill and Wang, 1993), 98–149.

12. Grace Thorpe interview.

13. Lemann, "Jim Thorpe."

14. *Jim Thorpe: All American* (1951), directed by Michael Curtiz (Burbank CA: Warner Home Video, 1992).

15. *Jim Thorpe: All American*.

16. Gene Schoor, *The Jim Thorpe Story: America's Greatest Athlete* (New York: Julian Messner, 1962), 75–76.

17. Schoor, *The Jim Thorpe Story*, 117–18.

18. Bob Bernotas, *Jim Thorpe: Sac and Fox Athlete* (New York: Chelsea House, 1992), 16–17.

19. Long, *Jim Thorpe*, 54.

20. Bernotas, *Jim Thorpe*, 17.

21. Michael Neill and Joseph Harmes, "Torch Bearer," *People* 45:1 (8 January 1996): 73.

22. Lomawaima, *They Called It Prairie Light*.

23. "Mother and Daughter Remember Alcatraz," *Indian Life* 17:6 (March/ April 1997): 11.

24. Grace Thorpe interview.

Epilogue

Native Athletes in Sport and Society is only a beginning, a suggestive foray into a long neglected and increasingly valuable subject. As such, the collected essays offer a reminder, occasions for reflection, and, we hope, an incitement to scholars working in the interdisciplinary fields of Native American studies and sports studies. Fundamentally it asks for more — additional research, alternative approaches, and further discussion. To close this collection, I want to point to a series of promising paths for future inquiry.

To begin a dialogue about the significance of Native American athletes, this volume emphasizes the lives and accomplishments of individuals within mainstream sports of Euro-American invention, played largely within intercultural contexts, during the twentieth century. Such a framing encourages a consideration of a set of key themes that resonate nicely with ongoing discussions in Native American and sports studies, particularly identity, power, racism, memory, and agency. However, it only begins to explore the subject. To fully address its diversity and complexity, as many of the contributors suggest, it is necessary to go outside dominant spaces and beyond renowned figures and commonsense assumptions. First, more traditional contexts demand greater attention. This will mean investigations of historical events and individuals to unravel the place and meaning of athletes in indigenous sport and society. It should also mean that scholars build the important work begun elsewhere by the likes of Kendall Blanchard, Vicky Paraschak, and John Bloom to make sense of athletes and athleticism in revived and reclaimed sports like lacrosse. Moreover, as Ann Cummins and her collaborators along with Ellen Staurowsky and Paraschak remind us in this volume, scholarship should think small. Because so many Indian athletes remain invisible, scholars would accomplish much by remembering the minor moments, less

245

well-known figures, and local heroes who make sport meaningful to so many indigenous athletes and audiences. At the same time, thinking small might mean thinking outside the pale and considering all-Indian leagues, tournaments, and competitions.

Regularly during the course of researching and writing about Native American athletes, I have turned to the worldwide Web, checking facts, locating photos, and communicating with contributors. In the process I have encountered wonderful sites devoted to Native Americans and sports. To be sure, they have taught me much about indigenous athletes, both famous and relatively obscure. More important, they have directed my attention away from the athletes themselves, their remarkable accomplishments, their struggles with racism, and their heroic and tragic lives and focused it on individuals and communities rarely discussed by scholars or journalists, namely indigenous fans and the subcultures they elaborate around athletes in high school gyms, within reservation communities, and through televised games. As Staurowsky, Bloom, and I suggest, indigenous audiences tell alternative stories about athletes, their careers, and their significance. In the process they often read mainstream sport and society against the grain, challenging its renderings of Indianness, value, and success. Finally, these interpretive communities have much to teach us about ethnic pride, racial identity, and collective memory in an increasingly mass-mediated Native America.

It is not simply that novel topics present themselves around athletes or sport and scholars should seize upon them to foster fuller dialogues about Indianness or the Native American experience. This is a good beginning and worthy task. More challenging and ultimately more rewarding is to locate new approaches to telling achievements. At its most basic, as undertaken by virtually all of the contributors, this concern for representation deconstructs anti-Indian stereotypes that inform popular understandings and media coverage, recording their history, unpacking their significance, underscoring their errors, and resisting their effects. It is not enough to interpret images and how they imprint identities and possibilities. It is equally important that indigenous perspectives, voices, and memories more actively enter into discourses surrounding sport and society. Here, Cummins and her collaborators initiate such a project as do Bloom and Smith and Peavy in slightly different ways. They allow the voices of Indian athletes and their relations to speak, at times unfettered and unconstrained by the pretense of interpretation, and at other times woven into beautiful narratives that counter commonsense presuppositions and mainstream preoccupations. Such endeavors need not be autobiographical; Sherman Alexie's fiction and poetry offer nuanced and evocative renderings of the meaning of playing sport for some contemporary American Indians. Creative writing, more generally, holds great promise. Brenda Zeman's imaginative biodocumentary fiction is one such example. Even more exciting is Todd Fuller's recent book on Mose YellowHorse. Fuller infuses a more or less conventional biography with his own powerful poetry, the recollections of Pawnee elders, and delightful analyses of popular culture (from journalist stereotypes about the ballplayer to the Dick Tracy comic strips that featured the Pawnee pitcher). What truly distinguishes Fuller's work, however, is his sensitive incorporation of Pawnee storytelling structures. In the end, he crafts a wonderfully dynamic mixed-genre text that outlines one promising way to challenge and open the telling of indigenous athletes' lives in context.

Clearly, athletes' lives invite scholars to ask familiar questions and forge novel lines of inquiry in sport studies and Native American studies. Not only have they taken leading roles in the creation of new worlds in the wake of Euro-American colonization (inter-Indian, intercultural, and decidedly hybrid), they also permit close readings of the problems and possibilities posed by these emergent worlds. Athletes, then, as the contributors to this volume clearly show, poignantly and powerfully illustrate processes central to the reconfiguration of Native America, including adaptation, assimilation, resurgence, and alienation. At the same time they permit a rethinking that concentrates on power (domination and resistance), agency, and identity.

Athletes afford unique understandings of the Native experience precisely because they have been better known than peers, often have been more visible than leaders, regularly are better liked than indigenous politicians and other public representatives, and have been understudied.

Epilogue

Sport has played a pivotal role in American efforts to make sense of race, power, and culture in the wake of the civil rights movement. It has emerged as a primary site of collective celebration and social struggle around these issues. Athletics facilitate simultaneously accepted accounts of integration and equality, popular notions linking race, body, criminality, and character, and critical renderings of stratification and exclusions. These stories and subversions have been almost invariably told in black and white. That is, they center on black-white relations, particularly blackness, and, though often held under erasure, whiteness. As the contributors continually remind readers, to fully appreciate the articulations of race and power in sport, Indians and Indianness must be considered as well. For well over a century and half, indigenous athletes have been marked as uncivilized, even savage, undisciplined, physically gifted yet psychologically weak, prone to be victims of modern life and its temptations, mystical children of nature, and so on. This repeated marking invariably has judged, (de)valued, marginalized, ranked, and racialized Native Americans. In effect, through sports, in often unrecognized ways, Native Americans (and not simply athletes) have been inscribed within the racial hierarchies at the heart of American society. In retelling and often reclaiming the lives of indigenous athletes contextually, then, the contributors to this volume have taken an important step toward rethinking sport and, in the process, have disrupted the taken-for-granted flattening of race and racialization.

These essays offer scholars a challenge: take the sporting experience of Native Americans seriously. Too often ignored in sport studies and public culture, Native American athletes deserve, nay demand, attention. We have only the most rudimentary understanding of sport in indigenous communities and sadly much of the emergent popular literature on the subject is riddled with clichés. Conceiving of sport as a contact zone, borderland, or middle ground, scholarship not only must attend to popular stereotypes in media coverage, but it also should interrogate heritage and tradition, exchanges and appropriations, assimilation and resistance, institutional contexts, audiences and fan culture. Fuller engagements with Native American athletes and athleticism surely would expand our sense of the means and meanings of sport in America and, more important, might be a useful way to reenergize the critical multicultural study of sport and society.

248

CONTRIBUTORS

CECILIA ANDERSON has worked in the health professions all of her adult life. She is currently an administrator at the Indian Public Health Hospital in Shiprock, New Mexico. Anderson has been an active athlete for over forty years. She began playing basketball and softball in her early teens and continues to play competitively on community teams in Farmington, New Mexico. An accomplished orator and business-woman, Anderson is also a member of the Navajo Tribe and the To-dacheene Clan.

DANIEL P. BARR is an assistant professor of history at Robert Morris University in Pittsburgh. His research interests include the early American frontier and Native American history. He is the author of *Unconquered: The Iroquois Confederacy at War in Colonial America* (Praeger), *A Colony Sprung from Hell: War and Society on the Pittsburgh Frontier, 1754–1794* (Kent State University Press), and editor of *The Boundaries between Us: Natives and Newcomers in the Old Northwest Territory* (Kent State University Press).

WILLIAM J. BAUER, JR. (Wailacki-Concow), completed his Ph.D. in history at the University of Oklahoma in 2003. He is an assistant professor of American Indian ethnohistory at the University of Wyoming. His dissertation is a study of Indians, agricultural labor, race, and federal policy on the Round Valley Reservation in northern California, where he grew up.

JOHN BLOOM teaches history at Shippensburg University. He has written widely about race and sports. His books include *A House of Cards: Baseball Card Collecting and Popular Culture* and *To Show What an Indian Can Do: Sports at Indian Boarding Schools*. He also edited *Sports Matters: Race, Recreation, and Culture*. He is currently working on a biography of Barry Bonds.

GEORGIA BRIGGS has been a public school educator for nearly twenty-five years. She received her bachelor's degree and teaching certification from Fort Lewis College in Durango, Colorado. She has accumulated hundreds of graduate-level college credits at a variety of institutions, but she has let her interests rather than a specific degree shape her education. Currently a fifth-grade teacher on the Southern Ute Indian Reservation in Ignacio, Colorado, Briggs is a veteran oral storyteller, an esteemed community leader, and a vital member of the Navajo Tribe. She is of the Todacheene Clan.

ANN CUMMINS is a professor of English at Northern Arizona University. She has published stories in *The New Yorker*, *McSweeney's*, and *The Best American Short Stories*, among numerous other publications. Her short story collection, *Red Ant House*, was published in spring 2003 as part of Houghton Mifflin's Best American Discovery Series. She was awarded a Lannan Foundation Literary Fellowship in 2002, Arizona Commission on the Arts Fellowships in 1990 and 1994, and an Arizona Humanities Council grant in 2000.

GERALD R. GEMS is a professor of health and physical education at North Central College, Illinois. He is the author of *For Pride, Profit, and Patriarchy: Football and the Incorporation of American Cultural Values* and *Windy City Wars: Labor, Leisure, and Sports in the Making of Chicago*.

C. RICHARD KING, an associate professor of comparative ethnic studies at Washington State University, has written extensively on race and sport, particularly the Native American mascot controversy. He is the author or editor of a number of books, including *Beyond the Cheers: Race as Spectacle in College Sports*, *Team Spirits: The Native American Mascot Controversy* (coedited with Charles Fruehling Springwood), and the *Encyclopedia of Native Americans and Sports*.

VICKY PARASCHAK is an associate professor of kinesiology at the University of Windsor. She has written extensively on race, gender, and sport in Canada and has been a leading figure in the study of indigenous peoples and sport for nearly two decades.

LINDA PEAVY and URSULA SMITH, independent scholars specializing in western women's history, have coauthored a dozen books, including *The Gold Rush Widows of Little Falls*, *Women in Waiting in the Westward Movement*, and *Pioneer Women*. Historical consultants for the PBS miniseries *Frontier House* (2002), they wrote the companion book for the series with producer Simon Shaw. Their forthcoming work on the girls' basketball team from Fort Shaw Indian School, supported in part by grants from the NEH, the Smithsonian Institution, and the Redd Center for Western Studies, has been greatly enriched by the memories and memorabilia shared by descendants and tribal kin of the players.

JEFFREY POWERS-BECK is a professor of English at East Tennessee State University in Johnson City. He is the author of *The American Indian Integration of Baseball*.

CHARLES FRUEHLING SPRINGWOOD is an associate professor of anthropology at Illinois Wesleyan University. He is the author or editor of several books, including *Cooperstown to Dyersville: A Geography of Baseball Nostalgia* and, with C. Richard King, *Team Spirits: The Native American Mascot Controversy*.

ELLEN J. STAUROWSKY is a professor of sport management and media at Ithaca College. A former college athlete, coach, and athletic director, she has actively researched social justice issues in sport for almost twenty years. She has recently published, with Allen L. Sack, *College Athletes for Hire: The Evolution and Legacy of the NCAA Amateur Myth*.

Index

CPSIA information can be obtained
at www.ICGtesting.com
Printed in the USA
LVOW13s0037120718

583393LV00017B/283/P